I0143045

# DEFINING FREEDOM

---

## WORKS BY
## AMERICA'S FOUNDING FATHERS

# DEFINING FREEDOM

WORKS BY
AMERICA'S FOUNDING FATHERS

Edited with introductions by
Noah T. Howard

WHITLOCK PUBLISHING
Alfred, New York

First Whitlock Publishing edition 2021

Whitlock Publishing
Alfred, New York
http://www.whitlockpublishing.com

Editorial Matter © Noah T. Howard

ISBN: 978-1-943115-40-2

This book was set in Adobe Garamond Pro on 50# acid-free paper
that meets ANSI standards for archival quality.

For my parents, Frank and Nicole Howard,
for my siblings, Christian and Mackenzie Howard,
and for my country.

# A Note on the Text

In editing these texts, I have essentially made no changes other than formatting. All spellings, abbreviations, etc. are true to the original documentss to preserve the exact words of the Founding Fathers. All images are public domain content from the Library of Congress, Flickr, and Wikimedia Commons.

# Table of Contents

# INTRODUCTION

*"If destruction be our lot, we must ourselves be its author and finisher. As a nation of freemen, we must live through all time, or die by suicide."*

–Abraham Lincoln

L IFE, LIBERTY, AND THE PURSUIT OF Happiness are the inalienable rights promised to us, the American Citizenry, by the Declaration of Independence and guaranteed by the U.S. Constitution. The Founding Fathers believed in the ability of these rights to protect against tyranny as they drew from these principles in order to craft a just and safeguarded nation which would ensure the preservation of the rights of its citizens. In recent years, though, many people feel that their individual liberties are being threatened. As the federal government's power has climbed through the country's short life, a growing portion of the citizenry continues to feel as though it is suffocating under the weight of an increasingly overbearing government. Given the importance of the liberties which we were granted, it's high time we revisit the minds of the men who built this nation and take another look at their image of it.

Today, many political factions have begun twisting the words of the Fathers in order to fit different, biased narratives. These increasing misrepresentations are further dividing our country and creating a sense of uncertainty with regards to the true roots of our nation. The very definitions of the liberties which we are granted are being skewed and stretched beyond recognition. During the COVID-19 pandemic, for example, the two main opposing sides argue over the physical freedoms of the people: one side is in favor of restricting travel between states and even towns, while the other feels they should be permitted to travel freely within their own nation. The growing and contentious gray areas regarding our rights is increasingly alarming. If we are to preserve the nation of free men that we inherited, we must be able to accurately understand the Founding Fathers' beliefs, hopes, and foundation for our country.

Fierce in their beliefs, and assertive in their methods, the Fathers began to plant the seeds of freedom within the minds of the colonists in the New World, using powerful language that sparked the American Revolution. Feeling oppressed, cheated, mistreated, and ignored, the Fathers sought to incorporate the ideas and sentiments of the many into the governing body of the few. While they didn't originally desire independence from Great Britain, the Fathers came to understand that it was not only becoming inevitable, but also necessary to safeguard the liberties which they thought intrinsic to humanity.

In the age of the pen, the Fathers took to paper, spreading their beliefs and expanding their influence through essays, newspapers, letters, and any other means of communication that they could. Many of these writings were preserved and documented, allowing us to access them to this day. Some of the most influential of these writings have been reprinted here to showcase the passion, ideas, and ideals of the Founding Fathers. These documents reveal that, while the Fathers were working towards a common cause, their ideas and political strategies sometimes differed greatly.

Some, like Alexander Hamilton and Thomas Paine, were more fervent than others. Hamilton was sometimes seen as brash, as he wasn't afraid of conflict; there were several times when he challenged others to an "affair of honor," or a duel. Though, he was still an eloquent and persuasive speaker and writer. While Paine was also a highly persuasive individual, he earned the image of being a pro-pagandist and a rabble-rouser. Thomas Jefferson was more quiet, reserved, and eloquent with his articulation. Ben Franklin was the moral man and inventor, while George Washington became the fig-urehead and leader of the entire movement, though he didn't want to be. James Madison's image was that of a short, quiet, weak man, yet powerful speaker. The majority of Americans mainly saw John Jay and John Adams as popular diplomats, without much of the other perceptions that followed other Fathers. When it came to political infrastructure, Hamilton favored the approach of a stronger government, while Jefferson was afraid of tyranny once again gripping the men of the nation. The Fathers were split on this issue and several of them changed their side as the nation's birth began. Regardless of their individual duties, each Father was relentless in his approach.

In the contemporary United States, the influence and guidance of the Fathers are becoming increasingly diminished. Their views and dreams for the nation are being erased from society. More and more, I hear my fellow American citizens say that the Founding Fathers would be rolling around in their graves if they knew what was happening to the country that they spent decades building. With the people continuing to diverge into polarized factions, the heart of the country is being squandered and forgotten. The people within these factions ignore certain aims of the Fathers in order to push their own agenda. An example of this is the Second Amendment, guaranteed in the Bill of Rights, which gives the people the right to keep and bear arms, meaning weapons. One side of the spectrum thinks that means that the people can have any weapon the government can, while the opposing side feels that the amendment is outdated, or that it can be manipulated. These debates are rising up more consistently in today's politically correct climate. The Fathers' efforts seemingly disappearing, how can we reignite the flame of freedom that began so bright and is now reaching the bottom of its candlestick?

It is obvious, and expected, that not every American will agree on every issue. In fact, many Americans are diametrically opposed on a whole slew of topics: abortion, gun control, immigration, LGBT movements, etc. This was the case with the Founding Fathers as well. But, how did they overcome such a challenge? How was it that the Fathers were able to craft a union of the People, by the People, and for the People, if not all of them agreed on what each of those ideas meant? It's simple. They succeeded then where we fail now: with compromise.

The Fathers originally avoided what we embrace today: a system of political parties and an increased participation in foreign affairs, among other blunders. The party system promotes division and polarizes the country so heavily that we refuse to respect one another solely because we belong to another party. We think that every issue is black and white; that every problem has two sides to it and there is nowhere in between. This mindset, this fallacy that the nation can thrive under such a system, is inherently erroneous. Each election year, we are force-fed only two candidates that have extreme differences of opinions on many issues. We're required to choose the one that is the closest to our beliefs. There are hundreds of millions of citizens in this country and there are millions that could do a better job than those that are appointed for us to "choose." Given this, yet another issue brought on by the polarization of the country, how are we to elect the most adequate leader who has the best intentions for the nation?

President George Washington would be appalled by the political climate of today's United States. He warned against a partisan approach to government and, the moment he was gone, that's exactly what our country descended into. The political parties of history, though, were not nearly as polarized as the ones that exist in 2021. Each year, we stray further from the intentions of the Fathers and closer to their fears. In taking a look back at the original words of the men who built this nation, we will be granted a much-needed reminder about what exactly our nation was created for: freedom, rights, and protection for the common man.

Luckily, though, the Fathers granted us a Bill of Rights within a Constitution that is meant to preserve our individual liberties and prevent a tyrannical grip from seizing our nation by the throat. Contained within this anthology are many works by several of the Founding Fathers that shed light on the beginning of our country and give us a better understanding of the true intentions of the Fathers. For, we are, and always have been, One Nation, Indivisible, with Liberty and Justice for all.

# Timeline

**1754: Benjamin Franklin publishes his "Join or Die" cartoon**

**1754–1763: French and Indian War**
Ended by the Treaty of Paris. The costs of the war contributed to the new taxes on the American colonies.

**March 22, 1765: Stamp Act**
Imposed to increase revenues to meet the costs of defending the enlarged British Empire. Colonists rioted.

**June 15–July 2, 1767: Townshend Acts**
Passed by the British Parliament to assert its authority over the colonies. Colonists resisted.

**October, 1768: Dispatch of troops**
In response to the resistance to the Townshend Acts, Parliament dispatched two regiments of the British army to Boston.

**March 5, 1770: Boston Massacre**
A small British army detachment, that was threatened by a mob, opened fire and killed five people.

**1771–1790: Benjamin Franklin writes his autobiography**

**December 16, 1773: Boston Tea Party**
Bostonians disguised as Mohawk people boarded ships at anchor and dumped about £10,000 worth of tea into the harbor.

**March–June 1774: Intolerable Acts**
Parliament enacted four measures that became the justification for convening the First Continental Congress later in 1774.

**September 5, 1774: First Continental Congress convenes**
Called in response to the Intolerable Acts, the First Continental Congress convened in Philadelphia. Fifty-six delegates represented all of the colonies, except for Georgia.

**December 1774: Alexander Hamilton publishes A Full Vindication of the Measures of Congress**

**March 23, 1775: Patrick Henry's "Give me liberty or give me death" speech**
Convinced that war was inevitable, Virginian Patrick Henry gave a speech that contained the famous words, "I know not what course others may take, but as for me, give me liberty or give me death!"

**April 18–19, 1775: Paul Revere's Ride and the Battles of Lexington and Concord**
Paul Revere rode from Charlestown to Lexington to warn that the British were marching from Boston to seize the colonial armory at Concord.

**June 17, 1775: Battle of Bunker Hill**
About 2,300 British troops cleared the hill of the Americans, but at the cost of more than 40 percent of their force. The battle was a moral victory for the Americans.

**January 1776: Thomas Paine's Common Sense published**
This publication swayed the view of the war from that of a civil war to one of independence. It sold more than 100,000 copies within a few months.

**Spring of 1776: John Adams' Thoughts on Government written**

**July 4, 1776: Declaration of Independence adopted**
Congress voted for independence on July 2 and adopted the Declaration of Independence on July 4.

**September 22, 1776: Nathan Hale executed**
American Capt. Nathan Hale was captured by the British and hanged

without trial. Before his death, Hale is credited with saying, "I only regret that I have but one life to lose for my country."

## December 25–26, 1776: Washington crosses the Delaware
George Washington and the Continental Army surprised the Hessians at Trenton at dawn, and took roughly 900 prisoners. This and the Battle of Princeton (January 3, 1777) kept the battle for independence alive.

## 1776-1783: Thomas Paine writes The American Crisis papers

## October 17, 1777: Burgoyne surrenders at Saratoga
A British force under Gen. John Burgoyne captured Fort Ticonderoga (July 5) before he failed at Bennington, Vermont (August 16), and Bemis Heights, New York (October 7). His forces having been depleted, Burgoyne surrendered.

## December 19, 1777–June 19, 1778: Washington winters at Valley Forge
Although its ranks were decimated by disease, semi-starvation, and the cold, the Continental Army emerged the following June as a well-disciplined and more efficient fighting force.

## February 6, 1778: France and the United States form an alliance
With the signing of the Treaty of Amity and Commerce and the Treaty of Alliance, the French and American alliance became official.

## September 23, 1779: John Paul Jones: "I have not yet begun to fight!"
With his ship being destroyed, the American commander, John Paul Jones, refused to surrender. He claimed, "I have not yet begun to fight!"

## September 1780: Benedict Arnold turns traitor
American Gen. Benedict Arnold conspired with the British to surrender the fort at West Point, New York. When found out, he took sanctuary with the British.

## March 1, 1781: Articles of Confederation ratified
The Articles became the stepping stones for the U.S. Constitution.

INTRODUCTION

## September–October 1781: Siege of Yorktown
Lord Cornwallis entered Virginia, setting up a base at Yorktown. Washington's army and allies, placed Yorktown under siege, and Cornwallis surrendered.

## September 3, 1783: Treaty of Paris ends the war
Britain recognized the independence of the United States with boundaries including the Mississippi River on the west. Britain held Canada but gave East and West Florida to Spain.

## Spring of 1787: John Jay's An Address to the People of the State of New York published

## October 1787–May 1788: Federalist Papers written
A series of 85 essays written by John Jay, James Madison, and Alexander Hamilton in support of the proposed Constitution.

## April 30, 1789: Washington delivers his first inaugural address

## September 1796: Washington's Farewell Address is published
President Washington decides to leave public office after two terms, to help set a precedent for future presidents, and details his best wishes and advice for the future of the country.

## March 4, 1801: Thomas Jefferson's First Inaugural Address is delivered

## 1802–1807: John Adams' Autobiography is written
Adams writes his autobiography not for the public, but mainly to share his experiences with his children and family.

# THOMAS JEFFERSON
## (1743-1826)

# THOMAS JEFFERSON
## (1743-1826)

THOMAS JEFFERSON WAS BORN ON APRIL 13, 1743, at the Shadwell plantation by Charlottesville, Virginia, as the third-born of 10 siblings. His mother, Jane Randolph Jefferson, held membership in the Randolph clan, who claimed to be descended from English and Scottish royalty. His father, Peter Jefferson, was a successful farmer and skillful cartographer, producing the first accurate map of the Province of Virginia.

Jefferson began formal education at the age of nine, and studied Latin and Greek at a private school run by the Reverend William Douglas. In 1757, aged 14, he started studying more of the classical languages as well as literature and mathematics with the Reverend James Maury.

In 1760, Jefferson began his education at the College of William and Mary and became distraught to see his classmates spending their time courting women, betting on horse races, and playing cards, rather than studying. He joined a circle of older scholars, including Professor William Small, Lieutenant Governor Francis Fauquier, and lawyer George Wythe. They gave him his true education.

Jefferson spent three years at William and Mary and, afterwards, decided to read law under Wythe. Jefferson underwent an extremely rigorous five-year course of study, which was more than double the typical duration. By the time Jefferson won admission to the Virginia bar in 1767, he was already one of the most learned lawyers in America.

From 1767 to 1774, Jefferson practiced law in Virginia, winning most of his cases. During this time, he also fell in love with Martha Wayles Skelton, a recent widow who happened to be one of the wealthiest women in Virginia. They married on January 1, 1772 and had six children together, but only two survived into adulthood: Martha, their firstborn, and Mary, their fourth.

Jefferson being one of the earliest and strongest supporters of the Revolution, he was elected to the Virginia House of Burgesses in 1768. In 1774, Jefferson wrote his first major political work, *A Summary View of the Rights of British America.* In 1775, Jefferson attended the Second Continental Congress, which created the Continental Army and appointed Jefferson's fellow Virginian, George Washington, as its commander-in-chief, leaving the Congress' more important works to Jefferson himself, such as the Declaration of Independence.

In June 1776, the Congress appointed a five-man committee (Jefferson, John Adams, Benjamin Franklin, Roger Sherman and Robert Livingston) to draft the Declaration of Independence. The committee chose Jefferson to author the first draft, selecting him for what Adams referred to as Jefferson's "happy talent for composition and singular felicity of expression." Although the version that was eventually adopted underwent heavy revisions, Jefferson's words remained his own. After this, Jefferson returned to Virginia where he served as a member of the Virginia House of Delegates from 1776 to 1779. He sought to revise Virginia's laws to fit the American ideals he outlined in the Declaration of Independence.

On June 1, 1779, Jefferson was elected as Virginia's second governor and, during this time, became torn between the Continental Army's pleas for more men and supplies and Virginians' desire to keep such resources for their own defense. Jefferson declined a third term as governor and stepped down on June 4, 1781. He intended to give up public life for good and returned to Monticello, where he planned to live out the rest of his days surrounded by his family, his farm, and his books.

When his wife died on September 6, 1782, Jefferson mourned before returning to public life in June 1783 to lead the Virginia delegation to the Confederation Congress. In 1785, he was appointed as Ben Franklin's replacement as minister to France. He returned to America in 1789 as Washington's Secretary of State. Jefferson became the head of the Republican party, which advocated for a weaker national government. Jefferson once again became frustrated with politics and resigned on January 5, 1794.

Jefferson was thrust into the presidential race in 1797 and became the vice president to his friend, John Adams. This presidency showed issues with the government, which prompted Jefferson to run in 1800 and, ultimately, become president until 1809. He believed in a strict interpretation of the Constitution and thought that the federal government was too powerful. During his presidency, he made large contributions to the country, such as stabilizing the economy and brokering the Louisiana Purchase of 1805 that essentially doubled the size of the nation at the time. He finally finished his life as a farmer in Monticello and died of unknown causes on July 4, 1826, the 50th anniversary of his new nation's independence. He and John Adams both passed within five hours of each other, leading some to suspect a divine connection between the two men.

# THE DECLARATION OF INDEPENDENCE

## In Congress, July 4, 1776

**The unanimous Declaration of the thirteen united States of America**, When in the Course of human events, it becomes necessary for one people to dissolve the political bands which have connected them with another, and to assume among the powers of the earth, the separate and equal station to which the Laws of Nature and of Nature's God entitle them, a decent respect to the opinions of mankind requires that they should declare the causes which impel them to the separation.

We hold these truths to be self-evident, that all men are created equal, that they are endowed by their Creator with certain unalienable Rights, that among these are Life, Liberty and the pursuit of Happiness.--That to secure these rights, Governments are instituted among Men, deriving their just powers from the consent of the governed, --That whenever any Form of Government becomes destructive of these ends, it is the Right of the People to alter or to abolish it, and to institute new Government, laying its foundation on such principles and organizing its powers in such form, as to them shall seem most likely to effect their Safety and Happiness. Prudence, indeed, will dictate that Governments long established should not be changed for light and transient causes; and accordingly all experience hath shewn, that mankind are more disposed to suffer, while evils are sufferable, than to right themselves by abolishing the forms to which they are accustomed. But when a long train of abuses and usurpations, pursuing invariably the same Object evinces a design to reduce them under absolute Despotism, it is their right, it is their duty, to throw off such Government, and to provide new Guards for their future security.--Such has been the patient sufferance of these Colonies; and such is now the necessity which constrains them to alter their former Systems of Government. The history of the present King of Great Britain is a history of repeated injuries and usurpations, all having in direct object the establishment of an absolute Tyranny over these States. To prove this, let Facts be submitted to a candid world.

He has refused his Assent to Laws, the most wholesome and necessary for the public good.

He has forbidden his Governors to pass Laws of immediate and pressing importance, unless suspended in their operation till his Assent should be obtained; and when so suspended, he has utterly neglected to attend to them.

He has refused to pass other Laws for the accommodation of large districts of people, unless those people would relinquish the right of Representation in the Legislature, a right inestimable to them and formidable to tyrants only.

He has called together legislative bodies at places unusual, uncomfortable, and distant from the depository of their public Records, for the sole purpose of fatiguing them into compliance with his measures.

He has dissolved Representative Houses repeatedly, for opposing with manly firmness his invasions on the rights of the people.

He has refused for a long time, after such dissolutions, to cause others to be elected; whereby the Legislative powers, incapable of Annihilation, have returned to the People at large for their exercise; the State remaining in the mean time exposed to all the dangers of invasion from without, and convulsions within.

He has endeavoured to prevent the population of these States; for that purpose obstructing the Laws for Naturalization of Foreigners; refusing to pass others to encourage their migrations hither, and raising the conditions of new Appropriations of Lands.

He has obstructed the Administration of Justice, by refusing his Assent to Laws for establishing Judiciary powers.

He has made Judges dependent on his Will alone, for the tenure of their offices, and the amount and payment of their salaries.

He has erected a multitude of New Offices, and sent hither swarms of Officers to harrass our people, and eat out their substance.

He has kept among us, in times of peace, Standing Armies without the Consent of our legislatures.

He has affected to render the Military independent of and superior to the Civil power.

He has combined with others to subject us to a jurisdiction foreign to our constitution, and unacknowledged by our laws; giving his Assent to their Acts of pretended Legislation:

For Quartering large bodies of armed troops among us:

For protecting them, by a mock Trial, from punishment for any Murders which they should commit on the Inhabitants of these States:

For cutting off our Trade with all parts of the world:

For imposing Taxes on us without our Consent:

For depriving us in many cases, of the benefits of Trial by Jury:

For transporting us beyond Seas to be tried for pretended offences

For abolishing the free System of English Laws in a neighbouring Province, establishing therein an Arbitrary government, and enlarging its Boundaries so as to render it at once an example and fit instrument for introducing the same absolute rule into these Colonies:

For taking away our Charters, abolishing our most valuable Laws, and altering fundamentally the Forms of our Governments:

For suspending our own Legislatures, and declaring themselves invested with power to legislate for us in all cases whatsoever.

He has abdicated Government here, by declaring us out of his Protection and waging War against us.

He has plundered our seas, ravaged our Coasts, burnt our towns, and destroyed the lives of our people.

He is at this time transporting large Armies of foreign Mercenaries to compleat the works of death, desolation and tyranny, already begun with circumstances of Cruelty & perfidy scarcely paralleled in the most barbarous ages, and totally unworthy the Head of a civilized nation.

He has constrained our fellow Citizens taken Captive on the high Seas to bear Arms against their Country, to become the executioners of their friends and Brethren, or to fall themselves by their Hands.

He has excited domestic insurrections amongst us, and has endeavoured to bring on the inhabitants of our frontiers, the merciless Indian Savages, whose known rule of warfare, is an undistinguished destruction of all ages, sexes and conditions.

In every stage of these Oppressions We have Petitioned for Redress in the most humble terms: Our repeated Petitions have been answered only by repeated injury. A Prince whose character is thus marked by every act which may define a Tyrant, is unfit to be the ruler of a free people.

Nor have We been wanting in attentions to our Brittish brethren. We have warned them from time to time of attempts by their legislature to extend an unwarrantable jurisdiction over us. We have reminded them of the circumstances of our emigration and settlement here. We have appealed to their native justice and magnanimity, and we have conjured them by the ties of our common kindred to disavow these usurpations, which, would inevitably interrupt our connections and correspondence. They too have been deaf to the voice of justice and of consanguinity. We must, therefore, acquiesce in the necessity, which denounces our Separation, and hold them, as we hold the rest of mankind, Enemies in War, in Peace Friends.

We, therefore, the Representatives of the united States of America, in General Congress, Assembled, appealing to the Supreme Judge of the world for the rectitude of our intentions, do, in the Name, and by Authority of the good People of these Colonies, solemnly publish and declare, That these United Colonies are, and of Right ought to be Free and Independent States; that they are Absolved from all Allegiance to the British Crown, and that all political connection between them and the State of Great Britain, is and ought to be totally dissolved; and that as Free and Independent States, they have full Power to levy War, conclude Peace, contract Alliances, establish Commerce, and to do all other Acts and Things which Independent States may of right do. And for the support of this Declaration, with a firm reliance on the protection of divine Providence, we mutually pledge to each other our Lives, our Fortunes and our sacred Honor.

# FIRST INAUGURAL ADDRESS

[March 4, 1801]

Friends & fellow citizens

Called upon to undertake the duties of the first Executive office of our country, I avail myself of the presence of that portion of my fellow citizens which is here assembled to express my grateful thanks for the favor with which they have been pleased to look towards me, to declare a sincere consciousness that the task is above my talents, & that I approach it wth yos anxs & awfl presenttms, wch ye greatns of ye charge, & ye weakns of my powrs so justly inspire.

A rising nation spread over a wide & fruitful land, traversing all the seas with the rich productions of their industry, engaged in commerce with nations who feel power and forget right, advancing rapidly to destinies beyond the reach of mortal eye; when I contemplate these transcendt objects, & see the honor, the happins, & the hopes of this beloved country committed to the issue & the auspices of this day, I shrink from the contemplation, & humble myself before the magnitude of the undertaking.

Utterly indeed should I despair, did not the presence of many whom I here see, remind me, yt in the othr high authorties providd by our constñ, I shll find resources of wsdm, of virt. & of zeal, on wch to rely undr all difficulties.

To you then, gent. who are chargd with the sovern functions of legisn. & to those associated with you, I look wth encorgmt for yt guidce & supprt wch m enable us to steer wth safety, ye vessl in wch w'r all mbkd amdst ye conflctg elemts of a troubld sea.

During the contest of opinion through which we have passed, the animation of discussions and of exertions, has sometimes worn an aspect which might impose on strangers unused to think freely, & to speak & to write what they think.

But this being now decided by the voice of the nation, enounced according to the rules of the constitution, all will of course arrange

11

themselves under the will of the law, & unite in common efforts for the common good. All too wll bear in mind ys sacrd principle yt yo ye will of ye Majorty is in all cases to prevail, that will, to be rightful, must be reasonable: that the Minorty possess yr equal rights, wch equal laws must protect, & to violate would be oppression.

Let us then, fellow citizens, unite with one heart & one mind; let us restore to social intercourse that harmony & affection, without which Liberty, & even Life itself, are but dreary things.

And let us reflect that havg banishd frm our land yt religious in-tolce undr wch mankind so long bled & suffered we hve yet gaind little, if we countence a politicl intolrce, as despotc as wickd & capable of as bitter & bloody persecution.

During the throes and convulsions of the antient world, durg the agonisd spasms of infuriatd man, seeking through blood & slaughter his long lost liberty, it was not wonderful that the agitation of the bil-lows should reach even this distant & peaceful shore: that ys shd be more felt & feard by some, & less by others, & shd divide opinions as to measures of safety.

But every difference of opinion, is not a difference of principle. We have called, by different names, brethren of the same principle. We are all republicans: we are all federalists.

If there be any among us who wish to dissolve this union, or to change its republican form, let them stand undisturbed, as monuments of the safety wth wch error of opinn m b toleratd whre reasn is left free to combat it.

I know indd yt some honest men hve feard yt a republican govmt cannt be strong; yt this govmt is not strong enough. But wd the hon-est patriot, in the full tide of successfl experiment abandon a govmt wch hs so far kept us free & firm on ye theoretic & visionary fear yt ys govmt, the world's best hope m, by possibilty, want energy to preserve itself?

I trust not. I believe this, on the contrary, the strongest government on earth.

I believe it the only one where every man, at the call of the law, would fly to the standard of the law; would meet invasions of public order, as his own personal concern.

Some times it is said yt Man cannt be trustd wth ye govmt of him-self.—Can he yn be trustd wth ye govmt of others? Or have we found an-gels in ye form of kings to govern him?—Let History answr this question.

Let us yn pursue wth courge & confidce our own federl & republ princ. our attamt to Union and Representative govmt.

Kindly separated by nature, & a wide ocean, from the exterminating havoc of one quarter of the globe,

Too high-minded to endure the degradations of the others;

Possessing a chosen country, with room enough for all descendts to the 1,000th & 1,000th generation;

Entertaining a due sense of our equal right, to ye use of our own faculties, to ye acqusitns of our own industry, to honr & confidce frm our fel. cit. resultg nt from birth, but frm our actions & their sense of them, enlightnd by a benign religion, professd indeed & practiced in various forms, yet all of ym inculcatg honesty, truth, temperce gratitude, & the love of man, acknolegg & adoring an overruling providence, which by all it's dispensations proves that it delights in the happiness of man here, & his greater happiness hereafter:

With all these blessings, what more is necessary to make us a happy and a prosperous people? Still one thing more, fel. cit. a wise & frugl govmt, wch shall restrain men from injuring one another, shall leave them otherwise free to regulate their own pursuits of industry & improvement, and shall not take from the mouth of labor the bread it has earned.

This is the sum of good govmt, & this is necessary to close the circle of our felicities.

About to enter fel. cit. on the exercise of duties, which comprehend everything dear & valuable to you, it is proper you should understand what I deem the essential principle of this govmt and consequently those which ought to shape it's administration.

I will compress them in ye narrowst compass y wll bear, statg the genl principle, but not all it's limitations.

Equal & exact justice to all men, of whatever state or persuasion, religious or political:

Peace, commerce, & honest friendship with all nations, entangling alliances with none:

The support of the State govmts in all their rights, as ye most competent admns for our domestic concerns, and the surest bulwarks against anti republican tendencies:

The preservn of the Genl govmt, in it's whole constnal vigor, as ye sheet anchor of our peace at home, & safety abroad.

A jealous care of the right of election by the people, a mild & safe corrective of abuses, wch r loppd by ye sword of revoln, where peaceable remedies are unprovided.

Absolute acquiescence in ye decisns of ye Majorty ye vitl princip. of republics, frm wch is no appeal bt to force, ye vitl princip. & mmedte part of despotism.

A well discipld militia, our best reliance in peace, & for ye first moments of war, till regulars may relieve them: The Supremacy of the Civil over the Military authority:

Economy in public expense, that labor may be lightly burthened:

The honest paiment of our debts and sacred preservation of the public faith:

Encouragement of Agriculture, & of Commerce as it's handmaid:

The diffusion of information, & arraignmt of all abuses at the bar of the public reason:

Freedom of Religion, freedom of the press, & freedom of Person under the protection of the Hab. corpus: And trial by juries, impartially selected.

These Principles form ye bright constelln wch hs gone before us, & guidd our steps, thro' an age of Revoln and Reformn: The wisdom of our Sages, & blood of our Heroes, have been devoted to their attainment: they should be the Creed of our political faith, the Text of civic instruction, the Touchstone by which to try the services of those we trust; and should we wander from them, in moments of error or alarm, let us hasten to retrace our steps and to regain the road which alone leads to Peace, Liberty & Safety.

I repair then, fellow citizens to the post which you have assigned me.

With experience enough in subordinate stations to know the difficulties of this the greatest of all, I have learnt to expect that it will rarely fall to the lot of imperfect man to retire from this station with the reputation & the favor which bring him into it.

Without pretensions to that high confidce you reposed in our first & greatest revolutiony character whose preeminent services had entitled him to the first place in his country's love, and had destined for him the fairest page in the volume of faithful history, I ask so much confidence only as may give firmness & effect to the legal admn of your affairs.

I shall often go wrong thro' defect of judgment: when right, I shall often be thought wrong by yos whse positns wll nt command a view of the whole ground.

I ask your indulgence for my own errors, which will never be intentional: & your support agnst the errors of others who may condemn wt they wd nt if seen in all it's parts.

The approbation implied by your suffrage, is a great consolation to me for the past; and my future solicitude will be to retain the good opinion of yos who hve bestowed it in advance, to conciliate that of others, by doing them all the good in my power, and to be instrumental to the happiness & freedom of all.

Relying then on the patronage of your good will, I advance with obedience to the work, ready to retire frm it whenevr you become sensible how mch better choice it is in your power to make.

And may that infinite power which rules the destinies of the universe lead our councils to what is best, and give ym a favorable issue for your peace & prosperity.

# JOHN ADAMS
## (1735-1826)

# JOHN ADAMS
## (1735-1826)

B
ORN ON OCTOBER 30, 1735, IN Braintree (now Quincy), Massachusetts, John Adams was the son of John Adams Sr. and Susanna Boylston Adams. John Adams Sr. was a farmer, town councilman, and Congregationalist deacon as well as a direct descendant of Henry Adams, a Puritan who emigrated to the colonies. Susana Boylston Adams was a descendant of the Boylstons of Brookline, a prominent Massachusetts family.

Adams earned a scholarship to Harvard at the age of 16 and graduated at the age of 20, in 1755. Upon graduation, and despite the fact that his father wanted him to enter the ministry, Adams studied law with James Putnam, . He earned his master's degree from Harvard and admittance to the bar in 1758. On October 25, 1764, Adams married his third cousin, Abigail Smith. Together, they had six children (one of whom was eventually elected president in 1825: John Quincy Adams). Despite his large family, Adams was often away from home due to his political endeavors.

Adams quickly chose the patriot cause when the Stamp Act of 1765 was instituted, pushing him to speak out publicly against it. Nevertheless, when the Boston Massacre occurred in 1770, Adams didn't hesitate to provide the defense for the British soldiers, arguing that the facts of a case were more important than how people felt about it. As a result, six of the eight soldiers were acquitted, while two were charged with manslaughter, and Adams' law practice suffered due to his unpopular decision to represent the soldiers. However, this helped to solidify his reputation later on.

Also in 1770, Adams was elected to the Massachusetts Assembly and was a representative at the First Continental Congress in 1774. He was one of the representatives to nominate George Washington as commander-in-chief of the Continental Army. In May of 1776, the Congress approved a resolution by Adams that proposed that the colonies would each adopt independent governments. He wrote the preamble to the resolution, which was approved on May 15. This helped set up for the passage of the Declaration of Independence, which Adams was among those chosen to help draft. Adams supported Richard Henry Lee's resolution of independence until it was adopted on July 2, 1776.

Adams served on nearly 90 committees in the new government, which was more than any other Congressman. In 1777, he became the head of the Board of War and Ordnance, which oversaw the Continental army. In 1779, Adams was sent to negotiate the Treaty of Paris (1783). After the war, he stayed in Europe and helped arrange treaties of commerce with multiple European nations. He became the first U.S. minister to England in 1785.

Adams stayed in Europe for nearly 10 years, finally returning home in 1788. He was placed on the ballot for the 1789 presidency and came second, behind George Washington, making him the vice president. This same outcome occurred in the 1792 election. Adams was frustrated with his position, as he did not have much political influence with his president. When Washington stepped down, Adams ran again and won as the Federalist nominee in 1796, (Thomas Jefferson was the Democratic-Republican nominee).

A war between the French and British caused political difficulties for the new United States. Adams focused the nation's efforts on France, who had suspended commercial relations. Adams sent three commissioners to France, but the French refused to negotiate unless the United States agreed to pay what was, essentially, a bribe. When this became publicly known, the nation called for war. However, Adams refused to declare war. By 1800, this scuffle had ended, and Adams had become much less popular with the public, losing to Thomas Jefferson for re-election in 1800.

After his political life, Adams retired to his farm in Quincy, continuing to correspond with his former vice-president, Thomas Jefferson. He died at the age of 90, on July 4, 1826, the 50th anniversary of the signing of the Declaration of Independence. Thomas Jefferson also died within five hours of Adams, creating an atmosphere of unease, as two prominent presidents passed on the same anniversary of independence.

# AUTOBIOGRAPHY

1775. September. [At the appointed time, we returned to Philadelphia, and Congress were reassembled. Mr. Richard Penn had sailed for England, and carried the petition, from which Mr. Dickinson and his party expected relief. I expected none, and was wholly occupied in measures to support the army and the expedition into Canada. Every important step was opposed, and carried by bare majorities, which obliged me to be almost constantly engaged in debate; but I was not content with all that was done, and almost every day I had something to say about advising the States to institute governments, to express my total despair of any good from the petition or any of those things which were called conciliatory measures. I constantly insisted that all such measures, instead of having any tendency to produce a reconciliation, would only be considered as proofs of our timidity and want of confidence in the ground we stood on, and would only encourage our enemies to greater exertions against us; that we should be driven to the necessity of declaring ourselves independent States, and that we ought now to be employed in preparing a plan of confederation for the Colonies, and treaties to be proposed to foreign powers, particularly to France and Spain; that all these measures ought to be maturely considered and carefully prepared, together with a declaration of independence; that these three measures, independence, confederation, and negotiations with foreign powers, particularly France, ought to go hand in hand, and be adopted all together; that foreign powers could not be expected to acknowledge us till we had acknowledged ourselves, and taken our station among them as a sovereign power and independent nation; that now we were distressed for want of artillery, arms, ammunition, clothing, and even for flints; that the people had no markets for their produce, wanted clothing and many other things, which foreign commerce alone could fully supply, and we could not expect commerce till we were independent; that the people were wonderfully well united, and extremely ardent. There was no danger of our wanting support from them, if we did not discourage them by checking and quenching their zeal; that there was no doubt of our ability to defend the country, to support the war, and maintain our independence. We had men enough, our people were brave, and every day improving in all the exercises and discipline of war; that we ought immediately to give permission to our merchants to fit out privateers and make reprisals on the enemy; that Congress ought to arm ships, and commission officers, and lay the foundation of a navy; that immense advantages might be derived from this resource; that not only West India articles, in great abundance, and British manufactures, of all kinds, might be obtained, but artillery ammunitions and all kinds of supplies for the army; that a system of measures, taken with unanimity and pursued with resolution, would insure us the friendship and assistance of France.

Some gentlemen doubted of the sentiments of France; thought she would frown upon us as rebels, and be afraid to countenance the example. I replied to those gentlemen, that I apprehended they had not attended to the relative situation of France and England; that it was the unquestionable interest of France that the British Continental Colonies should be independent; that Britain, by the conquest of Canada and her naval triumphs during the last war, and by her vast possessions in America and the East Indies, was exalted to a height of power and preëminence that France must envy and could not endure. But there was much more than pride and jealousy in the case. Her rank, her consideration in Europe, and even her safety and independence, were at stake. The navy of Great Britain was now mistress of the seas, all over the globe. The navy of France almost annihilated. Its inferiority was so great and obvious, that all the dominions of France, in the West Indies and in the East Indies, lay at the mercy of Great Britain, and must remain so as long as North America belonged to Great Britain, and afforded them so many harbors abounding with naval stores and resources of all kinds, and so many men and seamen ready to assist them and man their ships; that interest could not lie; that the interest of France was so obvious, and her motives so cogent, that nothing but a judicial infatuation of her councils could restrain her from embracing us; that our negotiations with France ought, however, to be conducted with great caution, and with all the foresight we could possibly obtain; that we ought not to enter into any alliance with her, which should entangle us in any future wars in Europe; that we ought to lay it down, as a first principle and a maxim never to be forgotten, to maintain an entire neutrality in all future European wars; that it never could be our interest to unite with France in the destruction of England, or in any measures to break her spirit, or reduce her to a situation in which she could not support her independence. On the other hand, it could never be our duty to unite with Britain in too great a humiliation of France; that our real, if not our nominal, independence, would consist in our neutrality. If we united with either nation, in any future war, we must become too subordinate and dependent on that nation, and should be involved in all European wars, as we had been hitherto; that foreign powers would find means to corrupt our people, to influence our councils, and, in fine, we should be little better than puppets, danced on the wires of the cabinets of Europe. We should be the sport of European intrigues and politics; that, therefore, in preparing treaties to be proposed to foreign powers, and in the instructions to be given to our ministers, we ought to confine ourselves strictly to a treaty of commerce; that such a treaty would be an ample compensation to France for all the aid we should want from her. The opening of American trade to her, would be a vast resource for her commerce and naval power, and a great assistance to her in protecting her East and West India possessions, as well as her fisheries; but that the bare dismemberment of the British empire would be to her an incalculable security and benefit, worth more than all the exertions we should require of her, even if it should draw her into another eight or ten years' war.

When I first made these observations in Congress, I never saw a greater impression made upon that assembly or any other. Attention and approbation were marked upon every countenance. Several gentlemen came to me afterwards, to thank me for that speech, particularly Mr. Cæsar Rodney, of Delaware, and Mr. Duane, of New York. I remember these two gentlemen in particular, because both of them said that I had considered the subject of foreign connections more maturely than any man they had ever heard in America; that I had perfectly digested the subject, and had removed, Mr. Rodney said, all, and Mr. Duane said, the greatest part of his objections to foreign negotiations. Even Mr. Dickinson said, to gentlemen out of doors, that I had thrown great light on the subject.

These and such as these, were my constant and daily topics, sometimes of reasoning and no doubt often of declamation, from the meeting of Congress in the autumn of 1775, through the whole winter and spring of 1776.

Many motions were made, and after tedious discussions, lost. I received little assistance from my colleagues in all these contests; three of them were either inclined to lean towards Mr. Dickinson's system, or at least chose to be silent, and the fourth spoke but rarely in Congress, and never entered into any extensive arguments, though, when he did speak, his sentiments were clear and pertinent and neatly expressed. Mr. Richard Henry Lee, of Virginia, Mr. Sherman, of Connecticut, and Mr. Gadsden, of South Carolina, were always on my side, and Mr. Chase, of Maryland, when he did speak at all, was always powerful, and generally with us. Mr. Johnson, of Maryland, was the most frequent speaker from that State, and, while he remained with us, was inclined to Mr. Dickinson for some time, but ere long he and all his State came cordially into our system. In the fall of 1776, his State appointed him General of militia, and he marched to the relief of General Washington in the Jerseys. He was afterwards chosen Governor of Maryland, and he came no more to Congress.

In the course of this winter appeared a phenomenon in Philadelphia, a disastrous meteor, I mean Thomas Paine. He came from England, and got into such company as would converse with him, and ran about picking up what information he could concerning our affairs, and finding the great question was concerning independence, he gleaned from those he saw the common-place arguments, such as the necessity of independence at some time or other; the peculiar fitness at this time; the justice of it; the provocation to it; our ability to maintain it, &c. &c. Dr. Rush put him upon writing on the subject, furnished him with the arguments which had been urged in Congress a hundred times, and gave him his title of "Common Sense." In the latter part of winter, or early in the spring, he came out with his pamphlet. The arguments in favor of independence I liked very well; but one third part of the book was filled with arguments, from the Old Testament, to prove the unlawfulness of monarchy, and another third, in planning a form of government for the separate States, in one assembly, and for the United States, in a Congress. His arguments from the Old Testament were ridiculous, but whether they proceeded from honest ignorance or foolish superstition on one hand, or from wilful sophistry and knavish hypocrisy on the other, I know not. The other third part, relative to a form of government, I considered as flowing from simple ignorance, and a mere desire to please the democratic party, in Philadelphia, at whose head were Mr. Matlack, Mr. Cannon, and Dr. Young. I regretted, however, to see so foolish a plan recommended to the people of the United States, who were all waiting only for the countenance of Congress to institute their State governments. I dreaded the effect so popular a pamphlet might have among the people, and determined to do all in my power to counteract the effect of it. My continual occupations in Congress allowed me no time to write any thing of any length; but I found moments to write a small pamphlet, which Mr. Richard Henry Lee, to whom I showed it, liked so well, that he insisted on my permitting him to publish it. He accordingly got Mr. Dunlap to print it, under the title of "Thoughts on Government, in a letter from a gentleman to his friend." Common Sense was published without a name, and I thought it best to suppress my name too. But as Common Sense, when it first appeared, was generally by the public ascribed to me or Mr. Samuel Adams, I soon regretted that my name did not appear. Afterwards I had a new edition of it printed, with my name and the name of Mr. Wythe, of Virginia, to whom the letter was at first intended to be addressed. The gentlemen of New York availed themselves of the ideas in this morsel, in the formation of the constitution of that State. And Mr. Lee sent it to the convention of Virginia, when they met to form their government, and it went to North Carolina, New Jersey, and other States. Matlack, Cannon, Young, and Paine, had influence enough, however, to get their plan adopted in substance in Georgia and Vermont, as well as Pennsylvania. These three States have since found them such systems of anarchy, if that expression is not a contradiction in terms, that they have altered them and made them more conformable to my plan.

Paine, soon after the appearance of my pamphlet, hurried away to my lodgings and spent an evening with me. His business was to reprehend me for publishing my pamphlet; said he was afraid it would do hurt, and that it was repugnant to the plan he had proposed in his Common Sense. I told him it was true it was repugnant, and for that reason I had written it and consented to the publication of it; for I was as much afraid of his work as he was of mine. His plan was so demo-cratical, without any restraints or even an attempt at any equilibrium or counterpoise, that it must produce confusion and every evil work. I told him further, that his reasoning from the Old Testament was ri-diculous, and I could hardly think him sincere. At this he laughed, and said he had taken his ideas in that part from Milton; and then expressed a contempt of the Old Testament, and indeed of the Bible at large, which surprised me. He saw that I did not relish this, and soon checked himself with these words: "However, I have some thoughts of publishing my thoughts on religion, but I believe it will be best to postpone it to the latter part of life." This conversation passed in good humor, without any harshness on either side; but I perceived in him a conceit of himself and a daring impudence, which have been developed more and more to this day.

The third part of Common Sense, which relates wholly to the ques-tion of independence, was clearly written, and contained a tolerable summary of the arguments which I had been repeating again and again in Congress for nine months. But I am bold to say there is not a fact nor a reason stated in it, which had not been frequently urged in Congress. The temper and wishes of the people supplied every thing at that time; and the phrases, suitable for an emigrant from Newgate, or one who had chiefly associated with such company, such as, "The Royal Brute of England," "The blood upon his soul," and a few others of equal delica-cy, had as much weight with the people as his arguments. It has been a general opinion that this pamphlet was of great importance in the Revolution. I doubted it at the time, and have doubted it to this day. It probably converted some to the doctrine of independence, and gave others an excuse for declaring in favor of it. But these would all have fol-lowed Congress with zeal; and on the other hand it excited many writers against it, particularly "Plain Truth," who contributed very largely to fortify and inflame the party against independence, and finally lost us the Allens, Penns, and many other persons of weight in the community.

Notwithstanding these doubts, I felt myself obliged to Paine for the pains he had taken, and for his good intentions to serve us, which I then had no doubt of. I saw he had a capacity and a ready pen; and, understanding he was poor and destitute, I thought we might put him into some employment where he might be useful and earn a living.

Congress appointed a Committee of Foreign Affairs, not long after, and they wanted a clerk. I nominated Thomas Paine, supposing him a ready writer and an industrious man. Dr. Witherspoon, the President of New Jersey College, and then a delegate from that State, rose and objected to it with an earnestness that surprised me. The Doctor said he would give his reasons; he knew the man and his communication; when he first came over, he was on the other side, and had written pieces against the American cause; that he had afterwards been employed by his friend, Robert Aitkin, and finding the tide of popularity run rapidly, he had turned about; that he was very intemperate, and could not write until he had quickened his thoughts with large draughts of rum and water; that he was, in short, a bad character, and not fit to be placed in such a situation. General Roberdeau spoke in his favor; no one confirmed Witherspoon's account, though the truth of it has since been sufficiently established. Congress appointed him; but he was soon obnoxious by his manners, and dismissed.

There was one circumstance in his conversation with me about the pamphlets, which I could not account for. He was extremely earnest to convince me that "Common Sense" was his first born; declared again and again that he had never written a line nor a word that had been printed, before "Common Sense." I cared nothing for this, and said nothing; but Dr. Witherspoon's account of his writing against us, brought doubts into my mind of his veracity, which the subsequent histories of his writings and publications in England, when he was in the custom-house, did not remove. At this day it would be ridiculous to ask any questions about Tom Paine's veracity, integrity, or any other virtue.

I was incessantly employed through the whole fall, winter, and spring of 1775 and 1776, in Congress during their sittings, and on committees on mornings and evenings, and unquestionably did more business than any other member of that house. In the beginning of May, I procured the appointment of a committee, to prepare a resolution recommending to the people of the States to institute governments. The committee, of whom I was one, requested me to draught a resolve, which I did, and by their direction reported it. Opposition was made to it, and Mr. Duane called it a machine to fabricate independence, but on the 15th of May, 1776, it passed. It was indeed, on all hands, considered by men of understanding as equivalent to a declaration of independence, though a formal declaration of it was still opposed by Mr. Dickinson and his party.

Not long after this, the three greatest measures of all were carried. Three committees were appointed, one for preparing a declaration of independence, another for reporting a plan of a treaty to be proposed to France, and a third to digest a system of articles of confederation to be proposed to the States. I was appointed on the committee of independence, and on that for preparing the form of a treaty with France. On the committee of confederation Mr. Samuel Adams was appointed. The committee of independence were Thomas Jefferson, John Adams, Benjamin Franklin, Roger Sherman, and Robert R. Livingston. Mr. Jefferson had been now about a year a member of Congress, but had attended his duty in the house a very small part of the time, and, when there, had never spoken in public. During the whole time I sat with him in Congress, I never heard him utter three sentences together. It will naturally be inquired how it happened that he was appointed on a committee of such importance. There were more reasons than one. Mr. Jefferson had the reputation of a masterly pen; he had been chosen a delegate in Virginia, in consequence of a very handsome public paper which he had written for the House of Burgesses, which had given him the character of a fine writer. Another reason was, that Mr. Richard Henry Lee was not beloved by the most of his colleagues from Virginia, and Mr. Jefferson was set up to rival and supplant him. This could be done only by the pen, for Mr. Jefferson could stand no competition with him or any one else in elocution and public debate.

Here I will interrupt the narration for a moment to observe, that, from all I have read of the history of Greece and Rome, England and France, and all I have observed at home and abroad, eloquence in public assemblies is not the surest road to fame or preferment, at least, unless it be used with caution, very rarely, and with great reserve. The examples of Washington, Franklin, and Jefferson, are enough to show that silence and reserve in public, are more efficacious than argumentation or oratory. A public speaker who inserts himself, or is urged by others, into the conduct of affairs, by daily exertions to justify his measures, and answer the objections of opponents, makes himself too familiar with the public, and unavoidably makes himself enemies. Few persons can bear to be outdone in reasoning or declamation or wit or sarcasm or repartee or satire, and all these things are very apt to grow out of public debate. In this way, in a course of years, a nation becomes full of a man's enemies, or at least, of such as have been galled in some controversy, and take a secret pleasure in assisting to humble and mortify him. So much for this digression. We will now return to our memoirs.

The committee had several meetings, in which were proposed the articles of which the declaration was to consist, and minutes made of them. The committee then appointed Mr. Jefferson and me to draw them up in form, and clothe them in a proper dress. The sub-committee met, and considered the minutes, making such observations on them as then occurred, when Mr. Jefferson desired me to take them to my lodgings, and make the draught. This I declined, and gave several reasons for declining. 1. That he was a Virginian, and I a Massachusettensian. 2. That he was a southern man, and I a northern one. 3. That I had been so obnoxious for my early and constant zeal in promoting the measure, that any draught of mine would undergo a more severe scrutiny and criticism in Congress, than one of his composition. 4. and lastly, and that would be reason enough if there were no other, I had a great opinion of the elegance of his pen, and none at all of my own. I therefore insisted that no hesitation should be made on his part. He accordingly took the minutes, and in a day or two produced to me his draught. Whether I made or suggested any correction, I remember not. The report was made to the committee of five, by them examined, but whether altered or corrected in any thing, I cannot recollect. But, in substance at least, it was reported to Congress, where, after a severe criticism, and striking out several of the most oratorical paragraphs, it was adopted on the fourth of July, 1776, and published to the world.

The committee for preparing the model of a treaty to be proposed to France, consisted of Mr. Dickinson, Mr. Franklin, Mr. John Adams, Mr. Harrison, and Mr. Robert Morris. When we met to deliberate on the subject, I contended for the same principles which I had before avowed and defended in Congress, namely, that we should avoid all alliance which might embarrass us in after times, and involve us in future European wars; that a treaty of commerce which would operate as a repeal of the British acts of navigation so far as respected us, and admit France into an equal participation of the benefits of our com-

merce, would encourage her manufactures, increase her exports of the
produce of her soil and agriculture, extend her navigation and trade,
augment her resources of naval power, raise her from her present deep
humiliation, distress, and decay, and place her on a more equal footing
with England, for the protection of her foreign possessions; and maintaining her independence at sea, would be an ample compensation to
France for acknowledging our independence, and for furnishing us, for
our money, or upon credit for a time, with such supplies of necessaries
as we should want, even if this conduct should involve her in a war; if a
war should ensue, which did not necessarily follow, for a bare acknowledgment of our independence, after we had asserted it, was not by the
law of nations an act of hostility, which would be a legitimate cause
of war. Franklin, although he was commonly as silent on committees
as in Congress, upon this occasion, ventured so far as to intimate his
concurrence with me in these sentiments; though, as will be seen hereafter, he shifted them as easily as the wind ever shifted, and assumed a
dogmatical tone in favor of an opposite system. The committee, after as
much deliberation upon the subject as they chose to employ, appointed
me to draw up a plan and report. Franklin had made some marks with
a pencil against some articles in a printed volume of treaties, which he
put into my hand. Some of these were judiciously selected, and I took
them, with others which I found necessary, into the draught, and made
my report to the committee at large, who, after a reasonable examination of it, agreed to report it. When it came before Congress, it occupied the attention of that body for several days. Many motions were
made to insert in it articles of entangling alliance, of exclusive privileges, and of warranties of possessions; and it was argued that the present
plan reported by the committee held out no sufficient temptation to
France, who would despise it and refuse to receive our Ambassador.
It was chiefly left to me to defend my report, though I had some able
assistance, and we did defend it with so much success that the treaty
passed without one particle of alliance, exclusive privilege, or warranty.

# Thoughts on Government

My dear Sir,—If I was equal to the task of forming a plan for the government of a colony, I should be flattered with your request, and very happy to comply with it; because, as the divine science of politics is the science of social happiness, and the blessings of society depend entirely on the constitutions of government, which are generally institutions that last for many generations, there can be no employment more agreeable to a benevolent mind than a research after the best.

Pope flattered tyrants too much when he said,

"For forms of government let fools contest,
That which is best administered is best."

Nothing can be more fallacious than this. But poets read history to collect flowers, not fruits; they attend to fanciful images, not the effects of social institutions. Nothing is more certain, from the history of nations and nature of man, than that some forms of government are better fitted for being well administered than others.

We ought to consider what is the end of government, before we determine which is the best form. Upon this point all speculative politicians will agree, that the happiness of society is the end of government, as all divines and moral philosophers will agree that the happiness of the individual is the end of man. From this principle it will follow, that the form of government which communicates ease, comfort, security, or, in one word, happiness, to the greatest number of persons, and in the greatest degree, is the best.

All sober inquirers after truth, ancient and modern, pagan and Christian, have declared that the happiness of man, as well as his dignity, consists in virtue. Confucius, Zoroaster, Socrates, Mahomet, not to mention authorities really sacred, have agreed in this.

If there is a form of government, then, whose principle and foundation is virtue, will not every sober man acknowledge it better calculated to promote the general happiness than any other form?

31

Fear is the foundation of most governments; but it is so sordid and brutal a passion, and renders men in whose breasts it predominates so stupid and miserable, that Americans will not be likely to approve of any political institution which is founded on it.

Honor is truly sacred, but holds a lower rank in the scale of moral excellence than virtue. Indeed, the former is but a part of the latter, and consequently has not equal pretensions to support a frame of government productive of human happiness.

The foundation of every government is some principle or passion in the minds of the people. The noblest principles and most generous affections in our nature, then, have the fairest chance to support the noblest and most generous models of government.

A man must be indifferent to the sneers of modern Englishmen, to mention in their company the names of Sidney, Harrington, Locke, Milton, Nedham, Neville, Burnet, and Hoadly. No small fortitude is necessary to confess that one has read them. The wretched condition of this country, however, for ten or fifteen years past, has frequently reminded me of their principles and reasonings. They will convince any candid mind, that there is no good government but what is republican. That the only valuable part of the British constitution is so; because the very definition of a republic is "an empire of laws, and not of men." That, as a republic is the best of governments, so that particular arrangement of the powers of society, or, in other words, that form of government which is best contrived to secure an impartial and exact execution of the laws, is the best of republics.

Of republics there is an inexhaustible variety, because the possible combinations of the powers of society are capable of innumerable variations.

As good government is an empire of laws, how shall your laws be made? In a large society, inhabiting an extensive country, it is impossible that the whole should assemble to make laws. The first necessary step, then, is to depute power from the many to a few of the most wise and good. But by what rules shall you choose your representatives? Agree upon the number and qualifications of persons who shall have the benefit of choosing, or annex this privilege to the inhabitants of a certain extent of ground.

The principal difficulty lies, and the greatest care should be employed, in constituting this representative assembly. It should be in miniature an exact portrait of the people at large. It should think, feel, reason, and act like them. That it may be the interest of this assembly to do strict justice at all times, it should be an equal representation, or, in other words, equal interests among the people should have equal interests in it. Great care should be taken to effect this, and to prevent unfair, partial, and corrupt elections. Such regulations, however, may be better made in times of greater tranquillity than the present; and they will spring up themselves naturally, when all the powers of government come to be in the hands of the people's friends. At present, it will be safest to proceed in all established modes, to which the people have been familiarized by habit.

A representation of the people in one assembly being obtained, a question arises, whether all the powers of government, legislative, executive, and judicial, shall be left in this body? I think a people cannot be long free, nor ever happy, whose government is in one assembly. My reasons for this opinion are as follow:—

1. A single assembly is liable to all the vices, follies, and frailties of an individual; subject to fits of humor, starts of passion, flights of enthusiasm, partialities, or prejudice, and consequently productive of hasty results and absurd judgments. And all these errors ought to be corrected and defects supplied by some controlling power.

2. A single assembly is apt to be avaricious, and in time will not scruple to exempt itself from burdens, which it will lay, without compunction, on its constituents.

3. A single assembly is apt to grow ambitious, and after a time will not hesitate to vote itself perpetual. This was one fault of the Long Parliament; but more remarkably of Holland, whose assembly first voted themselves from annual to septennial, then for life, and after a course of years, that all vacancies happening by death or otherwise, should be filled by themselves, without any application to constituents at all.

4. A representative assembly, although extremely well qualified, and absolutely necessary, as a branch of the legislative, is unfit to exercise the executive power, for want of two essential properties, secrecy and despatch.

5. A representative assembly is still less qualified for the judicial power, because it is too numerous, too slow, and too little skilled in the laws.

6. Because a single assembly, possessed of all the powers of government, would make arbitrary laws for their own interest, execute all laws arbitrarily for their own interest, and adjudge all controversies in their own favor.

But shall the whole power of legislation rest in one assembly? Most of the foregoing reasons apply equally to prove that the legislative power ought to be more complex; to which we may add, that if the legislative power is wholly in one assembly, and the executive in another, or in a single person, these two powers will oppose and encroach upon each other, until the contest shall end in war, and the whole power, legislative and executive, be usurped by the strongest.

The judicial power, in such case, could not mediate, or hold the balance between the two contending powers, because the legislative would undermine it. And this shows the necessity, too, of giving the executive power a negative upon the legislative, otherwise this will be continually encroaching upon that.

To avoid these dangers, let a distinct assembly be constituted, as a mediator between the two extreme branches of the legislature, that which represents the people, and that which is vested with the executive power.

Let the representative assembly then elect by ballot, from among themselves or their constituents, or both, a distinct assembly, which, for the sake of perspicuity, we will call a council. It may consist of any number you please, say twenty or thirty, and should have a free and independent exercise of its judgment, and consequently a negative voice in the legislature.

These two bodies, thus constituted, and made integral parts of the legislature, let them unite, and by joint ballot choose a governor, who, after being stripped of most of those badges of domination, called prerogatives, should have a free and independent exercise of his judgment, and be made also an integral part of the legislature. This, I know, is liable to objections; and, if you please, you may make him only president of the council, as in Connecticut. But as the governor is to be invested with the executive power, with consent of council, I think he ought to have a negative upon the legislative. If he is annually elective, as he ought to be, he will always have so much reverence and affection for the people, their representatives and counsellors, that, although you give him an independent exercise of his judgment, he will seldom use it in opposition to the two houses, except in cases the public utility of which would be conspicuous; and some such cases would happen.

In the present exigency of American affairs, when, by an act of Parliament, we are put out of the royal protection, and consequently discharged from our allegiance, and it has become necessary to assume government for our immediate security, the governor, lieutenant-governor, secretary, treasurer, commissary, attorney-general, should be chosen by joint ballot of both houses. And these and all other elections, especially of representatives and counsellors, should be annual, there not being in the whole circle of the sciences a maxim more infallible than this, "where annual elections end, there slavery begins."

These great men, in this respect, should be, once a year,

"Like bubbles on the sea of matter borne,
They rise, they break, and to that sea return."

This will teach them the great political virtues of humility, patience, and moderation, without which every man in power becomes a ravenous beast of prey.

This mode of constituting the great offices of state will answer very well for the present; but if by experiment it should be found inconvenient, the legislature may, at its leisure, devise other methods of creating them, by elections of the people at large, as in Connecticut, or it may enlarge the term for which they shall be chosen to seven years, or three years, or for life, or make any other alterations which the society shall find productive of its ease, its safety, its freedom, or, in one word, its happiness.

A rotation of all offices, as well as of representatives and counsellors, has many advocates, and is contended for with many plausible arguments. It would be attended, no doubt, with many advantages; and if the society has a sufficient number of suitable characters to supply the great number of vacancies which would be made by such a rotation, I can see no objection to it. These persons may be allowed to serve for three years, and then be excluded three years, or for any longer or shorter term.

Any seven or nine of the legislative council may be made a quorum, for doing business as a privy council, to advise the governor in the exercise of the executive branch of power, and in all acts of state.

The governor should have the command of the militia and of all your armies. The power of pardons should be with the governor and council.

Judges, justices, and all other officers, civil and military, should be nominated and appointed by the governor, with the advice and consent of council, unless you choose to have a government more popular; if you do, all officers, civil and military, may be chosen by joint ballot of both houses; or, in order to preserve the independence and importance of each house, by ballot of one house, concurred in by the other.

Sheriffs should be chosen by the freeholders of counties; so should registers of deeds and clerks of counties.

All officers should have commissions, under the hand of the governor and seal of the colony.

The dignity and stability of government in all its branches, the morals of the people, and every blessing of society depend so much upon an upright and skilful administration of justice, that the judicial power ought to be distinct from both the legislative and executive, and independent upon both, that so it may be a check upon both, as both should be checks upon that. The judges, therefore, should be always men of learning and experience in the laws, of exemplary morals, great patience, calmness, coolness, and attention. Their minds should not be distracted with jarring interests; they should not be dependent upon any man, or body of men. To these ends, they should hold estates for life in their offices; or, in other words, their commissions should be during good behavior, and their salaries ascertained and established by law. For misbehavior, the grand inquest of the colony, the house of representatives, should impeach them before the governor and council, where they should have time and opportunity to make their defence; but, if convicted, should be removed from their offices, and subjected to such other punishment as shall be thought proper.

A militia law, requiring all men, or with very few exceptions besides cases of conscience, to be provided with arms and ammunition, to be trained at certain seasons; and requiring counties, towns, or other small districts, to be provided with public stocks of ammunition and intrenching utensils, and with some settled plans for transporting provisions after the militia, when marched to defend their country against sudden invasions; and requiring certain districts to be provided with field-pieces, companies of matrosses, and perhaps some regiments of light-horse, is always a wise institution, and, in the present circumstances of our country, indispensable.

Laws for the liberal education of youth, especially of the lower class of people, are so extremely wise and useful, that, to a humane and generous mind, no expense for this purpose would be thought extravagant.

The very mention of sumptuary laws will excite a smile. Whether our countrymen have wisdom and virtue enough to submit to them, I know not; but the happiness of the people might be greatly promoted by them,

THOUGHTS ON GOVERNMENT 37

and a revenue saved sufficient to carry on this war forever. Frugality is a great revenue, besides curing us of vanities, levities, and fopperies, which are real antidotes to all great, manly, and warlike virtues.

But must not all commissions run in the name of a king? No. Why may they not as well run thus, "The colony of to A. B. greeting," and be tested by the governor?

Why may not writs, instead of running in the name of the king, run thus, "The colony of to the sheriff," &c., and be tested by the chief justice?

Why may not indictments conclude, "against the peace of the colony of and the dignity of the same?"

A constitution founded on these principles introduces knowledge among the people, and inspires them with a conscious dignity becoming freemen; a general emulation takes place, which causes good humor, sociability, good manners, and good morals to be general. That elevation of sentiment inspired by such a government, makes the common people brave and enterprising. That ambition which is inspired by it makes them sober, industrious, and frugal. You will find among them some elegance, perhaps, but more solidity; a little pleasure, but a great deal of business; some politeness, but more civility. If you compare such a country with the regions of domination, whether monarchical or aristocratical, you will fancy yourself in Arcadia or Elysium.

If the colonies should assume governments separately, they should be left entirely to their own choice of the forms; and if a continental constitution should be formed, it should be a congress, containing a fair and adequate representation of the colonies, and its authority should sacredly be confined to these cases, namely, war, trade, disputes between colony and colony, the post-office, and the unappropriated lands of the crown, as they used to be called.

These colonies, under such forms of government, and in such a union, would be unconquerable by all the monarchies of Europe.

You and I, my dear friend, have been sent into life at a time when the greatest lawgivers of antiquity would have wished to live. How few of the human race have ever enjoyed an opportunity of making an election of government, more than of air, soil, or climate, for themselves or their children! When, before the present epocha, had three millions of people full power and a fair opportunity to form and establish the wisest and happiest government that human wisdom can contrive? I hope you will avail yourself and your country of that extensive learning and indefatigable industry which you possess, to assist her in the formation of the happiest governments and the best character of a great people. For myself, I must beg you to keep my name out of sight; for this feeble attempt, if it should be known to be mine, would oblige me to apply to myself those lines of the immortal John Milton, in one of his sonnets:—

> "I did but prompt the age to quit their clogs
> By the known rules of ancient liberty,
> When straight a barbarous noise environs me
> Of owls and cuckoos, asses, apes, and dogs."

# JAMES MADISON
## (1751-1836)

# James Madison
## (1751-1836)

JAMES MADISON WAS BORN ON MARCH 16, 1751, in Port Conway, Virginia, though he grew up in Orange County. The eldest of 12 children and with a successful planter as a father, Madison was off to a strong start when he was sent to boarding school in 1762. He returned home after five years to receive private tutoring, because his father was concerned about his health. Madison stood at 5' 4" and weighed only about 100 pounds. He had a quiet voice, and people saw him as weak. Eventually, in 1769, Madison attended college at the College of New Jersey (now Princeton University). He studied Greek, Latin, philosophy, science, and other subjects before graduating in 1771.

Madison returned to Virginia in 1772 and was elected to the Orange County Committee of Safety in December of 1774. In 1775, he joined the Virginia militia at the rank of colonel. Drawing on his strength in writing, Madison impressed attendees at the Virginia Convention in 1776. It was around this time that he met Thomas Jefferson, who would become a lifelong friend. Working with George Mason, Madison made significant contributions to the Virginia Constitution.

In 1777, Madison ran for a seat on the Virginia Council, which he lost, but was eventually appointed to the Governor's Council. He strongly supported the alliance with France during the Revolutionary War and handled much of the Council's correspondence with the French. He also served as one of Virginia's representatives in the Continental Congress in 1780. In 1783, Madison returned to Virginia and once again served in the state's legislature where he helped advocate for religious freedom and separation of church and state. In 1787, Madison helped to craft the U.S. Constitution.

Madison is known as the Father of the Constitution because he birthed many of the ideas contained within it, such as a strong central government that consisted of three parts: executive, legislative, judicial.

In addition to this, given the heavy opposition that the Constitution received in several colonies, Madison joined John Jay and Alexander Hamilton to write a series of essays, known as *The Federalist Papers*, which were successful in helping to secure the ratification of the Constitution.

In 1789, Madison won a seat in the House of Representatives where he had an important role in the creation of the Bill of Rights, which protected the individual liberties of the U.S. citizenry. He originally supported George Washington but grew to dislike Washington's administration due to financial issues, including policies by Secretary of Treasury Hamilton, such as the proposition for a national bank. Around 1791, Madison and Jefferson split from the Federalist Party and created the Democratic-Republican Party.

Madison met and married his wife, Dolley, in 1794. He eventually tired of politics, returning to Virginia in 1797, but this didn't last long. In 1801, Madison became the Secretary of State for Jefferson's administration and supported the president in many of his ventures, such as the Louisiana Purchase in 1803. To prevent American merchants from being captured and forced into service by warring French and Britain, Madison campaigned for the highly unpopular Embargo Act of 1807, which prohibited American exports and trading with foreign ports. Surprisingly, though, in 1808, Madison ran for president and won. The Embargo Act of 1807 was repealed in 1809 and replaced with the Non-Intercourse Act, which only barred trading with France and Britain and it didn't help the growing tensions between the new nation and the older countries.

Given these tensions, many Americans began calling for war, which Madison didn't want, but knew that the country wouldn't stand for the attacks on its citizens. In June 1812, the U.S. declared war on Britain, now known as The War of 1812. Madison won his second bid for president in 1812, and the war continued through 1814 when the British invaded Maryland and burned many official buildings. The war finally ended in 1815.

Madison left office in 1817 and returned to his plantation, helping create the University of Virginia and assuming the role of leadership in 1826 when Jefferson, who was the rector at the time, passed away. In 1829, Madison served as a delegate to the state's Constitutional Convention and was active in the American Colonization Society, which he helped found in 1816. The aim of the Society was to return freed slaves to Africa. Madison became the president of the Society in 1833. On June 28, 1836, Madison died from heart failure.

# The Federalist Papers

## #39 (Conformity of the Plan to Republican Principles)

To the People of the State of New York:

THE last paper having concluded the observations which were meant to introduce a candid survey of the plan of government reported by the convention, we now proceed to the execution of that part of our undertaking.

The first question that offers itself is, whether the general form and aspect of the government be strictly republican. It is evident that no other form would be reconcilable with the genius of the people of America; with the fundamental principles of the Revolution; or with that honorable determination which animates every votary of freedom, to rest all our political experiments on the capacity of mankind for self-government. If the plan of the convention, therefore, be found to depart from the republican character, its advocates must abandon it as no longer defensible.

What, then, are the distinctive characters of the republican form? Were an answer to this question to be sought, not by recurring to principles, but in the application of the term by political writers, to the constitution of different States, no satisfactory one would ever be found. Holland, in which no particle of the supreme authority is derived from the people, has passed almost universally under the denomination of a republic. The same title has been bestowed on Venice, where absolute power over the great body of the people is exercised, in the most absolute manner, by a small body of hereditary nobles. Poland, which is a mixture of aristocracy and of monarchy in their worst forms, has been dignified with the same appellation. The government of England, which has one republican branch only, combined with an hereditary aristocracy and monarchy, has, with equal impropriety, been frequently placed on the list of republics. These examples, which are nearly as dissimilar to each other as to a genuine republic, show the extreme inaccuracy with which the term has been used in political disquisitions.

43

If we resort for a criterion to the different principles on which different forms of government are established, we may define a republic to be, or at least may bestow that name on, a government which derives all its powers directly or indirectly from the great body of the people, and is administered by persons holding their offices during pleasure, for a limited period, or during good behavior. It is ESSENTIAL to such a government that it be derived from the great body of the society, not from an inconsiderable proportion, or a favored class of it; otherwise a handful of tyrannical nobles, exercising their oppressions by a delegation of their powers, might aspire to the rank of republicans, and claim for their government the honorable title of republic. It is SUFFICIENT for such a government that the persons administering it be appointed, either directly or indirectly, by the people; and that they hold their appointments by either of the tenures just specified; otherwise every government in the United States, as well as every other popular government that has been or can be well organized or well executed, would be degraded from the republican character. According to the constitution of every State in the Union, some or other of the officers of government are appointed indirectly only by the people. According to most of them, the chief magistrate himself is so appointed. And according to one, this mode of appointment is extended to one of the co-ordinate branches of the legislature. According to all the constitutions, also, the tenure of the highest offices is extended to a definite period, and in many instances, both within the legislative and executive departments, to a period of years. According to the provisions of most of the constitutions, again, as well as according to the most respectable and received opinions on the subject, the members of the judiciary department are to retain their offices by the firm tenure of good behavior.

On comparing the Constitution planned by the convention with the standard here fixed, we perceive at once that it is, in the most rigid sense, conformable to it. The House of Representatives, like that of one branch at least of all the State legislatures, is elected immediately by the great body of the people. The Senate, like the present Congress, and the Senate of Maryland, derives its appointment indirectly from the people. The President is indirectly derived from the choice of the people, according to the example in most of the States. Even the judges, with all other officers of the Union, will, as in the several States, be the choice, though a remote choice, of the people themselves, the duration of the appointments is equally conformable to the republican standard, and to the model of State constitutions The House of Representatives is periodically elective, as in all the States; and for the period of two years, as in the State of South Carolina. The Senate is elective, for the period of six years; which is but one year more than the period of the Senate of Maryland, and but two more than that of the Senates of New York and Virginia. The President is to continue in office for the period of four years; as in New York and Delaware, the chief magistrate is elected for three years, and in South Carolina for two years. In the other States the election is annual. In several of the States, however, no constitutional provision is made for the impeachment of the chief magistrate. And in Delaware and Virginia he is not impeachable till out of office. The President of the United States is impeachable at any time during his continuance in office. The tenure by which the judges are to hold their places, is, as it unquestionably ought to be, that of good behavior. The tenure of the ministerial offices generally, will be a subject of legal regulation, conformably to the reason of the case and the example of the State constitutions.

Could any further proof be required of the republican complexion of this system, the most decisive one might be found in its absolute prohibition of titles of nobility, both under the federal and the State governments; and in its express guaranty of the republican form to each of the latter.

"But it was not sufficient," say the adversaries of the proposed Constitution, "for the convention to adhere to the republican form. They ought, with equal care, to have preserved the FEDERAL form, which regards the Union as a CONFEDERACY of sovereign states; instead of which, they have framed a NATIONAL government, which regards the Union as a CONSOLIDATION of the States." And it is asked by what authority this bold and radical innovation was undertaken? The handle which has been made of this objection requires that it should be examined with some precision.

Without inquiring into the accuracy of the distinction on which the objection is founded, it will be necessary to a just estimate of its force, first, to ascertain the real character of the government in question; secondly, to inquire how far the convention were authorized to propose such a government; and thirdly, how far the duty they owed to their country could supply any defect of regular authority.

First. In order to ascertain the real character of the government, it may be considered in relation to the foundation on which it is to be established; to the sources from which its ordinary powers are to be drawn; to the operation of those powers; to the extent of them; and to the authority by which future changes in the government are to be introduced.

On examining the first relation, it appears, on one hand, that the Constitution is to be founded on the assent and ratification of the people of America, given by deputies elected for the special purpose; but, on the other, that this assent and ratification is to be given by the people, not as individuals composing one entire nation, but as composing the distinct and independent States to which they respectively belong. It is to be the assent and ratification of the several States, derived from the supreme authority in each State, the authority of the people themselves. The act, therefore, establishing the Constitution, will not be a NATIONAL, but a FEDERAL act.

That it will be a federal and not a national act, as these terms are understood by the objectors; the act of the people, as forming so many independent States, not as forming one aggregate nation, is obvious from this single consideration, that it is to result neither from the decision of a MAJORITY of the people of the Union, nor from that of a MAJORITY of the States. It must result from the UNANIMOUS assent of the several States that are parties to it, differing no otherwise from their ordinary assent than in its being expressed, not by the legislative authority, but by that of the people themselves. Were the people regarded in this transaction as forming one nation, the will of the majority of the whole people of the United States would bind the minority, in the same manner as the majority in each State must bind the minority; and the will of the majority must be determined either by a comparison of the individual votes, or by considering the will of the majority of the States as evidence of the will of a majority of the people of the United States. Neither of these rules have been adopted. Each State, in ratifying the Constitution, is considered as a sovereign body, independent of all others, and only to be bound by its own voluntary act. In this relation, then, the new Constitution will, if established, be a FEDERAL, and not a NATIONAL constitution.

The next relation is, to the sources from which the ordinary powers of government are to be derived. The House of Representatives will derive its powers from the people of America; and the people will be represented in the same proportion, and on the same principle, as they are in the legislature of a particular State. So far the government is NATIONAL, not FEDERAL. The Senate, on the other hand, will derive its powers from the States, as political and coequal societies; and these will be represented on the principle of equality in the Senate, as they now are in the existing Congress. So far the government is FEDERAL, not NATIONAL. The executive power will be derived from a very compound source. The immediate election of the President is to be made by the States in their political characters. The votes allotted to them are in a compound ratio, which considers them partly as distinct and coequal societies, partly as unequal members of the same society. The eventual election, again, is to be made by that branch of the legislature which consists of the national representatives; but in this particular act they are to be thrown into the form of individual delegations, from so many distinct and coequal bodies politic. From this aspect of the government it appears to be of a mixed character, presenting at least as many FEDERAL as NATIONAL features.

The difference between a federal and national government, as it relates to the OPERATION OF THE GOVERNMENT, is supposed to consist in this, that in the former the powers operate on the political bodies composing the Confederacy, in their political capacities; in the latter, on the individual citizens composing the nation, in their individual capacities. On trying the Constitution by this criterion, it falls under the NATIONAL, not the FEDERAL character; though perhaps not so completely as has been understood. In several cases, and particularly in the trial of controversies to which States may be parties, they must be viewed and proceeded against in their collective and political capacities only. So far the national countenance of the government on this side seems to be disfigured by a few federal features. But this blemish is perhaps unavoidable in any plan; and the operation of the government on the people, in their individual capacities, in its ordinary and most essential proceedings, may, on the whole, designate it, in this relation, a NATIONAL government.

But if the government be national with regard to the OPERATION of its powers, it changes its aspect again when we contemplate it in relation to the EXTENT of its powers. The idea of a national government involves in it, not only an authority over the individual citizens, but an indefinite supremacy over all persons and things, so far as they are objects of lawful government. Among a people consolidated into one nation, this supremacy is completely vested in the national legislature. Among communities united for particular purposes, it is vested partly in the general and partly in the municipal legislatures. In the former case, all local authorities are subordinate to the supreme; and may be controlled, directed, or abolished by it at pleasure. In the latter, the local or municipal authorities form distinct and independent portions of the supremacy, no more subject, within their respective spheres, to the general authority, than the general authority is subject to them, within its own sphere. In this relation, then, the proposed government cannot be deemed a NATIONAL one; since its jurisdiction extends to certain enumerated objects only, and leaves to the several States a residuary and inviolable sovereignty over all other objects. It is true that in controversies relating to the boundary between the two jurisdictions, the tribunal which is ultimately to decide, is to be established under the general government. But this does not change the principle of the case. The decision is to be impartially made, according to the rules of the Constitution; and all the usual and most effectual precautions are taken to secure this impartiality. Some such tribunal is clearly essential to prevent an appeal to the sword and a dissolution of the compact; and that it ought to be established under the general rather than under the local governments, or, to speak more properly, that it could be safely established under the first alone, is a position not likely to be combated.

If we try the Constitution by its last relation to the authority by which amendments are to be made, we find it neither wholly NATIONAL nor wholly FEDERAL. Were it wholly national, the supreme and ultimate authority would reside in the MAJORITY of the people of the Union; and this authority would be competent at all times, like that of a majority of every national society, to alter or abolish its established government. Were it wholly federal, on the other hand, the concurrence of each State in the Union would be essential to every alteration that would be binding on all. The mode provided by the plan of the convention is not founded on either of these principles. In requiring more than a majority, and principles. In requiring more than a majority, and particularly in computing the proportion by STATES, not by CITIZENS, it departs from the NATIONAL and advances towards the FEDERAL character; in rendering the concurrence of less than the whole number of States sufficient, it loses again the FEDERAL and partakes of the NATIONAL character.

The proposed Constitution, therefore, is, in strictness, neither a national nor a federal Constitution, but a composition of both. In its foundation it is federal, not national; in the sources from which the ordinary powers of the government are drawn, it is partly federal and partly national; in the operation of these powers, it is national, not federal; in the extent of them, again, it is federal, not national; and, finally, in the authoritative mode of introducing amendments, it is neither wholly federal nor wholly national.

*PUBLIUS.*

# The Federalist Papers

## #49 (Method of Guarding Against the Encroachments of Any One Department of Government by Appealing to the People Through a Convention)

To the People of the State of New York:

THE author of the "Notes on the State of Virginia," quoted in the last paper, has subjoined to that valuable work the draught of a constitution, which had been prepared in order to be laid before a convention, expected to be called in 1783, by the legislature, for the establishment of a constitution for that commonwealth. The plan, like every thing from the same pen, marks a turn of thinking, original, comprehensive, and accurate; and is the more worthy of attention as it equally displays a fervent attachment to republican government and an enlightened view of the dangerous propensities against which it ought to be guarded.

One of the precautions which he proposes, and on which he appears ultimately to rely as a palladium to the weaker departments of power against the invasions of the stronger, is perhaps altogether his own, and as it immediately relates to the subject of our present inquiry, ought not to be overlooked. His proposition is, "that whenever any two of the three branches of government shall concur in opinion, each by the voices of two thirds of their whole number, that a convention is necessary for altering the constitution, or CORRECTING BREACHES OF IT, a convention shall be called for the purpose. "As the people are the only legitimate fountain of power, and it is from them that the constitutional charter, under which the several branches of government hold their power, is derived, it seems strictly consonant to the republican theory, to recur to the same original authority, not only whenever it may be necessary to enlarge, diminish, or new-model the powers of the government, but also whenever any one of the departments may commit encroachments on the chartered authorities of the others. The several departments being perfectly co-ordinate by the terms of their common commission, none of them, it is evident, can pretend to an exclusive or superior right of settling the boundaries between their respective powers; and how are the encroachments of the stronger to be prevented, or the wrongs of the weaker to be redressed, without an appeal to the people themselves, who, as the grantors of the commissions, can alone declare its true meaning, and enforce its observance? There is certainly great force in this reasoning, and it must be allowed to prove that a constitutional road to the decision of the people ought to be marked out and kept open, for certain great and extraordinary occasions. But there appear to be insuperable objections against the proposed recurrence to the people, as a provision in all cases for keeping the several departments of power within their constitutional limits. In the first place, the provision does not reach the case of a combination of two of the departments against the third. If the legislative authority, which possesses so many means of operating on the motives of the other departments, should be able to gain to its interest either of the others, or even one third of its members, the remaining department could derive no advantage from its remedial provision. I do not dwell, however, on this objection, because it may be thought to be rather against the modification of the principle, than against the principle itself. In the next place, it may be considered as an objection inherent in the principle, that as every appeal to the people would carry an implication of some defect in the government, frequent appeals would, in a great measure, deprive the government of that veneration which time bestows on every thing, and without which perhaps the wisest and freest governments would not possess the requisite stability. If it be true that all governments rest on opinion, it is no less true that the strength of opinion in each individual, and its practical influence on his conduct, depend much on the number which he supposes to have entertained the same opinion. The reason of man, like man himself, is timid and cautious when left alone, and acquires firmness and confidence in proportion to the number with which it is associated. When the examples which fortify opinion are ANCIENT as well as NUMEROUS, they are known to have a double effect. In a nation of philosophers, this consideration ought to be disregarded. A reverence for the laws would be sufficiently inculcated by the voice of an enlightened reason. But a nation of philosophers is as little to be expected as the philosophical race of kings wished for by Plato. And in every other nation, the most rational government will not find it a superfluous advantage to have the prejudices of the community on its side. The danger of disturbing the public tranquillity by interesting too strongly the public passions, is a still more serious objection against a frequent reference of constitutional questions to the decision of the whole society. Notwithstanding the success which has attended the revisions of our established forms of government, and which does so much honor to the virtue and intelligence of the people of America, it must be confessed that the experiments are of too ticklish a nature to be unnecessarily multiplied. We are to recollect that all the existing constitutions were formed in the midst of a danger which repressed the passions most unfriendly to order and concord; of an enthusiastic confidence of the people in their patriotic leaders, which stifled the ordinary diversity of opinions on great national questions; of a universal ardor for new and opposite forms, produced by a universal resentment and indignation against the ancient government; and whilst no spirit of party connected with the changes to be made, or the abuses to be reformed, could mingle its leaven in the operation. The future situations in which we must expect to be usually placed, do not present any equivalent security against the danger which is apprehended. But the greatest objection of all is, that the decisions which would probably result from such appeals would not answer the purpose of maintaining the constitutional equilibrium of the government. We have seen that the tendency of republican governments is to an aggrandizement of the legislative at the expense of the other departments. The appeals to the people, therefore, would usually be made by the executive and judiciary departments. But whether made by one side or the other, would each side enjoy equal advantages on the trial? Let us view their different situations. The members of the executive and judiciary departments are few in number, and can be personally known to a small part only of the people. The latter, by the mode of their appointment, as well as by the nature and permanency of it, are too far removed from the people to share much in their prepossessions. The former are generally the objects of jealousy, and their administration is always liable to be discolored and rendered unpopular. The members of the legislative department, on the other hand, are numberous. They are distributed and dwell among the people at large. Their connections of blood, of friendship, and of acquaintance embrace a great proportion of the most influential part of the society. The nature of their public trust implies a personal influence among the people, and that they are more immediately the confidential guardians of the rights and liberties of the people. With these advantages, it can hardly be supposed that the adverse party would have an equal chance for a favorable issue. But the legislative party would not only be able to plead their cause most successfully with the people. They would probably be constituted themselves the judges.

The same influence which had gained them an election into the legislature, would gain them a seat in the convention. If this should not be the case with all, it would probably be the case with many, and pretty certainly with those leading characters, on whom every thing depends in such bodies. The convention, in short, would be composed chiefly of men who had been, who actually were, or who expected to be, members of the department whose conduct was arraigned. They would consequently be parties to the very question to be decided by them. It might, however, sometimes happen, that appeals would be made under circumstances less adverse to the executive and judiciary departments. The usurpations of the legislature might be so flagrant and so sudden, as to admit of no specious coloring. A strong party among themselves might take side with the other branches. The executive power might be in the hands of a peculiar favorite of the people. In such a posture of things, the public decision might be less swayed by prepossessions in favor of the legislative party. But still it could never be expected to turn on the true merits of the question. It would inevitably be connected with the spirit of pre-existing parties, or of parties springing out of the question itself. It would be connected with persons of distinguished character and extensive influence in the community. It would be pronounced by the very men who had been agents in, or opponents of, the measures to which the decision would relate. The PASSIONS, therefore, not the REASON, of the public would sit in judgment. But it is the reason, alone, of the public, that ought to control and regulate the government. The passions ought to be controlled and regulated by the government.

We found in the last paper, that mere declarations in the written constitution are not sufficient to restrain the several departments within their legal rights. It appears in this, that occasional appeals to the people would be neither a proper nor an effectual provision for that purpose. How far the provisions of a different nature contained in the plan above quoted might be adequate, I do not examine. Some of them are unquestionably founded on sound political principles, and all of them are framed with singular ingenuity and precision.

*PUBLIUS.*

# The Federalist Papers

## #57 (The Alleged Tendency of the Plan to Elevate the Few at the Expense of the Many Considered in Connection with Representation)

To the People of the State of New York:

THE THIRD charge against the House of Representatives is, that it will be taken from that class of citizens which will have least sympathy with the mass of the people, and be most likely to aim at an ambitious sacrifice of the many to the aggrandizement of the few. Of all the objections which have been framed against the federal Constitution, this is perhaps the most extraordinary.

Whilst the objection itself is levelled against a pretended oligarchy, the principle of it strikes at the very root of republican government. The aim of every political constitution is, or ought to be, first to obtain for rulers men who possess most wisdom to discern, and most virtue to pursue, the common good of the society; and in the next place, to take the most effectual precautions for keeping them virtuous whilst they continue to hold their public trust. The elective mode of obtaining rulers is the characteristic policy of republican government. The means relied on in this form of government for preventing their degeneracy are numerous and various. The most effectual one, is such a limitation of the term of appointments as will maintain a proper responsibility to the people. Let me now ask what circumstance there is in the constitution of the House of Representatives that violates the principles of republican government, or favors the elevation of the few on the ruins of the many? Let me ask whether every circumstance is not, on the contrary, strictly conformable to these principles, and scrupulously impartial to the rights and pretensions of every class and description of citizens? Who are to be the electors of the federal representatives? Not the rich, more than the poor; not the learned, more than the ignorant; not the haughty heirs of distinguished names, more than the humble sons of obscurity and unpropitious fortune. The electors are to be the great body of the people of the United States. They are to be the same who exercise the right in every State of electing the corresponding branch of the legislature of the State. Who are to be the objects of popular choice? Every citizen whose merit may recommend him to the esteem and confidence of his country. No qualification of wealth, of birth, of religious faith, or of civil profession is permitted to fetter the judgement or disappoint the inclination of the people. If we consider the situation of the men on whom the free suffrages of their fellow-citizens may confer the representative trust, we shall find it involving every security which can be devised or desired for their fidelity to their constituents. In the first place, as they will have been distinguished by the preference of their fellow-citizens, we are to presume that in general they will be somewhat distinguished also by those qualities which entitle them to it, and which promise a sincere and scrupulous regard to the nature of their engagements. In the second place, they will enter into the public service under circumstances which cannot fail to produce a temporary affection at least to their constituents. There is in every breast a sensibility to marks of honor, of favor, of esteem, and of confidence, which, apart from all considerations of interest, is some pledge for grateful and benevolent returns.

Ingratitude is a common topic of declamation against human nature; and it must be confessed that instances of it are but too frequent and flagrant, both in public and in private life. But the universal and extreme indignation which it inspires is itself a proof of the energy and prevalence of the contrary sentiment.

In the third place, those ties which bind the representative to his constituents are strengthened by motives of a more selfish nature. His pride and vanity attach him to a form of government which favors his pretensions and gives him a share in its honors and distinctions. Whatever hopes or projects might be entertained by a few aspiring characters, it must generally happen that a great proportion of the men deriving their advancement from their influence with the people, would have more to hope from a preservation of the favor, than from innovations in the government subversive of the authority of the people. All these securities, however, would be found very insufficient without the restraint of frequent elections. Hence, in the fourth place, the House of Representatives is so constituted as to support in the members an habitual recollection of their dependence on the people. Before the sentiments impressed on their minds by the mode of their elevation can be effaced by the exercise of power, they will be compelled to anticipate the moment when their power is to cease, when their exercise of it is to be reviewed, and when they must descend to the level from which they were raised; there forever to remain unless a faithful discharge of their trust shall have established their title to a renewal of it. I will add, as a fifth circumstance in the situation of the House of Representatives, restraining them from oppressive measures, that they can make no law which will not have its full operation on themselves and their friends, as well as on the great mass of the society. This has always been deemed one of the strongest bonds by which human policy can connect the rulers and the people together. It creates between them that communion of interests and sympathy of sentiments, of which few governments have furnished examples; but without which every government degenerates into tyranny. If it be asked, what is to restrain the House of Representatives from making legal discriminations in favor of themselves and a particular class of the society? I answer: the genius of the whole system; the nature of just and constitutional laws; and above all, the vigilant and manly spirit which actuates the people of America, a spirit which nourishes freedom, and in return is nourished by it. If this spirit shall ever be so far debased as to tolerate a law not obligatory on the legislature, as well as on the people, the people will be prepared to tolerate any thing but liberty. Such will be the relation between the House of Representatives and their constituents. Duty, gratitude, interest, ambition itself, are the chords by which they will be bound to fidelity and sympathy with the great mass of the people.

It is possible that these may all be insufficient to control the caprice and wickedness of man. But are they not all that government will admit, and that human prudence can devise? Are they not the genuine and the characteristic means by which republican government provides for the liberty and happiness of the people? Are they not the identical means on which every State government in the Union relies for the attainment of these important ends? What then are we to understand by the objection which this paper has combated? What are we to say to the men who profess the most flaming zeal for republican government,

yet boldly impeach the fundamental principle of it; who pretend to
be champions for the right and the capacity of the people to choose
their own rulers, yet maintain that they will prefer those only who will
immediately and infallibly betray the trust committed to them? Were
the objection to be read by one who had not seen the mode prescribed
by the Constitution for the choice of representatives, he could suppose
nothing less than that some unreasonable qualification of property was
annexed to the right of suffrage; or that the right of eligibility was
limited to persons of particular families or fortunes; or at least that
the mode prescribed by the State constitutions was in some respect or
other, very grossly departed from. We have seen how far such a supposition would err, as to the two first points. Nor would it, in fact, be less
erroneous as to the last. The only difference discoverable between the
two cases is, that each representative of the United States will be elected by five or six thousand citizens; whilst in the individual States, the
election of a representative is left to about as many hundreds. Will it be
pretended that this difference is sufficient to justify an attachment to
the State governments, and an abhorrence to the federal government?
If this be the point on which the objection turns, it deserves to be examined. Is it supported by REASON?

This cannot be said, without maintaining that five or six thousand
citizens are less capable of choosing a fit representative, or more liable
to be corrupted by an unfit one, than five or six hundred. Reason, on
the contrary, assures us, that as in so great a number a fit representative
would be most likely to be found, so the choice would be less likely
to be diverted from him by the intrigues of the ambitious or the ambitious or the bribes of the rich. Is the CONSEQUENCE from this
doctrine admissible? If we say that five or six hundred citizens are as
many as can jointly exercise their right of suffrage, must we not deprive
the people of the immediate choice of their public servants, in every
instance where the administration of the government does not require
as many of them as will amount to one for that number of citizens? Is
the doctrine warranted by FACTS? It was shown in the last paper, that
the real representation in the British House of Commons very little
exceeds the proportion of one for every thirty thousand inhabitants.
Besides a variety of powerful causes not existing here, and which favor in that country the pretensions of rank and wealth, no person is

eligible as a representative of a county, unless he possess real estate of the clear value of six hundred pounds sterling per year; nor of a city or borough, unless he possess a like estate of half that annual value. To this qualification on the part of the county representatives is added another on the part of the county electors, which restrains the right of suffrage to persons having a freehold estate of the annual value of more than twenty pounds sterling, according to the present rate of money. Notwithstanding these unfavorable circumstances, and notwithstanding some very unequal laws in the British code, it cannot be said that the representatives of the nation have elevated the few on the ruins of the many. But we need not resort to foreign experience on this subject. Our own is explicit and decisive. The districts in New Hampshire in which the senators are chosen immediately by the people, are nearly as large as will be necessary for her representatives in the Congress. Those of Massachusetts are larger than will be necessary for that purpose; and those of New York still more so.

In the last State the members of Assembly for the cities and counties of New York and Albany are elected by very nearly as many voters as will be entitled to a representative in the Congress, calculating on the number of sixty-five representatives only. It makes no difference that in these senatorial districts and counties a number of representatives are voted for by each elector at the same time. If the same electors at the same time are capable of choosing four or five representatives, they cannot be incapable of choosing one. Pennsylvania is an additional example. Some of her counties, which elect her State representatives, are almost as large as her districts will be by which her federal representatives will be elected. The city of Philadelphia is supposed to contain between fifty and sixty thousand souls. It will therefore form nearly two districts for the choice of federal representatives. It forms, however, but one county, in which every elector votes for each of its representatives in the State legislature. And what may appear to be still more directly to our purpose, the whole city actually elects a SINGLE MEMBER for the executive council. This is the case in all the other counties of the State. Are not these facts the most satisfactory proofs of the fallacy which has been employed against the branch of the federal government under consideration? Has it appeared on trial that the senators of New Hampshire, Massachusetts, and New York, or the executive council of Pennsylvania, or the members of the

Assembly in the two last States, have betrayed any peculiar disposition to sacrifice the many to the few, or are in any respect less worthy of their places than the representatives and magistrates appointed in other States by very small divisions of the people? But there are cases of a stronger complexion than any which I have yet quoted.

One branch of the legislature of Connecticut is so constituted that each member of it is elected by the whole State. So is the governor of that State, of Massachusetts, and of this State, and the president of New Hampshire. I leave every man to decide whether the result of any one of these experiments can be said to countenance a suspicion, that a diffusive mode of choosing representatives of the people tends to elevate traitors and to undermine the public liberty.

*PUBLIUS.*

# JOHN JAY
## (1745-1829)

# John Jay
## (1745-1829)

BORN ON DECEMBER 12, 1745, IN New York City, John Jay spent much of his childhood nearby in Rye, New York. He was a member of a wealthy family of successful merchants and he attended King's College (now Columbia University). Jay graduated in 1764 and started a career as a lawyer.

Jay was a representative of New York at the Continental Congress in 1774. Like many of the colonists, Jay was initially in favor of keeping ties with Britain, but he ultimately wanted the colonists' rights protected, so he ended up supporting the Revolution. Jay went back to New York in 1776 and worked as the state's Chief Justice before returning to the Congress in 1778. He became president of the Continental Congress and then journeyed to Spain as the minister plenipotentiary in order to ascertain more support for the colonists' cause, though he was mostly unsuccessful. Afterwards, Jay traveled to Paris to meet up with Benjamin Franklin and to help negotiate the Treaty of Paris (1783).

Once the United States became a sovereign nation under the Articles of Confederation, Jay assumed the role of the foreign affairs secretary. He became frustrated with the limited powers of the government and grew to support a stronger central government, joining Alexander Hamilton and James Madison in writing *The Federalist Papers*. His "An Address to the People of the State of New York" also played a role in ratifying the Constitution.

In 1789, George Washington appointed Jay as the Supreme Court's first chief justice, where he remained until 1795. However, in 1794, Jay took a trip to Britain in order to negotiate a treaty over exports, occupation, and seizures between Britain and the U.S., which birthed the "Jay Treaty." While this treaty caused unrest in the U.S. because it was thought to favor the British, it helped to avoid a war.

Jay returned to the United States and learned that he had been appointed Governor of New York for which he resigned his seat on the Supreme Court. In 1800, Jay entered the presidential race, but lost substantially. He refused a second appointment to the Supreme Court and officially retired in 1801. He returned home to Bedford, New York where he died of a stroke on May 17, 1829.

# The Federalist Papers

## #2 (Concerning Dangers from Foreign Force and Influence)

To the People of the State of New York:

WHEN the people of America reflect that they are now called upon to decide a question, which, in its consequences, must prove one of the most important that ever engaged their attention, the propriety of their taking a very comprehensive, as well as a very serious, view of it, will be evident.

Nothing is more certain than the indispensable necessity of government, and it is equally undeniable, that whenever and however it is instituted, the people must cede to it some of their natural rights in order to vest it with requisite powers. It is well worthy of consideration therefore, whether it would conduce more to the interest of the people of America that they should, to all general purposes, be one nation, under one federal government, or that they should divide themselves into separate confederacies, and give to the head of each the same kind of powers which they are advised to place in one national government.

It has until lately been a received and uncontradicted opinion that the prosperity of the people of America depended on their continuing firmly united, and the wishes, prayers, and efforts of our best and wisest citizens have been constantly directed to that object. But politicians now appear, who insist that this opinion is erroneous, and that instead of looking for safety and happiness in union, we ought to seek it in a division of the States into distinct confederacies or sovereignties. However extraordinary this new doctrine may appear, it nevertheless has its advocates; and certain characters who were much opposed to it formerly, are at present of the number. Whatever may be the arguments or inducements which have wrought this change in the sentiments and declarations of these gentlemen, it certainly would not be wise in the people at large to adopt these new political tenets without being fully convinced that they are founded in truth and sound policy.

It has often given me pleasure to observe that independent America was not composed of detached and distant territories, but that one connected, fertile, widespreading country was the portion of our western sons of liberty. Providence has in a particular manner blessed it with a variety of soils and productions, and watered it with innumerable streams, for the delight and accommodation of its inhabitants. A succession of navigable waters forms a kind of chain round its borders, as if to bind it together; while the most noble rivers in the world, running at convenient distances, present them with highways for the easy communication of friendly aids, and the mutual transportation and exchange of their various commodities.

With equal pleasure I have as often taken notice that Providence has been pleased to give this one connected country to one united people--a people descended from the same ancestors, speaking the same language, professing the same religion, attached to the same principles of government, very similar in their manners and customs, and who, by their joint counsels, arms, and efforts, fighting side by side throughout a long and bloody war, have nobly established general liberty and independence.

This country and this people seem to have been made for each other, and it appears as if it was the design of Providence, that an inheritance so proper and convenient for a band of brethren, united to each other by the strongest ties, should never be split into a number of unsocial, jealous, and alien sovereignties.

Similar sentiments have hitherto prevailed among all orders and denominations of men among us. To all general purposes we have uniformly been one people each individual citizen everywhere enjoying the same national rights, privileges, and protection. As a nation we have made peace and war; as a nation we have vanquished our common enemies; as a nation we have formed alliances, and made treaties, and entered into various compacts and conventions with foreign states.

A strong sense of the value and blessings of union induced the people, at a very early period, to institute a federal government to preserve and perpetuate it. They formed it almost as soon as they had a political existence; nay, at a time when their habitations were in flames, when many of their citizens were bleeding, and when the progress of hostility and desolation left little room for those calm and mature inquiries and reflections which must ever precede the formation of a wise and wellbalanced government for a free people. It is not to be wondered at, that a government instituted in times so inauspicious, should on experiment be found greatly deficient and inadequate to the purpose it was intended to answer.

This intelligent people perceived and regretted these defects. Still continuing no less attached to union than enamored of liberty, they observed the danger which immediately threatened the former and more remotely the latter; and being pursuaded that ample security for both could only be found in a national government more wisely framed, they as with one voice, convened the late convention at Philadelphia, to take that important subject under consideration.

This convention composed of men who possessed the confidence of the people, and many of whom had become highly distinguished by their patriotism, virtue and wisdom, in times which tried the minds and hearts of men, undertook the arduous task. In the mild season of peace, with minds unoccupied by other subjects, they passed many months in cool, uninterrupted, and daily consultation; and finally, without having been awed by power, or influenced by any passions except love for their country, they presented and recommended to the people the plan produced by their joint and very unanimous councils.

Admit, for so is the fact, that this plan is only RECOMMENDED, not imposed, yet let it be remembered that it is neither recommended to BLIND approbation, nor to BLIND reprobation; but to that sedate and candid consideration which the magnitude and importance of the subject demand, and which it certainly ought to receive. But this (as was remarked in the foregoing number of this paper) is more to be wished than expected, that it may be so considered and examined. Experience on a former occasion teaches us not to be too sanguine in such hopes. It is not yet forgotten that well-grounded apprehensions of imminent danger induced the people of America to form the memorable Congress of 1774. That body recommended certain measures to their constituents, and the event proved their wisdom; yet it is fresh in our memories how soon the press began to teem with pamphlets and weekly papers against those very measures. Not only many of the officers of government, who obeyed the dictates of personal interest, but others, from a mistaken estimate of consequences, or the undue influence of former attachments, or whose ambition aimed at objects which did not correspond with the public good, were indefatigable in their efforts to pursuade the people to reject the advice of that patriotic Congress. Many, indeed, were deceived and deluded, but the great majority of the people reasoned and decided judiciously; and happy they are in reflecting that they did so.

They considered that the Congress was composed of many wise and experienced men. That, being convened from different parts of the country, they brought with them and communicated to each other a variety of useful information. That, in the course of the time they passed together in inquiring into and discussing the true interests of their country, they must have acquired very accurate knowledge on that head. That they were individually interested in the public liberty and prosperity, and therefore that it was not less their inclination than their duty to recommend only such measures as, after the most mature deliberation, they really thought prudent and advisable.

These and similar considerations then induced the people to rely greatly on the judgment and integrity of the Congress; and they took their advice, notwithstanding the various arts and endeavors used to deter them from it. But if the people at large had reason to confide in the men of that Congress, few of whom had been fully tried or generally known, still greater reason have they now to respect the judgment and advice of the convention, for it is well known that some of the most distinguished members of that Congress, who have been since tried and justly approved for patriotism and abilities, and who have grown old in acquiring political information, were also members of this convention, and carried into it their accumulated knowledge and experience.

It is worthy of remark that not only the first, but every succeeding Congress, as well as the late convention, have invariably joined with the people in thinking that the prosperity of America depended on its Union. To preserve and perpetuate it was the great object of the people in forming that convention, and it is also the great object of the plan which the convention has advised them to adopt. With what propriety, therefore, or for what good purposes, are attempts at this particular period made by some men to depreciate the importance of the Union? Or why is it suggested that three or four confederacies would be better than one? I am persuaded in my own mind that the people have always thought right on this subject, and that their universal and uniform attachment to the cause of the Union rests on great and weighty reasons, which I shall endeavor to develop and explain in some ensuing papers. They who promote the idea of substituting a number of distinct confederacies in the room of the plan of the convention, seem clearly to foresee that the rejection of it would put the continuance of the Union in the utmost jeopardy. That certainly would be the case, and I sincerely wish that it may be as clearly foreseen by every good citizen, that whenever the dissolution of the Union arrives, America will have reason to exclaim, in the words of the poet: "FAREWELL! A LONG FAREWELL TO ALL MY GREATNESS."

*PUBLIUS.*

# An Address to the People of the State of New York

*Friends and Fellow Citizens:*

There are times and seasons, when *general* evils spread general alarm and uneasiness, and yet arise from causes too complicated, and too little understood by many, to produce an unanimity of opinions respecting their remedies. Hence it is, that on such occasions, the conflict of arguments too often excites a conflict of passions, and introduces a degree of discord and animosity, which, by agitating the public mind dispose it to precipitation and extravagance. They who on the ocean have been unexpectedly enveloped with tempests, or suddenly entangled among rocks and shoals, know the value of that serene, self-possession and presence of mind, to which in such cases they owed their preservation; nor will the heroes who have given us victory and peace, hesitate to acknowledge that we are as much indebted for those blessings to the calm prevision, and cool intrepidity which planned and conducted our military measures, as to the glowing animation with which they were executed.

While reason retains her rule, while men are as ready to receive as to give advice, and as willing to be convinced themselves, as to convince others, there are few political evils from which a *free* and enlightened people cannot deliver themselves. It is unquestionably true, that the great body of the people love their country, and wish it prosperity; and this observation is particularly applicable to the people of a free country, for they have more and stronger reasons for loving it than others. It is not therefore to vicious motives that the unhappy divisions which sometimes prevail among them are to be imputed; the people at large always mean well, and although they may on certain occasions be misled by the counsels, or injured by the efforts of the few who expect more advantage from the wreck, than from the preservation of national prosperity, yet the motives of these few, are by no means to be confounded with those of the community in general.

That such seeds of discord and danger have been disseminated and begin to take root in America, as unless eradicated will soon poison our gardens and our fields, is a truth much to be lamented; and the more so, as their growth rapidly increases, while we are wasting the season in honestly but imprudently disputing, not whether they shall be pulled up, but by whom, in what manner, and with what instruments, the work shall be done.

When the king of Great Britain, misguided by men who did not merit his confidence, asserted the unjust claim of binding us in all cases whatsoever, and prepared to obtain our submission by force, the object which engrossed our attention, however important, was nevertheless plain and simple, "What shall we do?" was the question—the people answered, let us unite our counsels and our arms. They sent Delegates to Congress, and soldiers to the field. Confiding in the probity and wisdom of Congress, they received their recommendations as if they had been laws; and that ready acquiesence in their advice enabled those patriots to save their country. Then there was little leisure or disposition for controversy respecting the expediency of measures—hostile fleets soon filled our ports, and hostile armies spread desolation on our shores. Union was then considered as the most essential of human means and we almost worshipped it with as much fervor, as pagans in distress formerly implored the protection of their tutelar deities. That union was the child of wisdom—heaven blessed it, and it wrought out our political salvation.

That glorious war was succeeded by an advantageous peace. When danger disappeared, ease, tranquility, and a sense of security loosened the bands of union; and Congress and soldiers and good faith depreciated with their apparent importance. Recommendations lost their influence, and requisitions were rendered nugatory, not by their want of propriety, but by their want of power. The spirit of private gain expelled the spirit of public good, and men became more intent on the means of enriching and aggrandizing themselves, than of enriching and aggrandizing their country. Hence the war-worn veteran, whose reward for toils and wounds existed in written promises, found Congress without the means, and too many of the States without the disposition, to do him justice. Hard necessity compelled him, and others under similar circumstances, to sell their honest claims on the public for a little bread; and thus unmerited misfortunes and patriotic distresses became articles of speculation and commerce.

These and many other evils, too well known to require enumeration, imperceptibly stole in upon us, and acquired an unhappy influence on our public affairs. But such evils, like the worst of weeds, will naturally spring up in so rich a soil; and a good Government is as necessary to subdue the one, as an attentive gardner or husbandman is to destroy the other—Even the garden of Paradise required to be dressed, and while men continue to be constantly impelled to error and to wrong by innumerable circumstances and temptations, so long will society experience the unceasing necessity of government.

It is a pity that the expectations which actuated the authors of the existing confederation, neither have nor can be realized:—accustomed to see and admire the glorious spirit which moved all ranks of people in the most gloomy moments of the war, observing their steadfast attachment to Union, and the wisdom they so often manifested both in choosing and confiding in their rulers, those gentlemen were led to flatter themselves that the people of America only required to know what ought to be done, to do it. This amiable mistake induced them to institute a national government in such a manner, as though very fit to give advice, was yet destitute of power, and so constructed as to be very unfit to be trusted with it. They seem not to have been sensible that mere advice is a sad substitute for laws; nor to have recollected that the advice even of the allwise and best of Beings, has been always disregarded by a great majority of all the men that ever lived.

Experience is a severe preceptor, but it teaches useful truths, and however harsh, is always honest—Be calm and dispassionate, and listen to what it tells us.

Prior to the revolution we had little occasion to inquire or know much about national affairs, for although they existed and were managed, yet they were managed *for* us, but not *by* us. Intent on our domestic concerns, our internal legislative business, our agriculture, and our buying and selling, we were seldom anxious about what passed or was doing in foreign Courts. As we had nothing to do with that department of policy, so the affairs of it were not detailed to us, and we took as little pains to inform ourselves, as others did to inform us of them. War, and peace, alliances, and treaties, and commerce, and navigation, were conducted and regulated without our advice or controul. While we had liberty and justice, and in security enjoyed the fruits of our "vine and fig tree," we were in general too content and too much occupied, to be at the trouble of investigating the various political combinations in this department, or to examine and perceive how exceedingly important they often were to the advancement and protection of our prosperity. This habit and turn of thinking affords one reason why so much more care was taken, and so much more wisdom displayed, in forming our State Governments, than in forming our Federal or national one.

By the Confederation as it now stands, the direction of general and national affairs is committed to a single body of men, viz. the Congress. They may make war, but are not empowered to raise men or money to carry it on. They may make peace, but without power to see the terms of it observed—They may form alliances, but without ability to comply with the stipulations on their part—They may enter into treaties of commerce, but without power to enforce them at home or abroad—They may borrow money, but without having the means of repayment—They may partly regulate commerce, but without authority to execute their ordinances—They may appoint ministers and other officers of trust, but without power to try or punish them for misdemeanors—They may resolve, but cannot execute either with dispatch or with secrecy—In short, they may consult, and deliberate, and recommend, and make requisitions, and they who please, may regard them.

From this new and wonderful system of Government, it has come to pass, that almost every national object of every kind, is at this day unprovided for; and other nations taking the advantage of its imbecility, are daily multiplying commercial restraints upon us. Our fur trade is gone to Canada, and British garrisons keep the keys of it. Our shipyards have almost ceased to disturb the repose of the neighborhood by the noise of the axe and hammer; and while foreign flags fly triumphantly above our highest houses, the American Stars seldom do more than shed a few feeble rays about the humble masts of river sloops and coasting schooners. The greater part of our hardy seamen, are plowing the ocean in foreign pay; and not a few of our ingenious shipwrights are now building vessels on alien shores. Although our increasing agriculture and industry extend and multiply our productions, yet they constantly diminish in value; and although we permit all nations to fill our country with their merchandises, yet their best markets are shut against us. Is there an English, or a French, or a Spanish island or port in the West-Indies, to which an American vessel can carry a cargo of flour for sale? Not one. The Algerines exclude us from the Mediterranean, and adjacent countries; and we are neither able to purchase, nor to command the free use of those seas. Can our little towns or larger cities consume the immense productions of our fertile country? or will they without trade be able to pay a good price for the proportion which they do consume? The last season gave a very unequivocal answer to these questions—What numbers of fine cattle have returned from this city to the country for want of buyers? What great quantities of salted and other provisions still lie useless in the stores? To how much below the former price, is our corn, and wheat and flour and lumber rapidly falling? Our debts remain undiminished, and the interest on them accumulating—our credit abroad is nearly extinguished, and at home unrestored—they who had money have sent it beyond the reach of our laws, and scarcely any man can borrow of his neighbor. Nay, does not experience also tell us, that it is as difficult to pay as to borrow? That even our houses and lands cannot command money—that law suits and usurious contracts abound—that our farms sell on executions for less than half their value, and that distress in various forms, and in various ways, is approaching fast to the doors of our best citizens.

These things have been gradually coming upon us ever since the peace—they have been perceived and proclaimed, but the universal rage and pursuit of private gain conspired with other causes, to prevent any proper efforts being made to meliorate our condition by due attention to our national affairs, until the late Convention was convened for that purpose. From the result of their deliberations, the States expected to derive much good, and should they be disappointed, it will probably be not less their misfortune than their fault. That Convention was in general composed of excellent and tried men—men who had become conspicuous for their wisdom and public services, and whose names and characters will be venerated by posterity. Generous and *candid* minds cannot perceive without pain, the illiberal manner in which some have taken the liberty to treat them; nor forbear to impute it to impure and improper motives, zeal for public good, like zeal for religion, may sometimes carry men beyond the bounds of reason, but it is not conceivable, that on this occasion, it should find means so to inebriate any candid American, as to make him forget what he owed to truth and to decency, or induce him either to believe or to say, that the almost unanimous advice of the Convention, proceeded from a wicked combination and conspiracy against the liberties of their country. This is not the temper with which we should receive and consider their recommendations, nor the treatment that would be worthy either of us or them. Let us continue careful therefore that facts do not warrant historians to tell future generations, that envy, malice and uncharitableness pursued our patriotic benefactors to their graves, and that not even pre-eminence in virtue, nor lives devoted to the public, could shield them from obloquy and detraction. On the contrary, let our bosoms always retain a sufficient degree of honest indignation to disappoint and discourage those who expect our thanks or applause for calumniating our most faithful and meritorious friends.

The Convention concurred in opinion with the people, that a national government, *competent to every national object*, was indispensibly necessary; and it was as plain to them, as it now is to all America, that the present confederation does not provide for such a government. These points being agreed, they proceeded to consider how and in what manner such a government could be formed, as on the one hand, should be sufficiently energetic to raise us from our prostrate and distressed situation, and on the other be perfectly consistent with the liberties of the people of every State. Like men to whom the experience of other ages and countries had taught wisdom, they not only determined that it should be erected by, and depend on the people; but remembering the many instances in which governments vested solely in one man, or one body of men, had degenerated into tyrannies, they judged it most prudent that the three great branches of power should be committed to different hands, and therefore that the executive should be separated from the legislative, and the judicial from both. Thus far the propriety of their work is easily seen and understood, and therefore is thus far *almost* universally approved—for no one man or thing under the sun ever yet pleased every body.

The next question was, what particular powers should be given to these three branches? Here the different views and interests of the different states, as well as the different abstract opinions of their members on such points, interposed many difficulties. Here the business became complicated, and presented a wide field for investigation; too wide for every eye to take a quick and comprehensive view of it.

It is said that "in a multitude of counsellors there is safety," because in the first place, there is greater security for probity; and in the next, if every member cast in only his mite of information and argument, their joint stock of both will thereby become greater than the stock possessed by any one single man out of doors. Gentlemen out of doors therefore should not be hasty in condemning a system, which probably rests on more good reasons than they are aware of, especially when formed under such advantages, and recommended by so many men of distinguished worth and abilities.

The difficulties before mentioned occupied the Convention a long time and it was not without mutual concessions that they were at last surmounted. These concessions serve to explain to us the reason why some parts of the system please in some states, which displease in others; and why many of the objections which have been made to it, are so contradictory and inconsistent with one another. It does great credit to the temper and talents of the Convention, that they were able so to reconcile the different views and interests of the different States, and the clashing opinions of their members as to unite with such singular and almost perfect unanimity in any plan whatever, on a subject so intricate and perplexed. It shews that it must have been thoroughly discussed and understood; and probably if the community at large had the same lights and reasons before them, they would, if equally candid and uninfluenced, be equally unanimous.

It would be arduous, and indeed impossible, to comprise within the limits of this address, a full discussion of every part of the plan. Such a task would require a volume, and few men have leisure or inclination to read volumes on any subject. The objections made to it are almost without number, and many of them without reason—some of them are real and honest, and others merely ostensible. There are friends to Union and a national Government who have serious doubts, who wish to be informed, and to be convinced; and there are others who, neither wishing for union, nor any national Government at all, will oppose and object to any plan that can be contrived.

We are told, among other strange things, that the liberty of the press is left insecure by the proposed Constitution, and yet that Constitution says neither more nor less about it, than the Constitution of the State of New York does. We are told that it deprives us of trial by jury, whereas the fact is, that it expressly secures it in certain cases, and takes it away in none—it is absurd to construe the silence of this, or of our own constitution, relative to a great number of our rights, into a total extinction of them—silence and blank paper neither grant nor take away anything. Complaints are also made that the proposed constitution is not accompanied by a bill of rights; and yet they who would make these complaints, know and are content that no bill of rights accompanied the Constitution of this State. In days and countries, where Monarchs and their subjects were frequently disputing about prerogative and privileges, the latter often found it necessary, as it were to run out the line between them, and oblige the former to admit by solemn acts, called bills of rights, that certain enumerated rights belonged to the people, and were not comprehended in the royal prerogative. But thank God we have no such disputes—we have no Monarchs to contend with, or demand admission from—the proposed Government is to be the government of the people—all its officers are to be their officers, and to exercise no rights but such as the people commit to them. The Constitution only serves to point out that part of the people's business, which they think proper by it to refer to the management of the persons therein designated—those persons are to receive that business to manage, not for themselves and as their own, but as agents and overseers for the people to whom they are constantly responsible, and by whom only they are to be appointed

But the design of this address is not to investigate the merits of the plan, nor of the objections to it. They who seriously contemplate the present state of our affairs will be convinced that other considerations of at least equal importance demand their attention. Let it be admitted that this plan, like everything else devised by man, has its imperfections: That it does not please every body is certain and there is little reason to expect one that will. It is a question of great moment to you, whether the probability of your being able seasonably to obtain a better, is such as to render it prudent and advisable to reject this, and run the risque. Candidly to consider this question is the design of this address.

As the importance of this question must be obvious to every man, whatever his private opinions respecting it may be, it becomes us all to treat it in that calm and temperate manner, which a subject so deeply interesting to the future welfare of our country and prosperity requires. Let us therefore as much as possible repress and compose that irritation in our minds, which to warm disputes about it may have excited. Let us endeavour to forget that this or that man, is on this or that side; and that we ourselves, perhaps without sufficient reflection, have classed ourselves with one or the other party. Let us remember that this is not a matter to be regarded as a matter that only touches our local parties, but as one so great, so general, and so extensive in its future consequences to America, that for our deciding upon it according to the best of our unbiassed judgment, we must be highly responsible both here and hereafter.

The question now before us now naturally leads to *three* enquiries:

1. Whether it is probable that a better plan can be obtained?
2. Whether, if attainable, it is likely to be in season?
3. What would be our situation, if after rejecting this, all our efforts to obtain a better should prove fruitless?

The men, who formed this plan are Americans, who had long deserved and enjoyed our confidence, and who are as much interested in having a good government as any of us are, or can be. They were appointed to that business at a time when the States had become very sensible of the derangement of our national affairs, and of the impossibility of retrieving them under the existing Confederation. Although well persuaded that nothing but a good national government could oppose and divert the tide of evils that was flowing in upon us, yet those gentlemen met in Convention with minds perfectly unprejudiced in favour of any particular plan. The minds of their Constituents were at that time equally unbiased, cool and dispassionate. All agreed in the necessity of doing something, but no one ventured to say decidedly what precisely ought to be done—opinions were then fluctuating and unfixed, and whatever might have been the wishes of a few individuals, yet while the Convention deliberated, the people remained in silent suspense. Neither wedded to favourite systems of their own, nor influenced by popular ones abroad, the members were more desirous to receive light from, than to impress their private sentiments on, one another. These circumstances naturally opened the door to that spirit of candour, of calm enquiry, of mutual accommodation, and mutual respect, which entered into the Convention with them, and regulated their debates and proceedings.

The impossibility of agreeing upon any plan that would exactly quadrate with the local policy and objects of every State, soon became evident; and they wisely thought it better mutually to concede, and accommodate, and in that way to fashion their system as much as possible by the circumstances and wishes of different States, than by pertinaciously adhering, each to his own ideas, oblige the Convention to rise without doing anything. They were sensible that obstacles arising from local circumstances, would not cease while those circumstances continued to exist; and so far as those circumstances depended on differences of climate, productions, and commerce, that no change was to be expected. They were likewise sensible that on a subject so comprehensive, and involving such a variety of points and questions, the most able, the most candid, and the most honest men will differ in opinion. The same proposition seldom strikes many minds exactly in the same point of light; different habits of thinking, different degrees and modes of education, different prejudices and opinions early formed and long entertained, conspire with a multitude of other circumstances, to produce among men a diversity and contrariety of opinions on questions of difficulty. Liberality therefore as well as prudence, induced them to treat each other's opinions with tenderness, to argue without asperity, and to endeavor to convince the judgment without hurting the feelings of each other. Although many weeks were passed in these discussions, some points remained, on which a unison of opinions could not be effected. Here again that same happy disposition to unite and conciliate, induced them to meet each other; and enabled them, by mutual concessions, finally to complete and agree to the plan they have recommended, and that too with a degree of unanimity which, considering the variety of discordant views and ideas, they had to reconcile, is really astonishing.

They tell us very honestly that this plan is the result of accommodation—they do not hold it up as the best of all possible ones, but only as the best which they could unite in, and agree to. If such men, appointed and meeting under such auspicious circumstances, and so sincerely disposed to conciliation, could go no further in their endeavors to please every State, and every body, what reason have we at present to expect any system that would give more general satisfaction?

Suppose this plan to be rejected, what measures would you propose for obtaining a better? Some will answer, let us appoint another Convention, and as everything has been said and written that can well be said and written on the subject, they will be better informed than the former one was, and consequently be better able to make and agree upon a more eligible one.

This reasoning is fair, and as far as it goes has weight; but it nevertheless takes one thing for granted, which appears very doubtful; for although the new Convention might have more information, and perhaps equal abilities, yet it does not from thence follow that they would be equally *disposed to agree*. The contrary of this position is the most probable. You must have observed that the same temper and equanimity which prevailed among the people on the former occasion, no longer exists. We have unhappily become divided into parties; and this important subject has been handled with such indiscreet and offensive acrimony, and with so many little unhandsome artifices and misrepresentations, that pernicious heats and animosities have been kindled, and spread their flames far and wide among us. When therefore it becomes a question who shall be deputed to the new Convention; we cannot flatter ourselves that the talents and integrity of the candidates will determine who shall be elected. Federal electors will vote for Fœderal deputies, and anti-Fœderal electors for anti-Fœderal ones. Nor will either party prefer the most moderate of their adherents, for as the most staunch and active partizans will be the most popular, so the men most willing and able to carry points, to oppose, and divide, and embarrass their opponents, will be chosen. A Convention formed at such a season, and of such men, would be but too exact an epitome of the great body that named them. The same party views, the same propensity to opposition, the same distrusts and jealousies, and the same unaccommodating spirit which prevail without, would be concentred and ferment with still greater violence within. Each deputy would recollect *who* sent him, and *why* he was sent; and be too apt to consider himself bound in honor, to contend and act vigorously under the standard of his party, and not hazard their displeasure by prefering compromise to victory. As vice does not sow the seeds of virtue, so neither does passion cultivate the fruits of reason. Suspicions and resentments create no disposition to conciliate, nor do they infuse a desire of making partial

and personal objects bend to general union and the common good.
The utmost efforts of that excellent disposition were necessary to enable the late Convention to perform their task; and although contrary
causes sometimes operate similar effects, yet to expect that discord and
animosity should produce the fruits of confidence and agreement, is to
expect "grapes from thorns, and figs from thistles."

The States of Georgia, Delaware, Jersey, and Connecticut, have
adopted the present plan with unexampled unanimity; they are content with it as it is, and consequently their deputies, being apprized
of the sentiments of their Constituents, will be little inclined to make
alterations, and cannot be otherwise than averse to changes which
they have no reason to think would be agreeable to their people—
some other States, tho' less unanimous, have nevertheless adopted it
by very respectable majorities; and for reasons so evidently cogent,
that even the minority in one of them, have nobly pledged themselves
for its promotion and support. From these circumstances, the new
Convention would derive and experience difficulties unknown to the
former. Nor are these the only additional difficulties they would have
to encounter. Few are ignorant that there has lately sprung up a sect
of politicians who teach and profess to believe that the extent of our
nation is too great for the superintendance of one national Government, and on that principle argue that it ought to be divided into
two or three. This doctrine, however mischievous in its tendency and
consequences, has its advocates; and, should any of them be sent to
the Convention, it will naturally be their policy rather to cherish than
to prevent divisions; for well knowing that the institution of any national Government, would blast their favourite system, no measures
that lead to it can meet with their aid or approbation.

Nor can we be certain whether or not any and what foreign influence would, on such an occasion, be indirectly exerted, nor for what
purposes—delicacy forbids an ample discussion of this question. Thus
much may be said, without error or offence, viz. That such foreign nations as desire the prosperity of America, and would rejoice to see her
become great and powerful, under the auspices of a Government wisely
calculated to extend her commerce, to encourage her navigation and
marine, and to direct the whole weight of her power and resources as
her interest and honour may require, will doubtless be friendly to the

Union of the States, and to the establishment of a Government able to perpetuate, protect and dignify it. Such other foreign nations, if any such their be, who, jealous of our growing importance, and fearful that our commerce and navigation should impair their own—who behold our rapid population with regret, and apprehend that the enterprising spirit of our people, when seconded by power and probability of success, may be directed to objects not consistent with their policy or interests, cannot fail to wish that we may continue a weak and a divided people.

These considerations merit much attention, and candid men will judge how far they render it probable that a new Convention would be able either to agree in a better plan, or with tolerable unanimity, in any plan at all. Any plan forcibly carried by a slender majority, must expect numerous opponents among the people, who, especially in their present temper, would be more inclined to reject than adopt any system so made and carried. We should in such case again see the press teeming with publications for and against it; for as the minority would take pains to justify their dissent, so would the majority be industrious to display the wisdom of their proceedings. Hence new divisions, new parties, and new distractions would ensue, and no one can foresee or conjecture when or how they would terminate.

Let those who are sanguine in their expectations of a better plan from a new Convention, also reflect on the delays and risque to which it would expose us. Let them consider whether we ought, by continuing much longer in our present humiliated condition, to give other nations further time to perfect their restrictive systems of commerce, to reconcile their own people to them, and to fence and guard and strengthen them by all those regulations and contrivances in which a jealous policy is ever fruitful. Let them consider whether we ought to give further opportunities to discord to alienate the hearts of our citizens from one another, and thereby encourage new Cromwells to bold exploits. Are we certain that our foreign creditors will continue patient, and ready to proportion their forbearance to our delays? Are we sure that our distresses, dissentions and weakness will neither invite hostility nor insult? If they should, how ill prepared shall we be for defence! without Union, without Government, without money, and without credit!

It seems necessary to remind you, that some time must yet elapse, before all the States will have decided on the present plan. If they reject it, some time must also pass before the measure of a new Convention, can be brought about and generally agreed to. A further space of time will then be requisite to elect their deputies, and send them on to Convention. What time they may expend when met, cannot be divined, and it is equally uncertain how much time the several States may take to deliberate and decide on any plan they may recommend—if adopted, still a further space of time will be necessary to organize and set it in motion:—In the mean time our affairs are daily going on from bad to worse, and it is not rash to say that our distresses are accumulating like compound interest.

But if for the reasons already mentioned, and others that we cannot now perceive, the new Convention, instead of producing a better plan, should give us only a history of their disputes, or should offer us one still less pleasing than the present, where should we be then? The old Confederation has done its best, and cannot help us; and is now so relaxed and feeble, that in all probability it would not survive so violent a shock. Then "to your tents Oh Israel!" would be the word. Then every band of union would be severed. Then every State would be a little nation, jealous of its neighbors, and anxious to strengthen itself by foreign alliances, against its former friends. Then farewell to fraternal affection, unsuspecting intercourse; and mutual participation in commerce, navigation and citizenship. Then would arise mutual restrictions and fears, mutual garrisons,—and standing armies, and all those dreadful evils which for so many ages plagued England, Scotland, Wales, and Ireland, while they continued disunited, and were played off against each other.

Consider my fellow citizens what you are about, before it is too late—consider what in such an event would be your particular case. You know the geography of your State, and the consequences of your local position. Jersey and Connecticut, to whom your impost laws have been unkind—Jersey and Connecticut, who have adopted the present plan, and expect much good from it—will impute its miscarriage and all the consequent evils to you. They now consider your opposition as dictated more by your fondness for your impost, than for those rights to which they have never been behind you in attachment. They cannot, they will not love you—they border upon you, and are your neighbors; but you will soon cease to regard their neighborhood as a blessing. You have but one port and outlet to your commerce, and how you are to keep that outlet free and uninterrupted, merits consideration.—What advantage

Vermont in combination with others, might take of you, may easily be conjectured; nor will you be at a loss to perceive how much reason the people of Long Island, whom you cannot protect, have to deprecate being constantly exposed to the depredations of every invader.

These are short hints—they ought not to be more developed—you can easily in your own mind dilate and trace them through all their relative circumstances and connections.—Pause then for a moment, and reflect whether the matters you are disputing about, are of sufficient moment to justify your running such extravagant risques. Reflect that the present plan comes recommended to you by men and fellow citizens who have given you the highest proofs that men can give, of their justice, their love for liberty and their country of their prudence, of their application, and of their talents. They tell you it is the best that they could form; and that in their opinion, it is necessary to redeem you from those calamities which already begin to be heavy upon us all. You find that not only those men, but others of similar characters, and of whom you have also had very ample experience, advise you to adopt it. You find that whole States concur in the sentiment, and among them are your next neighbors; both whom have shed much blood in the cause of liberty, and have manifested as strong and constant a predilection for a free Republican Government as any State in the Union, and perhaps in the world. They perceive not those latent mischiefs in it, with which some double-sighted politicians endeavor to alarm you. You cannot but be sensible that this plan or constitution will always be in the hands and power of the people, and that if on experiment, it should be found defective or incompetent, they may either remedy its defects, or substitute another in its room. The objectionable parts of it are certainly very questionable, for otherwise there would not be such a contrariety of opinions about them. Experience will better determine such questions than theoretical arguments, and so far as the danger of abuses is urged against the institution of a Government, remember that a power to do good, always involves a power to do harm. We must in the business of Government as well as in all other business, have some degree of confidence, as well as a great degree of caution. Who on a sick bed would refuse medicines from a physician, merely because it is as much in his power to administer deadly poisons, as salutary remedies.

You cannot be certain, that by rejecting the proposed plan you would not place yourself in a very awkward situation. Suppose nine States should nevertheless adopt it, would you not in that case be obliged either to separate from the Union or rescind your dissent? The first would not be eligible, nor could the latter be pleasant—A mere hint is sufficient on this topic—You cannot but be aware of the consequences.

Consider then, how weighty and how many considerations advise and persuade the people of America to remain in the safe and easy path of Union; to continue to move and act as they hitherto have done, as a *band of brothers*; to have confidence in themselves and in one another; and since all cannot see with the same eyes, at least to give the proposed Constitution a fair trial, and to mend it as time, occasion and experience may dictate. It would little become us to verify the predictions of those who ventured to prophecy, that *peace*: instead of blessing us with happiness and tranquility, would serve only as the signal for factions, discords and civil contentions to rage in our land, and overwhelm it with misery and distress.

Let us also be mindful that the cause of freedom greatly depends on the use we make of the singular opportunities we enjoy of governing ourselves wisely; for if the event should prove, that the people of this country either cannot or will not govern themselves, who will hereafter be advocates for systems, which however charming in theory and prospect. are not reducible to practice. If the people of our nation, instead of consenting to be governed by laws of their own making, and rulers of their own choosing, should let licentiousness, disorder, and confusion reign over them, the minds of men every where, will insensibly become alienated from republican forms, and prepared to prefer and acquiesce in Governments, which, though less friendly to liberty, afford more peace and security.

*Receive this Address with the same candor with which it is written; and may the spirit of wisdom and patriotism direct and distinguish your councils and your conduct.*

*A citizen of New York.*

# Thomas Paine
## (1737-1809)

# THOMAS PAINE
## (1737-1809)

THOMAS PAINE WAS BORN ON FEBRUARY 9, 1737, in Thetford, England, to a Quaker father and Anglican mother. Though Paine didn't receive much of formal education, he did learn arithmetic, as well as how to read and write. When he was 13, he started to work with his father to make stays for ships. Later on, Paine served as an officer that hunted smugglers and collected taxes. He was not very successful in any job he held prior to leaving England.

Around 1760, Paine's wife died in childbirth, losing the baby, and his business failed. In 1772, Paine published "The Case of the Officers of Excise," which argued for higher pay for excise officers. He personally handed out 4,000 copies of the work. In 1774, Paine was fired, and soon afterwards, he met Benjamin Franklin, who told Paine that he should travel to the colonies and begin a life there. On November 30, 1774, Paine arrived in Philadelphia, PA, where he helped to edit the *Pennsylvania Magazine*. He started to write his own works under pseudonyms, condemning the slave trade and advocating for human rights as a whole.

After the Battle of Lexington and Concord on April 19, 1775, which was the first battle of the Revolutionary War, Paine believed that the colonists should acquire independence from Britain, rather than revolt against taxation. In support of this belief, Paine wrote his 50-page pamphlet, "Common Sense," which was printed in 1776 and sold more than 500,000 copies in just a few months.

During the war, Paine volunteered as a personal assistant to General Nathanael Greene. To help the revolutionary cause, Paine wrote his 16 "Crisis" papers, from 1776-1783. The first paper was published on December 19, 1776 and was so inspiring that George Washington had it read to the Continental Army at Valley Forge, hoping to help motivate them.

In 1777, Congress appointed Paine to be the secretary to the Committee for Foreign Affairs. This lasted only until 1779, however, due to actions that Paine took to reveal a scandal in which a member of the Continental Congress was trying to personally profit from foreign aid. Paine quoted secret documents to the public and alluded to secret negotiation in his pamphlets.

Afterwards, Paine became the clerk of the General Assembly of Pennsylvania. In his new position, he noticed that many American troops were receiving little to no pay, and rarely had any supplies. He began a drive at his home, as well as one in France, in order to help garner support for the troops, which helped the Americans finish out the war. Seeing success in his endeavors, he appealed to the states to pool their resources together to support the nation as a whole. Paine then wrote "Public Good" in 1780, advocating for a convention that would replace the weak Articles of Confederation with a new constitution.

Paine decided to return to England in April of 1787. Soon after arriving, the French Revolution began and he turned his attention to supporting its democratic ideals. Seeing other individuals attacking the Revolution, Paine wrote his book, *Rights of Man*, in 1791. Though, in the book, Paine's ideas went further than the French Revolution and began speaking of many aspects of European society, leading to the book being banned in Britain and Paine being accused of treason.

Traveling to France and escaping prosecution, Paine, who was eventually named an honorary citizen of France, ended up supporting a cause that called for preserving the life of Louis XVI. When Robespierre took over, Paine was imprisoned for nearly a year (1793-1794). During this time, he wrote the beginning part of *The Age of Reason*, which criticized institutional religion. Again, this book was banned in Britain. After his release, Paine remained in France and finished the book before returning to the United States at the invitation of President Jefferson.

In addition to his writing skills, Paine was also an inventor. Among his developments were a crane to lift objects, a smokeless candle. He also attempted to use gunpowder to generate power. He built several bridges in both the U.S. and England, creating the Sunderland Bridge in Wearmonth, England, which was the second iron bridge ever built and was the largest in the world at the time. It was renovated in 1857 and ultimately replaced in 1927.

Paine again returned to the U.S. in 1802 or 1803 to find that his work and reputation had been forgotten, leaving him to be viewed as a rabble-rouser. It wouldn't be for another hundred years before his tarnished name would be redeemed.

Thomas Paine died alone of an unknown illness on June 8, 1809. Only six people attended his funeral. In his obituary, the *New York Citizen*, wrote that "[h]e had lived long, did some good and much harm." It wasn't until 1937 that the *Times of London* called him the "English Voltaire," helping reinstate Paine's rightful place as one of the Founding Fathers.

# COMMON SENSE

## INTRODUCTION.

Perhaps the sentiments contained in the following pages, are not *yet* sufficiently fashionable to procure them general Favor; a long Habit of not thinking a Thing *wrong*, gives it a superficial appearance of being *right*, and raises at first a formidable outcry in defence of Custom. But the Tumult soon subsides. Time makes more Converts than Reason.

As a long and violent abuse of power is generally the means of calling the right of it in question, (and in matters too which might never have been thought of, had not the sufferers been aggravated into the inquiry,) and as the King of England hath undertaken in his *own right*, to support the Parliament in what he calls *Theirs*, and as the good People of this Country are grievously oppressed by the Combination, they have an undoubted privilege to enquire into the Pretensions of both, and equally to reject the Usurpation of *either*.

In the following Sheets, the Author hath studiously avoided every thing which is personal among ourselves. Compliments as well as censure to individuals make no part thereof. The wise and the worthy need not the triumph of a Pamphlet; and those whose sentiments are injudicious or unfriendly will cease of themselves, unless too much pains is bestowed upon their conversions.

The cause of America is in a great measure the cause of all mankind. Many circumstances have, and will arise, which are not local, but universal, and through which the principles of all lovers of mankind are affected, and in the event of which their affections are interested. The laying a country desolate with fire and sword, declaring war against the natural rights of all mankind, and extirpating the defenders thereof from the face of the earth, is the concern of every man to whom nature hath given the power of feeling; of which class, regardless of party censure, is

The Author.

*Postscript to Preface in the third edition.*

P. S. The Publication of this new Edition hath been delayed, with a view of taking notice (had it been necessary) of any attempt to refute the Doctrine of Independence: As no answer hath yet appeared, it is now presumed that none will, the time needful for getting such a Performance ready for the Public being considerably past.

Who the Author of this Production is, is wholly unnecessary to the Public, as the Object for Attention is the *Doctrine itself*, not the *Man*. Yet it may not be unnecessary to say, That he is unconnected with any party, and under no sort of Influence, public or private, but the influence of reason and principle.

Philadelphia,

February 14, 1776

## COMMON SENSE. ON THE ORIGIN AND DESIGN OF GOVERNMENT IN GEN- ERAL, WITH CONCISE RE-MARKS ON THE ENGLISH CONSTITUTION.

Some writers have so confounded society with government, as to leave little or no distinction between them; whereas they are not only different, but have different origins. Society is produced by our wants, and government by our wickedness; the former promotes our happiness *positively* by uniting our affections, the latter *negatively* by restraining our vices. The one encourages intercourse, the other creates distinctions. The first is a patron, the last a punisher.

Society in every state is a blessing, but Government, even in its best state, is but a necessary evil; in its worst state an intolerable one: for when we suffer, or are exposed to the same miseries *by a Government*, which we might expect in a country *without Government*, our calamity is heightened by reflecting that we furnish the means by which we suffer. Government, like dress, is the badge of lost innocence; the palaces of kings are built upon the ruins of the bowers of paradise. For were the impulses of conscience clear, uniform and irresistibly obeyed, man would need no other law-giver; but that not being the case, he finds it necessary to surrender up a part of his property to furnish means for the protection of the rest; and this he is induced to do by the same prudence which in every other case advises him, out of two evils to choose the least. Wherefore, security being the true design and end of government, it unanswerably follows that whatever form thereof appears most likely to ensure it to us, with the least expence and greatest benefit, is preferable to all others.

In order to gain a clear and just idea of the design and end of government, let us suppose a small number of persons settled in some sequestered part of the earth, unconnected with the rest; they will then represent the first peopling of any country, or of the world. In this state of natural liberty, society will be their first thought. A thousand motives will excite them thereto; the strength of one man is so unequal to his wants, and his mind so unfitted for perpetual solitude, that he is soon obliged to seek assistance and relief of another, who in his turn requires the same. Four or five united would be able to raise a tolerable dwelling in the midst of a wilderness, but one man might labour out the common period of life without accomplishing any thing; when he had felled his timber he could not remove it, nor erect it after it was removed; hunger in the mean time would urge him to quit his work, and every different want would call him a different way. Disease, nay even misfortune, would be death; for though neither might be mortal, yet either would disable him from living, and reduce him to a state in which he might rather be said to perish than to die.

Thus necessity, like a gravitating power, would soon form our newly arrived emigrants into society, the reciprocal blessings of which would supercede, and render the obligations of law and government unnecessary while they remained perfectly just to each other; but as nothing but Heaven is impregnable to vice, it will unavoidably happen that in proportion as they surmount the first difficulties of emigration, which bound them together in a common cause, they will begin to relax in their duty and attachment to each other: and this remissness will point out the necessity of establishing some form of government to supply the defect of moral virtue.

Some convenient tree will afford them a State House, under the branches of which the whole Colony may assemble to deliberate on public matters. It is more than probable that their first laws will have the title only of Regulations and be enforced by no other penalty than public disesteem. In this first parliament every man by natural right will have a seat.

But as the Colony encreases, the public concerns will encrease likewise, and the distance at which the members may be separated, will render it too inconvenient for all of them to meet on every occasion as at first, when their number was small, their habitations near, and the public concerns few and trifling. This will point out the convenience of their consenting to leave the legislative part to be managed by a select number chosen from the whole body, who are supposed to have the same concerns at stake which those have who appointed them, and who will act in the same manner as the whole body would act were they present. If the colony continue encreasing, it will become necessary to augment the number of representatives, and that the interest of every part of the colony may be attended to, it will be found best to divide the whole into convenient parts, each part sending its proper number: and that the *elected* might never form to themselves an interest separate from the *electors*, prudence will point out the propriety of having elections often: because as the *elected* might by that means return and mix again with the general body of the *electors* in a few months, their fidelity to the public will be secured by the prudent reflection of not making a rod for themselves. And as this frequent interchange will establish a common interest with every part of the community, they will mutually and naturally support each other, and on this, (not on the unmeaning name of king,) depends the *strength of government, and the happiness of the governed.*

Here then is the origin and rise of government; namely, a mode rendered necessary by the inability of moral virtue to govern the world; here too is the design and end of government, viz. Freedom and security. And however our eyes may be dazzled with show, or our ears deceived by sound; however prejudice may warp our wills, or interest darken our understanding, the simple voice of nature and reason will say, 'tis right.

I draw my idea of the form of government from a principle in nature which no art can overturn, viz. that the more simple any thing is, the less liable it is to be disordered, and the easier repaired when disordered; and with this maxim in view I offer a few remarks on the so much boasted constitution of England That it was noble for the dark and slavish times in which it was erected, is granted. When the world was overrun with tyranny the least remove therefrom was a glorious rescue. But that it is imperfect, subject to convulsions, and incapable of producing what it seems to promise, is easily demonstrated.

Absolute governments, (tho' the disgrace of human nature) have this advantage with them, they are simple; if the people suffer, they know the head from which their suffering springs; know likewise the remedy; and are not bewildered by a variety of causes and cures. But the constitution of England is so exceedingly complex, that the nation may suffer for years together without being able to discover in which part the fault lies; some will say in one and some in another, and every political physician will advise a different medicine.

I know it is difficult to get over local or long standing prejudices, yet if we will suffer ourselves to examine the component parts of the English constitution, we shall find them to be the base remains of two ancient tyrannies, compounded with some new Republican materials.

*First.*—The remains of Monarchical tyranny in the person of the King.

*Secondly.*—The remains of Aristocratical tyranny in the persons of the Peers.

*Thirdly.*—The new Republican materials, in the persons of the Commons, on whose virtue depends the freedom of England.

The two first, by being hereditary, are independent of the People; wherefore in a *constitutional sense* they contribute nothing towards the freedom of the State.

To say that the constitution of England is an *union* of three powers, reciprocally *checking* each other, is farcical; either the words have no meaning, or they are flat contradictions.

To say that the Commons is a check upon the King, presupposes two things.

*First.*—That the King is not to be trusted without being looked after, or in other words, that a thirst for absolute power is the natural disease of monarchy.

*Secondly.*—That the Commons, by being appointed for that purpose, are either wiser or more worthy of confidence than the Crown.

But as the same constitution which gives the Commons a power to check the King by withholding the supplies, gives afterwards the King a power to check the Commons, by empowering him to reject their other bills; it again supposes that the King is wiser than those whom it has already supposed to be wiser than him. A mere absurdity!

There is something exceedingly ridiculous in the composition of Monarchy; it first excludes a man from the means of information, yet empowers him to act in cases where the highest judgment is required. The state of a king shuts him from the World, yet the business of a king requires him to know it thoroughly; wherefore the different parts, by unnaturally opposing and destroying each other, prove the whole character to be absurd and useless.

Some writers have explained the English constitution thus: the King, say they, is one, the people another; the Peers are a house in behalf of the King, the commons in behalf of the people; but this hath all the distinctions of a house divided against itself; and though the expressions be pleasantly arranged, yet when examined they appear idle and ambiguous; and it will always happen, that the nicest construction that words are capable of, when applied to the description of something which either cannot exist, or is too incomprehensible to be within the compass of description, will be words of sound only, and though they may amuse the ear, they cannot inform the mind: for this explanation includes a previous question, viz. *how came the king by a power which the people are afraid to trust, and always obliged to check?* Such a power could not be the gift of a wise people, neither can any power, *which needs checking*, be from God; yet the provision which the constitution makes supposes such a power to exist.

But the provision is unequal to the task; the means either cannot or will not accomplish the end, and the whole affair is a *Felo de se*: for as the greater weight will always carry up the less, and as all the wheels of a machine are put in motion by one, it only remains to know which power in the constitution has the most weight, for that will govern: and tho' the others, or a part of them, may clog, or, as the phrase is, check the rapidity of its motion, yet so long as they cannot stop it, their endeavours will be ineffectual: The first moving power will at last have its way, and what it wants in speed is supplied by time.

That the crown is this overbearing part in the English constitution needs not be mentioned, and that it derives its whole consequence merely from being the giver of places and pensions is self-evident; wherefore, though we have been wise enough to shut and lock a door against absolute Monarchy, we at the same time have been foolish enough to put the Crown in possession of the key.

The prejudice of Englishmen, in favour of their own government, by King, Lords and Commons, arises as much or more from
national pride than reason. Individuals are undoubtedly safer in England than in some other countries: but the will of the king is as
much the law of the land in Britain as in France, with this difference,
that instead of proceeding directly from his mouth, it is handed to
the people under the formidable shape of an act of parliament. For
the fate of Charles the First hath only made kings more subtle—not
more just.

Wherefore, laying aside all national pride and prejudice in favour
of modes and forms, the plain truth is that *it is wholly owing to the constitution of the people, and not to the constitution of the government* that
the crown is not as oppressive in England as in Turkey.

An inquiry into the *constitutional errors* in the English form of
government, is at this time highly necessary; for as we are never in a
proper condition of doing justice to others, while we continue under
the influence of some leading partiality, so neither are we capable of doing it to ourselves while we remain fettered by any obstinate prejudice.
And as a man who is attached to a prostitute is unfitted to choose or
judge of a wife, so any prepossession in favour of a rotten constitution
of government will disable us from discerning a good one.

## OF MONARCHY AND HEREDITARY SUCCESSION.

Mankind being originally equals in the order of creation, the
equality could only be destroyed by some subsequent circumstance: the distinctions of rich and poor may in a great measure
be accounted for, and that without having recourse to the harsh
ill-sounding names of oppression and avarice. Oppression is often
the *consequence*, but seldom or never the *means* of riches; and tho'
avarice will preserve a man from being necessitously poor, it generally makes him too timorous to be wealthy.

But there is another and greater distinction for which no truly
natural or religious reason can be assigned, and that is the distinction
of men into KINGS and SUBJECTS. Male and female are the distinctions of nature, good and bad the distinctions of Heaven; but how a
race of men came into the world so exalted above the rest, and distin-

guished like some new species, is worth inquiring into, and whether they are the means of happiness or of misery to mankind.

In the early ages of the world, according to the scripture chronology there were no kings; the consequence of which was, there were no wars; it is the pride of kings which throws mankind into confusion. Holland, without a king hath enjoyed more peace for this last century than any of the monarchical governments in Europe. Antiquity favours the same remark; for the quiet and rural lives of the first Patriarchs have a happy something in them, which vanishes when we come to the history of Jewish royalty.

Government by kings was first introduced into the world by the Heathens, from whom the children of Israel copied the custom. It was the most prosperous invention the Devil ever set on foot for the promotion of idolatry. The Heathens paid divine honours to their deceased kings, and the Christian World hath improved on the plan by doing the same to their living ones. How impious is the title of sacred Majesty applied to a worm, who in the midst of his splendor is crumbling into dust!

As the exalting one man so greatly above the rest cannot be justified on the equal rights of nature, so neither can it be defended on the authority of scripture; for the will of the Almighty as declared by Gideon, and the prophet Samuel, expressly disapproves of government by Kings. All anti-monarchical parts of scripture, have been very smoothly glossed over in monarchical governments, but they undoubtedly merit the attention of countries which have their governments yet to form. *Render unto Cesar the things which are Cesar's*, is the scripture doctrine of courts, yet it is no support of monarchical government, for the Jews at that time were without a king, and in a state of vassalage to the Romans.

Near three thousand years passed away, from the Mosaic account of the creation, till the Jews under a national delusion requested a king. Till then their form of government (except in extraordinary cases where the Almighty interposed) was a kind of Republic, administered by a judge and the elders of the tribes. Kings they had none, and it was held sinful to acknowledge any being under that title but the Lord of Hosts. And when a man seriously reflects on the idolatrous homage which is paid to the persons of kings, he need not wonder that the Almighty, ever jealous of his honour, should disapprove a form of government which so impiously invades the prerogative of Heaven.

Monarchy is ranked in scripture as one of the sins of the Jews, for which a curse in reserve is denounced against them. The history of that transaction is worth attending to.

The children of Israel being oppressed by the Midianites, Gideon marched against them with a small army, and victory thro' the divine interposition decided in his favour. The Jews, elate with success, and attributing it to the generalship of Gideon, proposed making him a king, saying, *Rule thou over us, thou and thy son, and thy son's son.* Here was temptation in its fullest extent; not a kingdom only, but an hereditary one; but Gideon in the piety of his soul replied, *I will not rule over you, neither shall my son rule over you.* THE LORD SHALL RULE OVER YOU. Words need not be more explicit; Gideon doth not decline the honour, but denieth their right to give it; neither doth he compliment them with invented declarations of his thanks, but in the positive stile of a prophet charges them with disaffection to their proper Sovereign, the King of Heaven.

About one hundred and thirty years after this, they fell again into the same error. The hankering which the Jews had for the idolatrous customs of the Heathens, is something exceedingly unaccountable; but so it was, that laying hold of the misconduct of Samuel's two sons, who were intrusted with some secular concerns, they came in an abrupt and clamorous manner to Samuel, saying, *Behold thou art old, and thy sons walk not in thy ways, now make us a king to judge us like all the other nations.* And here we cannot but observe that their motives were bad, viz. that they might be *like* unto other nations, i. e. the Heathens, whereas their true glory lay in being as much *unlike* them as possible. *But the thing displeased Samuel when they said, give us a King to judge us; and Samuel prayed unto the Lord, and the Lord said unto Samuel, hearken unto the voice of the people in all that they say unto thee, for they have not rejected thee, but they have rejected me,* THAT I SHOULD NOT REIGN OVER THEM. *According to all the works which they have done since the day that I brought them up out of Egypt even unto this day, wherewith they have forsaken me, and served other Gods: so do they also unto thee. Now therefore hearken unto their voice, howbeit, protest solemnly unto them and show them the manner of the King that shall reign over them,* i. e. not of any particular King, but the general manner of the Kings of the earth whom Israel was so eagerly copying after. And notwithstanding the great distance of time and difference of manners, the character is still in fashion. *And Samuel told all the words of the Lord unto the people, that asked of him a King. And he said, This shall be the manner of the King that shall reign over you. He will take your sons and appoint them for himself for his chariots and to be his horsemen, and some shall run before his chariots* (this description agrees with the present mode of impressing men) *and he will appoint him captains over thousands and captains over fifties, will set them to ear his ground and to reap his harvest, and to make his instruments of war, and instruments of his chariots. And he will take your daughters to be confectionaries, and to be cooks, and to be bakers* (this describes the expense and luxury as well as the oppression of Kings) *and he will take your fields and your vineyards, and your olive yards, even the best of them, and give them to his servants. And he will take the tenth of your seed, and of your vineyards, and give them to his officers and to his servants* (by which we see that bribery, corruption, and favouritism, are the standing vices of Kings) *and he will take the tenth of your men servants, and your maid servants, and your goodliest young men, and your asses, and put them to his work: and he will take the tenth of your sheep, and ye shall be his servants, and ye shall cry out in that day because of your king which ye shall have chosen,* AND THE LORD WILL NOT HEAR YOU IN THAT DAY. This accounts for the continuation of Monarchy; neither do the characters of the few good kings which have lived since, either sanctify the title, or blot out the sinfulness of the origin; the high encomium given of David takes no notice of him *officially as a King*, but only as a *Man* after God's own heart. *Nevertheless the people refused to obey the voice of Samuel, and they said, Nay but we will have a king over us, that we may be like all the nations, and that our king may judge us, and go out before us and fight our battles.* Samuel continued to reason with them but to no purpose; he set before them their ingratitude, but all would not avail; and seeing them fully bent on their folly, he cried out, *I will call unto the Lord, and he shall send thunder and rain* (which was then a punishment, being in the time of wheat harvest) *that ye may perceive and see that your wickedness is great which ye have done in the sight of the Lord,* IN ASKING YOU A KING. *So Samuel called unto the Lord, and the Lord sent thunder and rain that day, and all the people greatly feared the Lord and Samuel. And all the people said unto Samuel, Pray for thy servants unto the Lord thy God that we die not, for* WE HAVE ADDED UNTO OUR SINS THIS EVIL, TO ASK A KING. These portions of scripture are direct and positive. They admit of no equivocal construction. That the Almighty hath here entered his protest against monarchical government is true, or the scripture is false. And a man hath good reason to believe that there is as much of kingcraft as priestcraft in withholding the scripture from the public in popish countries. For monarchy in every instance is the popery of government.

To the evil of monarchy we have added that of hereditary succession; and as the first is a degradation and lessening of ourselves, so the second, claimed as a matter of right, is an insult and imposition on posterity. For all men being originally equals, no one by birth could have a right to set up his own family in perpetual preference to all others for ever, and tho' himself might deserve some decent degree of honours of his cotemporaries, yet his descendants might be far too unworthy to inherit them. One of the strongest natural proofs of the folly of hereditary right in Kings, is that nature disapproves it, otherwise she would not so frequently turn it into ridicule, by giving mankind an *Ass for a Lion.*

Secondly, as no man at first could possess any other public honors than were bestowed upon him, so the givers of those honors could have no power to give away the right of posterity, and though they might say "We choose you for our head," they could not without manifest injustice to their children say "that your children and your children's children shall reign over ours forever." Because such an unwise, unjust, unnatural compact might (perhaps) in the next succession put them under the government of a rogue or a fool. Most wise men in their private sentiments have ever treated hereditary right with contempt; yet it is one of those evils which when once established is not easily removed: many submit from fear, others from superstition, and the more powerful part shares with the king the plunder of the rest.

This is supposing the present race of kings in the world to have had an honorable origin: whereas it is more than probable, that, could we take off the dark covering of antiquity and trace them to their first rise, we should find the first of them nothing better than the principal ruffian of some restless gang, whose savage manners or pre-eminence in subtilty obtained him the title of chief among plunderers: and who by increasing in power and extending his depredations, overawed the quiet and defenceless to purchase their safety by frequent contributions. Yet his electors could have no idea of giving hereditary right to his descendants, because such a perpetual exclusion of themselves was incompatible with the free and unrestrained principles they professed to live by. Wherefore, hereditary succession in the early ages of monarchy could not take place as a matter of claim, but as something casual or complemental; but as few or no records were extant in those days, and traditionary history stuff'd with fables, it was very easy, after the lapse of a few generations, to trump up some superstitious tale conveniently timed, Mahomet-like, to cram hereditary right down the throats of the vulgar. Perhaps the disorders which threatened, or seemed to threaten, on the decease of a leader and the choice of a new one (for elections among ruffians could not be very orderly) induced many at first to favour hereditary pretensions; by which means it happened, as it hath happened since, that what at first was submitted to as a convenience was afterwards claimed as a right.

England since the conquest hath known some few good monarchs, but groaned beneath a much larger number of bad ones: yet no man in his senses can say that their claim under William the Conqueror is a very honourable one. A French bastard landing with an armed Banditti and establishing himself king of England against the consent of the natives, is in plain terms a very paltry rascally original. It certainly hath no divinity in it. However it is needless to spend much time in exposing the folly of hereditary right; if there are any so weak as to believe it, let them promiscuously worship the Ass and the Lion, and welcome. I shall neither copy their humility, nor disturb their devotion.

Yet I should be glad to ask how they suppose kings came at first? The question admits but of three answers, viz. either by lot, by election, or by usurpation. If the first king was taken by lot, it establishes a precedent for the next, which excludes hereditary succession. Saul was by lot, yet the succession was not hereditary, neither does it appear from that transaction that there was any intention it ever should. If the first king of any country was by election, that likewise establishes a precedent for the next; for to say, that the right of all future generations is taken away, by the act of the first electors, in their choice not only of a king but of a family of kings for ever, hath no parallel in or out of scripture but the doctrine of original sin, which supposes the free will of all men lost in Adam; and from such comparison, and it will admit of no other, hereditary succession can derive no glory. For as in Adam all sinned, and as in the first electors all men obeyed; as in the one all mankind were subjected to Satan, and in the other to sovereignty; as our innocence was lost in the first, and our authority in the last; and as both disable us from re-assuming some former state and privilege, it unanswerably follows that original sin and hereditary succession are parallels. Dishonourable rank! inglorious connection! yet the most subtle sophist cannot produce a juster simile.

As to usurpation, no man will be so hardy as to defend it; and that William the Conqueror was an usurper is a fact not to be contradicted. The plain truth is, that the antiquity of English monarchy will not bear looking into.

But it is not so much the absurdity as the evil of hereditary succession which concerns mankind. Did it ensure a race of good and wise men it would have the seal of divine authority, but as it opens a door to the *foolish*, the *wicked*, and the *improper*, it hath in it the nature of oppression. Men who look upon themselves born to reign, and others to obey, soon grow insolent. Selected from the rest of mankind, their minds are early poisoned by importance; and the world they act in differs so materially from the world at large, that they have but little opportunity of knowing its true interests, and when they succeed to the government are frequently the most ignorant and unfit of any throughout the dominions.

Another evil which attends hereditary succession is, that the throne is subject to be possessed by a minor at any age; all which time the regency acting under the cover of a king have every opportunity and inducement to betray their trust. The same national misfortune happens when a king worn out with age and infirmity enters the last stage of human weakness. In both these cases the public becomes a prey to every miscreant who can tamper successfully with the follies either of age or infancy.

The most plausible plea which hath ever been offered in favor of hereditary succession is, that it preserves a nation from civil wars; and were this true, it would be weighty; whereas it is the most bare-faced falsity ever imposed upon mankind. The whole history of England disowns the fact. Thirty kings and two minors have reigned in that distracted kingdom since the conquest, in which time there has been (including the revolution) no less than eight civil wars and nineteen Rebellions. Wherefore instead of making for peace, it makes against it, and destroys the very foundation it seems to stand upon.

The contest for monarchy and succession, between the houses of York and Lancaster, laid England in a scene of blood for many years. Twelve pitched battles besides skirmishes and sieges were fought between Henry and Edward. Twice was Henry prisoner to Edward, who in his turn was prisoner to Henry. And so uncertain is the fate of war and the temper of a nation, when nothing but personal matters are the ground of a quarrel, that Henry was taken in triumph from a prison to a palace, and Edward obliged to fly from a palace to a foreign land; yet, as sudden transitions of temper are seldom lasting, Henry in his turn was driven from the throne, and Edward re-called to succeed him. The parliament always following the strongest side.

This contest began in the reign of Henry the Sixth, and was not entirely extinguished till Henry the Seventh, in whom the families were united. Including a period of 67 years, viz. from 1422 to 1489.

In short, monarchy and succession have laid (not this or that kingdom only) but the world in blood and ashes. 'Tis a form of government which the word of God bears testimony against, and blood will attend it.

If we enquire into the business of a King, we shall find that in some countries they may have none; and after sauntering away their lives without pleasure to themselves or advantage to the nation, withdraw from the scene, and leave their successors to tread the same idle round. In absolute monarchies the whole weight of business civil and military lies on the King; the children of Israel in their request for a king urged this plea, "that he may judge us, and go out before us and fight our battles." But in countries where he is neither a Judge nor a General, as in England, a man would be puzzled to know what is his business.

The nearer any government approaches to a Republic, the less business there is for a King. It is somewhat difficult to find a proper name for the government of England. Sir William Meredith calls it a Republic; but in its present state it is unworthy of the name, because the corrupt influence of the Crown, by having all the places in its disposal, hath so effectually swallowed up the power, and eaten out the virtue of the House of Commons (the Republican part in the constitution) that the government of England is nearly as monarchical as that of France or Spain. Men fall out with names without understanding them. For 'tis the Republican and not the Monarchical part of the constitution of England which Englishmen glory in, viz. the liberty of choosing an House of Commons from out of their own body—and it is easy to see that when Republican virtues fails, slavery ensues. Why is the constitution of England sickly, but because monarchy hath poisoned the Republic; the Crown hath engrossed the Commons.

In England a King hath little more to do than to make war and give away places; which, in plain terms, is to empoverish the nation and set it together by the ears. A pretty business indeed for a man to be allowed eight hundred thousand sterling a year for, and worshipped into the bargain! Of more worth is one honest man to society, and in the sight of God, than all the crowned ruffians that ever lived.

## THOUGHTS ON THE PRESENT STATE OF AMERICAN AFFAIRS.

In the following pages I offer nothing more than simple facts, plain arguments, and common sense: and have no other preliminaries to settle with the reader, than that he will divest himself of prejudice and prepossession, and suffer his reason and his feelings to determine for themselves: that he will put on, or rather that he will not put off, the true character of a man, and generously enlarge his views beyond the present day.

Volumes have been written on the subject of the struggle between England and America. Men of all ranks have embarked in the controversy, from different motives, and with various designs; but all have been ineffectual, and the period of debate is closed. Arms as the last resource decide the contest; the appeal was the choice of the King, and the Continent has accepted the challenge.

It hath been reported of the late Mr. Pelham (who tho' an able minister was not without his faults) that on his being attacked in the House of Commons on the score that his measures were only of a temporary kind, replied, *"they will last my time."* Should a thought so fatal and unmanly possess the Colonies in the present contest, the name of ancestors will be remembered by future generations with detestation.

The Sun never shined on a cause of greater worth. 'Tis not the affair of a City, a County, a Province, or a Kingdom; but of a Continent—of at least one eighth part of the habitable Globe. 'Tis not the concern of a day, a year, or an age; posterity are virtually involved in the contest, and will be more or less affected even to the end of time, by the proceedings now. Now is the seed-time of Continental union, faith and honour. The least fracture now will be like a name engraved with the point of a pin on the tender rind of a young oak; the wound would enlarge with the tree, and posterity read it in full grown characters.

By referring the matter from argument to arms, a new æra for politics is struck—a new method of thinking hath arisen. All plans, proposals, &c. prior to the nineteenth of April, *i.e.* to the commencement of hostilities, are like the almanacks of the last year; which tho' proper then, are superceded and useless now. Whatever was advanced by the advocates on either side of the question then, terminated in one and the same point, viz. a union with Great Britain; the only difference between the parties was the method of effecting it; the one proposing force, the other friendship; but it hath so far happened that the first hath failed, and the second hath withdrawn her influence.

As much hath been said of the advantages of reconciliation, which, like an agreeable dream, hath passed away and left us as we were, it is but right that we should examine the contrary side of the argument, and enquire into some of the many material injuries which these Colonies sustain, and always will sustain, by being connected with and dependant on Great-Britain. To examine that connection and dependance, on the principles of nature and common sense, to see what we have to trust to, if separated, and what we are to expect, if dependant.

I have heard it asserted by some, that as America has flourished under her former connection with Great-Britain, the same connection is necessary towards her future happiness, and will always have the same effect. Nothing can be more fallacious than this kind of argument. We may as well assert that because a child has thrived upon milk, that it is never to have meat, or that the first twenty years of our lives is to become a precedent for the next twenty. But even this is admitting more than is true; for I answer roundly, that America would have flourished as much, and probably much more, had no European power taken any notice of her. The commerce by which she hath enriched herself are the necessaries of life, and will always have a market while eating is the custom of Europe.

But she has protected us, say some. That she hath engrossed us is true, and defended the Continent at our expense as well as her own, is admitted; and she would have defended Turkey from the same motive, *viz.* for the sake of trade and dominion.

Alas! we have been long led away by ancient prejudices and made large sacrifices to superstition. We have boasted the protection of Great Britain, without considering, that her motive was *interest* not *attachment*; and that she did not protect us from *our enemies* on *our account*; but from *her enemies* on *her own account*, from those who had no quarrel with us on any *other account*, and who will always be our enemies on the *same account*. Let Britain waive her pretensions to the Continent, or the Continent throw off the dependance, and we should be at peace with France and Spain, were they at war with Britain. The miseries of Hanover last war ought to warn us against connections.

It hath lately been asserted in parliament, that the Colonies have no relation to each other but through the Parent Country, *i.e.* that Pennsylvania and the Jerseys, and so on for the rest, are sister Colonies by the way of England; this is certainly a very roundabout way of proving relationship, but it is the nearest and only true way of proving enmity (or enemyship, if I may so call it.) France and Spain never were, nor perhaps ever will be, our enemies as *Americans*, but as our being the *subjects of Great Britain*.

But Britain is the parent country, say some. Then the more shame upon her conduct. Even brutes do not devour their young, nor savages make war upon their families; Wherefore, the assertion, if true, turns to her reproach; but it happens not to be true, or only partly so, and the phrase *parent* or *mother country* hath been jesuitically adopted by the King and his parasites, with a low papistical design of gaining an unfair bias on the credulous weakness of our minds. Europe, and not England, is the parent country of America. This new World hath been the asylum for the persecuted lovers of civil and religious liberty from *every part* of Europe. Hither have they fled, not from the tender embraces of the mother, but from the cruelty of the monster; and it is so far true of England, that the same tyranny which drove the first emigrants from home, pursues their descendants still.

In this extensive quarter of the globe, we forget the narrow limits of three hundred and sixty miles (the extent of England) and carry our friendship on a larger scale; we claim brotherhood with every European Christian, and triumph in the generosity of the sentiment.

It is pleasant to observe by what regular gradations we surmount the force of local prejudices, as we enlarge our acquaintance with the World. A man born in any town in England divided into parishes, will naturally associate most with his fellow parishioners (because their interests in many cases will be common) and distinguish him by the name of *neighbour*; if he meet him but a few miles from home, he drops the narrow idea of a street, and salutes him by the name of *townsman*; if he travel out of the county and meet him in any other, he forgets the minor divisions of street and town, and calls him *countryman, i. e. countyman*: but if in their foreign excursions they should associate in France, or any other part of Europe, their local remembrance would be enlarged into that of *Englishmen*. And by a just parity of reasoning, all Europeans meeting in America, or any other quarter of the globe, are *countrymen*; for England, Holland, Germany, or Sweden, when compared with the whole, stand in the same places on the larger scale, which the divisions of street, town, and county do on the smaller ones; Distinctions too limited for Continental minds. Not one third of the inhabitants, even of this province, [Pennsylvania], are of English descent. Wherefore, I reprobate the phrase of Parent or Mother Country applied to England only, as being false, selfish, narrow and ungenerous.

But, admitting that we were all of English descent, what does it amount to? Nothing. Britain, being now an open enemy, extinguishes every other name and title: and to say that reconciliation is our duty, is truly farcical. The first king of England, of the present line (William the Conqueror) was a Frenchman, and half the peers of England are descendants from the same country; wherefore, by the same method of reasoning, England ought to be governed by France.

Much hath been said of the united strength of Britain and the Colonies, that in conjunction they might bid defiance to the world: But this is mere presumption; the fate of war is uncertain, neither do the expressions mean any thing; for this continent would never suffer itself to be drained of inhabitants, to support the British arms in either Asia, Africa, or Europe.

Besides, what have we to do with setting the world at defiance? Our plan is commerce, and that, well attended to, will secure us the peace and friendship of all Europe; because it is the interest of all Europe to have America a free port. Her trade will always be a protection, and her barrenness of gold and silver secure her from invaders.

I challenge the warmest advocate for reconciliation to show a single advantage that this continent can reap by being connected with Great Britain. I repeat the challenge; not a single advantage is derived. Our corn will fetch its price in any market in Europe, and our imported goods must be paid for buy them where we will.

But the injuries and disadvantages which we sustain by that connection, are without number; and our duty to mankind at large, as well as to ourselves, instruct us to renounce the alliance: because, any submission to, or dependance on, Great Britain, tends directly to involve this Continent in European wars and quarrels, and set us at variance with nations who would otherwise seek our friendship, and against whom we have neither anger nor complaint. As Europe is our market for trade, we ought to form no partial connection with any part of it. It is the true interest of America to steer clear of European contentions, which she never can do, while, by her dependance on Britain, she is made the make-weight in the scale of British politics.

Europe is too thickly planted with Kingdoms to be long at peace, and whenever a war breaks out between England and any foreign power, the trade of America goes to ruin, *because of her connection with Britain.* The next war may not turn out like the last, and should it not, the advocates for reconciliation now will be wishing for separation then, because neutrality in that case would be a safer convoy than a man of war. Every thing that is right or reasonable pleads for separation. The blood of the slain, the weeping voice of nature cries, 'TIS TIME TO PART. Even the distance at which the Almighty hath placed England and America is a strong and natural proof that the authority of the one over the other, was never the design of Heaven. The time likewise at which the Continent was discovered, adds weight to the argument, and the manner in which it was peopled, encreases the force of it. The Reformation was preceded by the discovery of America: As if the Almighty graciously meant to open a sanctuary to the persecuted in future years, when home should afford neither friendship nor safety.

The authority of Great Britain over this continent, is a form of government, which sooner or later must have an end: And a serious mind can draw no true pleasure by looking forward, under the painful and positive conviction that what he calls "the present constitution" is merely temporary. As parents, we can have no joy, knowing that this government is not sufficiently lasting to ensure any thing which we may bequeath to posterity: And by a plain method of argument, as we are running the next generation into debt, we ought to do the work of it, otherwise we use them meanly and pitifully. In order to discover the line of our duty rightly, we should take our children in our hand, and fix our station a few years farther into life; that eminence will present a prospect which a few present fears and prejudices conceal from our sight.

Though I would carefully avoid giving unnecessary offence, yet I am inclined to believe, that all those who espouse the doctrine of reconciliation, may be included within the following descriptions.

Interested men, who are not to be trusted, weak men who *cannot* see, prejudiced men who will not see, and a certain set of moderate men who think better of the European world than it deserves; and this last class, by an ill-judged deliberation, will be the cause of more calamities to this Continent than all the other three.

It is the good fortune of many to live distant from the scene of present sorrow; the evil is not sufficiently brought to their doors to make them feel the precariousness with which all American property is possessed. But let our imaginations transport us a few moments to Boston; that seat of wretchedness will teach us wisdom, and instruct us for ever to renounce a power in whom we can have no trust. The inhabitants of that unfortunate city who but a few months ago were in ease and affluence, have now no other alternative than to stay and starve, or turn out to beg. Endangered by the fire of their friends if they continue within the city, and plundered by the soldiery if they leave it, in their present situation they are prisoners without the hope of redemption, and in a general attack for their relief they would be exposed to the fury of both armies.

Men of passive tempers look somewhat lightly over the offences of Great Britain, and, still hoping for the best, are apt to call out, *Come, come, we shall be friends again for all this.* But examine the passions and feelings of mankind: bring the doctrine of reconciliation to the touchstone of nature, and then tell me whether you can hereafter love, honour, and faithfully serve the power that hath carried fire and sword into your land? If you cannot do all these, then are you only deceiving yourselves, and by your delay bringing ruin upon posterity. Your future connection with Britain, whom you can neither love nor honour, will be forced and unnatural, and being formed only on the plan of present convenience, will in a little time fall into a relapse more wretched than the first. But if you say, you can still pass the violations over, then I ask, hath your house been burnt? Hath your property been destroyed before your face? Are your wife and children destitute of a bed to lie on, or bread to live on? Have you lost a parent or a child by their hands, and yourself the ruined and wretched survivor? If you have not, then are you not a judge of those who have. But if you have, and can still shake hands with the murderers, then are you unworthy the name of husband, father, friend, or lover, and whatever may be your rank or title in life, you have the heart of a coward, and the spirit of a sycophant.

This is not inflaming or exaggerating matters, but trying them by those feelings and affections which nature justifies, and without which we should be incapable of discharging the social duties of life, or enjoying the felicities of it. I mean not to exhibit horror for the purpose of provoking revenge, but to awaken us from fatal and unmanly slumbers, that we may pursue determinately some fixed object. 'Tis not in the power of Britain or of Europe to conquer America, if she doth not conquer herself by delay and timidity. The present winter is worth an age if rightly employed, but if lost or neglected the whole Continent will partake of the misfortune; and there is no punishment which that man doth not deserve, be he who, or what, or where he will, that may be the means of sacrificing a season so precious and useful.

'Tis repugnant to reason, to the universal order of things, to all examples from former ages, to suppose that this Continent can long remain subject to any external power. The most sanguine in Britain doth not think so. The utmost stretch of human wisdom cannot, at this time, compass a plan, short of separation, which can promise the continent even a year's security. Reconciliation is *now* a fallacious dream. Nature hath deserted the connection, and art cannot supply her place. For, as Milton wisely expresses, "never can true reconcilement grow where wounds of deadly hate have pierced so deep."

Every quiet method for peace hath been ineffectual. Our prayers have been rejected with disdain; and hath tended to convince us that nothing flatters vanity or confirms obstinacy in Kings more than repeated petitioning—and nothing hath contributed more than that very measure to make the Kings of Europe absolute. Witness Denmark and Sweden. Wherefore, since nothing but blows will do, for God's sake let us come to a final separation, and not leave the next generation to be cutting throats under the violated unmeaning names of parent and child.

To say they will never attempt it again is idle and visionary; we thought so at the repeal of the stamp act, yet a year or two undeceived us; as well may we suppose that nations which have been once defeated will never renew the quarrel.

As to government matters, 'tis not in the power of Britain to do this continent justice: the business of it will soon be too weighty and intricate to be managed with any tolerable degree of convenience, by a power so distant from us, and so very ignorant of us; for if they cannot conquer us, they cannot govern us. To be always running three or four thousand miles with a tale or a petition, waiting four or five months for an answer, which, when obtained, requires five or six more to explain it in, will in a few years be looked upon as folly and childishness. There was a time when it was proper, and there is a proper time for it to cease.

Small islands not capable of protecting themselves are the proper objects for government to take under their care; but there is something absurd, in supposing a Continent to be perpetually governed by an island. In no instance hath nature made the satellite larger than its primary planet; and as England and America, with respect to each other, reverse the common order of nature, it is evident that they belong to different systems. England to Europe: America to itself.

I am not induced by motives of pride, party, or resentment to espouse the doctrine of separation and independence; I am clearly, positively, and conscientiously persuaded that it is the true interest of this Continent to be so; that every thing short of *that* is mere patchwork, that it can afford no lasting felicity,—that it is leaving the sword to our children, and shrinking back at a time when a little more, a little further, would have rendered this Continent the glory of the earth.

As Britain hath not manifested the least inclination towards a compromise, we may be assured that no terms can be obtained worthy the acceptance of the Continent, or any ways equal to the expence of blood and treasure we have been already put to.

The object contended for, ought always to bear some just proportion to the expense. The removal of North, or the whole detestable

junto, is a matter unworthy the millions we have expended. A temporary stoppage of trade was an inconvenience, which would have sufficiently ballanced the repeal of all the acts complained of, had such
repeals been obtained; but if the whole Continent must take up arms,
if every man must be a soldier, 'tis scarcely worth our while to fight
against a contemptible ministry only. Dearly, dearly do we pay for the
repeal of the acts, if that is all we fight for; for, in a just estimation
'tis as great a folly to pay a Bunker-hill price for law as for land. As I
have always considered the independancy of this continent, as an event
which sooner or later must arrive, so from the late rapid progress of the
Continent to maturity, the event cannot be far off. Wherefore, on the
breaking out of hostilities, it was not worth the while to have disputed
a matter which time would have finally redressed, unless we meant
to be in earnest: otherwise it is like wasting an estate on a suit at law,
to regulate the trespasses of a tenant whose lease is just expiring. No
man was a warmer wisher for a reconciliation than myself, before the
fatal nineteenth of April, 1775, but the moment the event of that day
was made known, I rejected the hardened, sullen-tempered Pharaoh of
England for ever; and disdain the wretch, that with the pretended title
of FATHER OF HIS PEOPLE can unfeelingly hear of their slaughter,
and composedly sleep with their blood upon his soul.

But admitting that matters were now made up, what would be the
event? I answer, the ruin of the Continent. And that for several reasons.

*First.* The powers of governing still remaining in the hands of the
King, he will have a negative over the whole legislation of this Continent.
And as he hath shown himself such an inveterate enemy to liberty, and
discovered such a thirst for arbitrary power, is he, or is he not, a proper
person to say to these colonies, *You shall make no laws but what I please!?*
And is there any inhabitant of America so ignorant as not to know, that
according to what is called the *present constitution,* this Continent can
make no laws but what the king gives leave to; and is there any man so
unwise as not to see, that (considering what has happened) he will suffer no law to be made here but such as suits *his* purpose? We may be as
effectually enslaved by the want of laws in America, as by submitting to
laws made for us in England. After matters are made up (as it is called)
can there be any doubt, but the whole power of the crown will be exerted
to keep this continent as low and humble as possible? Instead of going

forward we shall go backward, or be perpetually quarrelling, or ridiculously petitioning. We are already greater than the King wishes us to be, and will he not hereafter endeavor to make us less? To bring the matter to one point, Is the power who is jealous of our prosperity, a proper power to govern us? Whoever says *No*, to this question, is an Independant for independency means no more than this, whether we shall make our own laws, or, whether the King, the greatest enemy this continent hath, or can have, shall tell us *there shall be no laws but such as I like.*

But the King, you will say, has a negative in England; the people there can make no laws without his consent. In point of right and good order, it is something very ridiculous that a youth of twenty-one (which hath often happened) shall say to several millions of people older and wiser than himself, "I forbid this or that act of yours to be law." But in this place I decline this sort of reply, though I will never cease to expose the absurdity of it, and only answer that England being the King's residence, and America not so, makes quite another case. The King's negative here is ten times more dangerous and fatal than it can be in England; for there he will scarcely refuse his consent to a bill for putting England into as strong a state of defense as possible, and in America he would never suffer such a bill to be passed.

America is only a secondary object in the system of British politics. England consults the good of this country no further than it answers her own purpose. Wherefore, her own interest leads her to suppress the growth of ours in every case which doth not promote her advantage, or in the least interferes with it. A pretty state we should soon be in under such a second hand government, considering what has happened! Men do not change from enemies to friends by the alteration of a name: And in order to show that reconciliation now is a dangerous doctrine, I affirm, *that it would be policy in the King at this time to repeal the acts, for the sake of reinstating himself in the government of the provinces;* In order that HE MAY ACCOMPLISH BY CRAFT AND SUBTLETY, IN THE LONG RUN, WHAT HE CANNOT DO BY FORCE AND VIOLENCE IN THE SHORT ONE. Reconciliation and ruin are nearly related.

*Secondly.* That as even the best terms which we can expect to obtain can amount to no more than a temporary expedient, or a kind of government by guardianship, which can last no longer than till the

Colonies come of age, so the general face and state of things in the interim will be unsettled and unpromising. Emigrants of property will not choose to come to a country whose form of government hangs but by a thread, and who is every day tottering on the brink of commotion and disturbance; and numbers of the present inhabitants would lay hold of the interval to dispose of their effects, and quit the Continent.

But the most powerful of all arguments is, that nothing but independance, *i. e.* a Continental form of government, can keep the peace of the Continent and preserve it inviolate from civil wars. I dread the event of a reconciliation with Britain now, as it is more than probable that it will be followed by a revolt some where or other, the consequences of which may be far more fatal than all the malice of Britain.

Thousands are already ruined by British barbarity; (thousands more will probably suffer the same fate.) Those men have other feelings than us who have nothing suffered. All they now possess is liberty; what they before enjoyed is sacrificed to its service, and having nothing more to lose they disdain submission. Besides, the general temper of the Colonies, towards a British government will be like that of a youth who is nearly out of his time; they will care very little about her: And a government which cannot preserve the peace is no government at all, and in that case we pay our money for nothing; and pray what is it that Britain can do, whose power will be wholly on paper, should a civil tumult break out the very day after reconciliation? I have heard some men say, many of whom I believe spoke without thinking, that they dreaded an independance, fearing that it would produce civil wars: It is but seldom that our first thoughts are truly correct, and that is the case here; for there is ten times more to dread from a patched up connection than from independance. I make the sufferer's case my own, and I protest, that were I driven from house and home, my property destroyed, and my circumstances ruined, that as a man, sensible of injuries, I could never relish the doctrine of reconciliation, or consider myself bound thereby.

The Colonies have manifested such a spirit of good order and obedience to Continental government, as is sufficient to make every reasonable person easy and happy on that head. No man can assign the least pretence for his fears, on any other grounds, than such as are truly childish and ridiculous, viz., that one colony will be striving for superiority over another.

Where there are no distinctions there can be no superiority; perfect equality affords no temptation. The Republics of Europe are all (and we may say always) in peace. Holland and Switzerland are without wars, foreign or domestic: Monarchical governments, it is true, are never long at rest: the crown itself is a temptation to enterprising ruffians at home; and that degree of pride and insolence ever attendant on regal authority, swells into a rupture with foreign powers in instances where a republican government, by being formed on more natural principles, would negociate the mistake.

If there is any true cause of fear respecting independance, it is because no plan is yet laid down. Men do not see their way out. Wherefore, as an opening into that business I offer the following hints; at the same time modestly affirming, that I have no other opinion of them myself, than that they may be the means of giving rise to something better. Could the straggling thoughts of individuals be collected, they would frequently form materials for wise and able men to improve into useful matter.

Let the assemblies be annual, with a president only. The representation more equal, their business wholly domestic, and subject to the authority of a Continental Congress.

Let each Colony be divided into six, eight, or ten, convenient districts, each district to send a proper number of Delegates to Congress, so that each Colony send at least thirty. The whole number in Congress will be at least 390. Each congress to sit and to choose a President by the following method. When the Delegates are met, let a Colony be taken from the whole thirteen Colonies by lot, after which let the Congress choose (by ballot) a president from out of the Delegates of that Province. In the next Congress, let a Colony be taken by lot from twelve only, omitting that Colony from which the president was taken in the former Congress, and so proceeding on till the whole thirteen shall have had their proper rotation. And in order that nothing may pass into a law but what is satisfactorily just, not less than three fifths of the Congress to be called a majority. He that will promote discord, under a government so equally formed as this, would have joined Lucifer in his revolt.

But as there is a peculiar delicacy from whom, or in what manner, this business must first arise, and as it seems most agreeable and consistent that it should come from some intermediate body between the governed and the governors, that is, between the Congress and the People, let a Continental Conference be held in the following manner, and for the following purpose,

A Committee of twenty six members of congress, *viz.* Two for each Colony. Two Members from each House of Assembly, or Provincial Convention; and five Representatives of the people at large, to be chosen in the capital city or town of each Province, for, and in behalf of the whole Province, by as many qualified voters as shall think proper to attend from all parts of the Province for that purpose; or, if more convenient, the Representatives may be chosen in two or three of the most populous parts thereof. In this conference, thus assembled, will be united the two grand principles of business, *knowledge* and *power*. The Members of Congress, Assemblies, or Conventions, by having had experience in national concerns, will be able and useful counsellors, and the whole, being impowered by the people, will have a truly legal authority.

The conferring members being met, let their business be to frame a Continental Charter, or Charter of the United Colonies; (answering to what is called the Magna Charta of England) fixing the number and manner of choosing Members of Congress, Members of Assembly, with their date of sitting; and drawing the line of business and jurisdiction between them: Always remembering, that our strength is Continental, not Provincial. Securing freedom and property to all men, and above all things, the free exercise of religion, according to the dictates of conscience; with such other matter as it is necessary for a charter to contain. Immediately after which, the said conference to dissolve, and the bodies which shall be chosen conformable to the said charter, to be the Legislators and Governors of this Continent for the time being: Whose peace and happiness, may GOD preserve. AMEN.

Should any body of men be hereafter delegated for this or some similar purpose, I offer them the following extracts from that wise observer on Governments, Dragonetti. "The science," says he, "of the Politician consists in fixing the true point of happiness and freedom. Those men would deserve the gratitude of ages, who should discover a mode of government that contained the greatest sum of individual happiness, with the least national expense." (Dragonetti on "Virtues and Reward.")

But where, say some, is the King of America? I'll tell you, friend, he reigns above, and doth not make havoc of mankind like the Royal Brute of Great Britain. Yet that we may not appear to be defective even in earthly honours, let a day be solemnly set apart for proclaiming the Charter; let it be brought forth placed on the Divine Law, the Word of God; let a crown be placed thereon, by which the world may know, that so far as we approve of monarchy, that in America the law is king. For as in absolute governments the King is law, so in free countries the law ought to be king; and there ought to be no other. But lest any ill use should afterwards arise, let the Crown at the conclusion of the ceremony be demolished, and scattered among the people whose right it is.

A government of our own is our natural right: and when a man seriously reflects on the precariousness of human affairs, he will become convinced, that it is infinitely wiser and safer, to form a constitution of our own in a cool deliberate manner, while we have it in our power, than to trust such an interesting event to time and chance. If we omit it now, some Massanello* may hereafter arise, who, laying hold of popular disquietudes, may collect together the desperate and the discontented, and by assuming to themselves the powers of government, finally sweep away the liberties of the Continent like a deluge. Should the government of America return again into the hands of Britain, the tottering situation of things will be a temptation for some desperate adventurer to try his fortune; and in such a case, what relief can Britain give? Ere she could hear the news, the fatal business might be done; and ourselves suffering like the wretched Britons under the oppression of the Conqueror. Ye that oppose independance now, ye know not what ye do: ye are opening a door to eternal tyranny, by keeping vacant the seat of government. There are thousands and tens of thousands, who would think it glorious to expel from the Continent, that barbarous and hellish power, which hath stirred up the Indians and the Negroes to destroy us; the cruelty hath a double guilt, it is dealing brutally by us, and treacherously by them.

To talk of friendship with those in whom our reason forbids us to have faith, and our affections wounded thro' a thousand pores instruct us to detest, is madness and folly. Every day wears out the little remains of kindred between us and them; and can there be any reason to hope, that as the relationship expires, the affection will encrease, or that we shall agree better when we have ten times more and greater concerns to quarrel over than ever?

Ye that tell us of harmony and reconciliation, can ye restore to us the time that is past? Can ye give to prostitution its former innocence? neither can ye reconcile Britain and America. The last cord now is broken, the people of England are presenting addresses against us. There are injuries which nature cannot forgive; she would cease to be nature if she did. As well can the lover forgive the ravisher of his mistress, as the Continent forgive the murders of Britain. The Almighty hath implanted in us these unextinguishable feelings for good and wise purposes. They are the Guardians of his Image in our hearts. They distinguish us from the herd of common animals. The social compact would dissolve, and justice be extirpated from the earth, or have only a casual existence were we callous to the touches of affection. The robber and the murderer would often escape unpunished, did not the injuries which our tempers sustain, provoke us into justice.

O! ye that love mankind! Ye that dare oppose not only the tyranny but the tyrant, stand forth! Every spot of the old world is overrun with oppression. Freedom hath been hunted round the Globe. Asia and Africa have long expelled her. Europe regards her like a stranger, and England hath given her warning to depart. O! receive the fugitive, and prepare in time an asylum for mankind.

## OF THE PRESENT ABILITY OF AMERICA: WITH SOME MISCELLANEOUS REFLECTIONS.

I Have never met with a man, either in England or America, who hath not confessed his opinion, that a separation between the countries would take place one time or other: And there is no instance in which we have shown less judgment, than in endeavoring to describe, what we call, the ripeness or fitness of the Continent for independance.

As all men allow the measure, and vary only in their opinion of the time, let us, in order to remove mistakes, take a general survey of things, and endeavor if possible to find out the very time. But I need not go far, the inquiry ceases at once, for the *time hath found us*. The general concurrence, the glorious union of all things, proves the fact.

'Tis not in numbers but in unity that our great strength lies: yet our present numbers are sufficient to repel the force of all the world. The Continent hath at this time the largest body of armed and disciplined men of any power under Heaven: and is just arrived at that pitch of strength, in which no single colony is able to support itself, and the whole, when united, is able to do anything. Our land force is more than sufficient, and as to Naval affairs, we cannot be insensible that Britain would never suffer an American man of war to be built, while the Continent remained in her hands. Wherefore, we should be no forwarder an hundred years hence in that branch than we are now; but the truth is, we should be less so, because the timber of the Country is every day diminishing, and that which will remain at last, will be far off or difficult to procure.

Were the Continent crowded with inhabitants, her sufferings under the present circumstances would be intolerable. The more seaport-towns we had, the more should we have both to defend and to lose. Our present numbers are so happily proportioned to our wants, that no man need be idle. The diminution of trade affords an army, and the necessities of an army create a new trade.

Debts we have none: and whatever we may contract on this account will serve as a glorious memento of our virtue. Can we but leave posterity with a settled form of government, an independant constitution of its own, the purchase at any price will be cheap. But to expend millions for the sake of getting a few vile acts repealed, and routing the present ministry only, is unworthy the charge, and is using posterity with the utmost cruelty; because it is leaving them the great work to do, and a debt upon their backs from which they derive no advantage. Such a thought's unworthy a man of honour, and is the true characteristic of a narrow heart and a pidling politician.

The debt we may contract doth not deserve our regard if the work be but accomplished. No nation ought to be without a debt. A national debt is a national bond; and when it bears no interest, is in no case a grievance. Britain is oppressed with a debt of upwards of one hundred and forty millions sterling, for which she pays upwards of four millions interest. And as a compensation for her debt, she has a large navy; America is without a debt, and without a navy; yet for the twentieth part of the English national debt, could have a navy as large again. The navy of England is not worth at this time more than three millions and a half sterling.

The first and second editions of this pamphlet were published
without the following calculations, which are now given as a proof
that the above estimation of the navy is a just one. See Entic's "Naval
History," Intro., p. 56.

The charge of building a ship of each rate, and furnishing her with
masts, yards, sails, and rigging, together with a proportion of eight
months boatswain's and carpenter's sea-stores, as calculated by Mr.
Burchett, Secretary to the navy.

| For a ship of 100 guns, | . | . | 35,553 *l.* |
|---|---|---|---|
| 90 | . | . | 29,886 |
| 80 | . | . | 23,638 |
| 70 | . | . | 17,785 |
| 60 | . | . | 14,197 |
| 50 | . | . | 10,606 |
| 40 | . | . | 7,558 |
| 30 | . | . | 5,846 |
| 20 | . | . | 3,710 |

And hence it is easy to sum up the value, or cost, rather, of the
whole British navy, which, in the year 1757, when it was at its greatest
glory, consisted of the following ships and guns.

No country on the globe is so happily situated, or so internally capable of raising a fleet as America. Tar, timber, iron, and cordage are her
natural produce. We need go abroad for nothing. Whereas the Dutch,
who make large profits by hiring out their ships of war to the Spaniards
and Portugese, are obliged to import most of the materials they use. We
ought to view the building a fleet as an article of commerce, it being
the natural manufactory of this country. 'Tis the best money we can lay
out. A navy when finished is worth more than it cost: And is that nice
point in national policy, in which commerce and protection are united. Let us build; if we want them not, we can sell; and by that means
replace our paper currency with ready gold and silver.

In point of manning a fleet, people in general run into great
errors; it is not necessary that one fourth part should be sailors. The
Terrible privateer, captain Death, stood the hottest engagement of

any ship last war, yet had not twenty sailors on board, though her complement of men was upwards of two hundred. A few able and social sailors will soon instruct a sufficient number of active landsmen in the common work of a ship. Wherefore we never can be more capable of beginning on maritime matters than now, while our timber is standing, our fisheries blocked up, and our sailors and shipwrights out of employ. Men of war, of seventy and eighty guns, were built forty years ago in New England, and why not the same now? Ship building is America's greatest pride, and in which she will, in time, excel the whole world. The great empires of the east are mostly inland, and consequently excluded from the possibility of rivalling her. Africa is in a state of barbarism; and no power in Europe, hath either such an extent of coast, or such an internal supply of materials. Where nature hath given the one, she hath withheld the other; to America only hath she been liberal to both. The vast empire of Russia is almost shut out from the sea; wherefore her boundless forests, her tar, iron, and cordage are only articles of commerce.

In point of safety, ought we to be without a fleet? We are not the little people now, which we were sixty years ago; at that time we might have trusted our property in the streets, or fields rather, and slept securely without locks or bolts to our doors and windows. The case is now altered, and our methods of defence ought to improve with our encrease of property. A common pirate, twelve months ago, might have come up the Delaware, and laid the city of Philadelphia under contribution for what sum he pleased; and the same might have happened to other places. Nay, any daring fellow, in a brig of fourteen or sixteen guns, might have robbed the whole Continent, and carried off half a million of money. These are circumstances which demand our attention, and point out the necessity of naval protection.

Some perhaps will say, that after we have made it up with Britain, she will protect us. Can they be so unwise as to mean, that she will keep a navy in our Harbours for that purpose? Common sense will tell us, that the power which hath endeavoured to subdue us, is of all others, the most improper to defend us. Conquest may be effected under the pretence of friendship; and ourselves, after a long and brave resistance, be at last cheated into slavery. And if her ships are not to be admitted into our harbours, I would ask, how is she to protect us? A navy three or four thousand miles off can be of little use, and on sudden emergencies, none at all. Wherefore if we must hereafter protect ourselves, why not do it for ourselves? Why do it for another?

The English list of ships of war, is long and formidable, but not a tenth part of them are at any one time fit for service, numbers of them are not in being; yet their names are pompously continued in the list, if only a plank be left of the ship: and not a fifth part of such as are fit for service, can be spared on any one station at one time. The East and West Indies, Mediterranean, Africa, and other parts, over which Britain extends her claim, make large demands upon her navy. From a mixture of prejudice and inattention, we have contracted a false notion respecting the navy of England, and have talked as if we should have the whole of it to encounter at once, and, for that reason, supposed that we must have one as large; which not being instantly practicable, has been made use of by a set of disguised Tories to discourage our beginning thereon. Nothing can be further from truth than this; for if America had only a twentieth part of the naval force of Britain, she would be by far an over-match for her; because, as we neither have, nor claim any foreign dominion, our whole force would be employed on our own coast, where we should, in the long run, have two to one the advantage of those who had three or four thousand miles to sail over, before they could attack us, and the same distance to return in order to refit and recruit. And although Britain, by her fleet, hath a check over our trade to Europe, we have as large a one over her trade to the West Indies, which, by laying in the neighborhood of the Continent, lies entirely at its mercy.

Some method might be fallen on to keep up a naval force in time of peace, if we should not judge it necessary to support a constant navy. If premiums were to be given to Merchants to build and employ in their service, ships mounted with twenty, thirty, forty, or fifty guns, (the premiums to be in proportion to the loss of bulk to the merchant,) fifty or sixty of those ships, with a few guardships on constant duty, would keep up a sufficient navy, and that without burdening ourselves with the evil so loudly complained of in England, of suffering their fleet in time of peace to lie rotting in the docks. To unite the sinews of commerce and defence is sound policy; for when our strength and our riches play into each other's hand, we need fear no external enemy.

In almost every article of defence we abound. Hemp flourishes even to rankness, so that we need not want cordage. Our iron is superior to that of other countries. Our small arms equal to any in the world. Cannon we can cast at pleasure. Saltpetre and gunpowder we are every day producing. Our knowledge is hourly improving. Resolution is our inherent character, and courage hath never yet forsaken us. Wherefore, what is it that we want? Why is it that we hesitate? From Britain we can expect nothing but ruin. If she is once admitted to the government of America again, this Continent will not be worth living in. Jealousies will be always arising; insurrections will be constantly happening; and who will go forth to quell them? Who will venture his life to reduce his own countrymen to a foreign obedience? The difference between Pennsylvania and Connecticut, respecting some unlocated lands, shows the insignificance of a British government, and fully proves that nothing but Continental authority can regulate Continental matters.

Another reason why the present time is preferable to all others, is, that the fewer our numbers are, the more land there is yet unoccupied, which, instead of being lavished by the king on his worthless dependants, may be hereafter applied, not only to the discharge of the present debt, but to the constant support of government. No nation under Heaven hath such an advantage as this.

The infant state of the Colonies, as it is called, so far from being against, is an argument in favour of independance. We are sufficiently numerous, and were we more so we might be less united. 'Tis a matter worthy of observation, that the more a country is peopled, the smaller their armies are. In military numbers, the ancients far exceeded the moderns: and the reason is evident, for trade being the consequence of population, men became too much absorbed thereby to attend to any thing else. Commerce diminishes the spirit both of patriotism and military defence. And history sufficiently informs us, that the bravest achievements were always accomplished in the non-age of a nation. With the increase of commerce England hath lost its spirit. The city of London, notwithstanding its numbers, submits to continued insults with the patience of a coward. The more men have to lose, the less willing are they to venture. The rich are in general slaves to fear, and submit to courtly power with the trembling duplicity of a spaniel.

Youth is the seed-time of good habits as well in nations as in individuals. It might be difficult, if not impossible, to form the Continent into one Government half a century hence. The vast variety of interests, occasioned by an increase of trade and population, would create confusion. Colony would be against Colony. Each being able would scorn each other's assistance: and while the proud and foolish gloried in their little distinctions, the wise would lament that the union had not been formed before. Wherefore the present time is the true time for establishing it. The intimacy which is contracted in infancy, and the friendship which is formed in misfortune, are of all others the most lasting and unalterable. Our present union is marked with both these characters: we are young, and we have been distressed; but our concord hath withstood our troubles, and fixes a memorable Æra for posterity to glory in.

The present time, likewise, is that peculiar time which never happens to a nation but once, viz. the time of forming itself into a government. Most nations have let slip the opportunity, and by that means have been compelled to receive laws from their conquerors, instead of making laws for themselves. First, they had a king, and then a form of government; whereas the articles or charter of government should be formed first, and men delegated to execute them afterwards: but from the errors of other nations let us learn wisdom, and lay hold of the present opportunity—*to begin government at the right end.*

When William the Conqueror subdued England, he gave them law at the point of the sword; and, until we consent that the seat of government in America be legally and authoritatively occupied, we shall be in danger of having it filled by some fortunate ruffian, who may treat us in the same manner, and then, where will be our freedom? where our property?

As to religion, I hold it to be the indispensable duty of government to protect all conscientious professors thereof, and I know of no other business which government hath to do therewith. Let a man throw aside that narrowness of soul, that selfishness of principle, which the niggards of all professions are so unwilling to part with, and he will be at once delivered of his fears on that head. Suspicion is the companion of mean souls, and the bane of all good society. For myself, I fully and conscientiously believe, that it is the will of the

Almighty that there should be a diversity of religious opinions among us. It affords a larger field for our Christian kindness: were we all of one way of thinking, our religious dispositions would want matter for probation; and on this liberal principle I look on the various denominations among us, to be like children of the same family, differing only in what is called their Christian names.

In page I threw out a few thoughts on the propriety of a Continental Charter (for I only presume to offer hints, not plans) and in this place, I take the liberty of re-mentioning the subject, by observing, that a charter is to be understood as a bond of solemn obligation, which the whole enters into, to support the right of every separate part, whether of religion, professional freedom, or property. A firm bargain and a right reckoning make long friends.

I have heretofore likewise mentioned the necessity of a large and equal representation; and there is no political matter which more deserves our attention. A small number of electors, or a small number of representatives, are equally dangerous. But if the number of the representatives be not only small, but unequal, the danger is encreased. As an instance of this, I mention the following; when the petition of the associators was before the House of Assembly of Pennsylvania, twenty-eight members only were present; all the Bucks county members, being eight, voted against it, and had seven of the Chester members done the same, this whole province had been governed by two counties only; and this danger it is always exposed to. The unwarrantable stretch likewise, which that house made in their last sitting, to gain an undue authority over the Delegates of that Province, ought to warn the people at large, how they trust power out of their own hands. A set of instructions for their Delegates were put together, which in point of sense and business would have dishonoured a school-boy, and after being approved by a few, a very few, without doors, were carried into the house, and there passed *in behalf of the whole Colony*; whereas, did the whole colony know with what ill will that house had entered on some necessary public measures, they would not hesitate a moment to think them unworthy of such a trust.

Immediate necessity makes many things convenient, which if continued would grow into oppressions. Expedience and right are different things. When the calamities of America required a consultation, there was no method so ready, or at that time so proper, as to appoint persons from the several houses of Assembly for that purpose; and the wisdom with which they have proceeded hath preserved this Continent from ruin. But as it is more than probable that we shall never be without a CONGRESS, every well wisher to good order must own that the mode for choosing members of that body, deserves consideration. And I put it as a question to those who make a study of mankind, whether representation and election is not too great a power for one and the same body of men to possess? When we are planning for posterity, we ought to remember that virtue is not hereditary.

It is from our enemies that we often gain excellent maxims, and are frequently surprised into reason by their mistakes. Mr. Cornwall (one of the Lords of the Treasury) treated the petition of the New York Assembly with contempt, because *that* house, he said, consisted but of twenty-six members, which trifling number, he argued, could not with decency be put for the whole. We thank him for his involuntary honesty.*

TO CONCLUDE, however strange it may appear to some, or however unwilling they may be to think so, matters not, but many strong and striking reasons may be given to show, that nothing can settle our affairs so expeditiously as an open and determined declaration for independance. Some of which are,

*First*—It is the custom of Nations, when any two are at war, for some other powers, not engaged in the quarrel, to step in as mediators, and bring about the preliminaries of a peace: But while America calls herself the subject of Great Britain, no power, however well disposed she may be, can offer her mediation. Wherefore, in our present state we may quarrel on for ever.

*Secondly*—It is unreasonable to suppose, that France or Spain will give us any kind of assistance, if we mean only to make use of that assistance for the purpose of repairing the breach, and strengthening the connection between Britain and America; because, those powers would be sufferers by the consequences.

*Thirdly*—While we profess ourselves the subjects of Britain, we must, in the eyes of foreign nations, be considered as Rebels. The precedent is somewhat dangerous to their peace, for men to be in arms under the name of subjects: we, on the spot, can solve the paradox; but to unite resistance and subjection, requires an idea much too refined for common understanding.

*Fourthly*—Were a manifesto to be published, and despatched to foreign Courts, setting forth the miseries we have endured, and the peaceful methods which we have ineffectually used for redress; declaring at the same time, that not being able any longer to live happily or safely under the cruel disposition of the British Court, we had been driven to the necessity of breaking off all connections with her; at the same time, assuring all such Courts of our peaceable disposition towards them, and of our desire of entering into trade with them: such a memorial would produce more good effects to this Continent, than if a ship were freighted with petitions to Britain.

Under our present denomination of British subjects, we can neither be received nor heard abroad: the custom of all Courts is against us, and will be so, until by an independance we take rank with other nations.

These proceedings may at first seem strange and difficult, but like all other steps which we have already passed over, will in a little time become familiar and agreeable: and until an independance is declared, the Continent will feel itself like a man who continues putting off some unpleasant business from day to day, yet knows it must be done, hates to set about it, wishes it over, and is continually haunted with the thoughts of its necessity.

## APPENDIX TO COMMON SENSE.

Since the publication of the first edition of this pamphlet, or rather, on the same day on which it came out, the King's Speech made its appearance in this city [Philadelphia]. Had the spirit of prophecy directed the birth of this production, it could not have brought it forth at a more seasonable juncture, or at a more necessary time. The bloody-mindedness of the one, shows the necessity of pursuing the doctrine of the other. Men read by way of revenge. And the Speech, instead of terrifying, prepared a way for the manly principles of Independance.

Ceremony, and even silence, from whatever motives they may arise, have a hurtful tendency when they give the least degree of countenance to base and wicked performances; wherefore, if this maxim be admitted, it naturally follows, that the King's Speech, as being a piece of finished villany, deserved and still deserves, a general execration, both by the Congress and the people. Yet, as the domestic tranquillity of a nation, depends greatly on the *chastity* of what might properly be called NA-TIONAL MANNERS, it is often better to pass some things over in silent disdain, than to make use of such new methods of dislike, as might introduce the least innovation on that guardian of our peace and safety. And, perhaps, it is chiefly owing to this prudent delicacy, that the King's Speech hath not before now suffered a public execution. The Speech, if it may be called one, is nothing better than a wilful audacious libel against the truth, the common good, and the existence of mankind; and is a formal and pompous method of offering up human sacrifices to the pride of tyrants. But this general massacre of mankind, is one of the privileges and the certain consequences of Kings; for as nature knows them *not*, they know *not her*, and although they are beings of our *own* creating, they know not *us*, and are become the Gods of their creators. The speech hath one good quality, which is, that it is not calculated to deceive, neither can we, even if we would, be deceived by it. Brutality and tyranny appear on the face of it. It leaves us at no loss: And every line convinces, even in the moment of reading, that he who hunts the woods for prey, the naked and untutored Indian, is less Savage than the King of Britain.

Sir John Dalrymple, the putative father of a whining jesuitical piece, fallaciously called, "*The address of the people of* England *to the inhabitants of* America," hath perhaps from a vain supposition that the people *here* were to be frightened at the pomp and description of a king, given (though very unwisely on his part) the real character of the present one: "But," says this writer, "if you are inclined to pay compliments to an administration, which we do not complain of (meaning the Marquis of Rockingham's at the repeal of the Stamp Act) it is very unfair in you to withhold them from that prince, *by whose* NOD ALONE *they were permitted to do any thing.*" This is toryism with a witness! Here is idolatry even without a mask: And he who can calmly hear and digest such doctrine, hath forfeited his claim to rationality—an apostate from the order of manhood—and ought to be considered as one who hath not only given up the proper dignity of man, but sunk himself beneath the rank of animals, and contemptibly crawls through the world like a worm.

However, it matters very little now what the king of England either says or does; he hath wickedly broken through every moral and human obligation, trampled nature and conscience beneath his feet, and by a steady and constitutional spirit of insolence and cruelty procured for himself an universal hatred. It is *now* the interest of America to provide for herself. She hath already a large and young family, whom it is more her duty to take care of, than to be granting away her property to support a power who is become a reproach to the names of men and christians—YE, whose office it is to watch the morals of a nation, of whatsoever sect or denomination ye are of, as well as ye who are more immediately the guardians of the public liberty, if ye wish to preserve your native country uncontaminated by European corruption, ye must in secret wish a separation. But leaving the moral part to private reflection, I shall chiefly confine my further remarks to the following heads:

First, That it is the interest of America to be separated from Britain.

Secondly, Which is the easiest and most practicable plan, RECON-CILIATION or INDEPENDENCE with some occasional remarks.

In support of the first, I could, if I judged it proper, produce the opinion of some of the ablest and most experienced men on this continent: and whose sentiments on that head, are not yet publicly known. It is in reality a self-evident position: for no nation in a state of foreign dependance, limited in its commerce, and cramped and fettered in its legislative powers, can ever arrive at any material eminence. America doth not yet know what opulence is; and although the progress which she hath made stands unparalleled in the history of other nations, it is but childhood compared with what she would be capable of arriving at, had she, as she ought to have, the legislative powers in her own hands. England is at this time proudly coveting what would do her no good were she to accomplish it; and the continent hesitating on a matter which will be her final ruin if neglected. It is the commerce and not the conquest of America by which England is to be benefited, and that would in a great measure continue, were the countries as independant of each other as France and Spain; because in many articles neither can go to a better market. But it is the independance of this country of Britain, or any other, which is now the main and only object worthy of contention, and which, like all other truths discovered by necessity, will appear clear and stronger every day.

First, Because it will come to that one time or other.

Secondly, Because the longer it is delayed, the harder it will be to accomplish.

I have frequently amused myself both in public and private companies, with silently remarking the specious errors of those who speak without reflecting. And among the many which I have heard, the following seems the most general, viz. that had this rupture happened forty or fifty years hence, instead of now, the continent would have been more able to have shaken off the dependance. To which I reply, that our military ability, *at this time*, arises from the experience gained in the last war, and which in forty or fifty years time, would be totally extinct. The continent would not, by that time, have a general, or even a military officer left; and we, or those who may succeed us, would be as ignorant of martial matters as the ancient Indians: and this single position, closely attended to, will unanswerably prove that the present time is preferable to all others. The argument turns thus: At the conclusion of the last war, we had experience, but wanted numbers; and forty or fifty years hence, we shall have numbers, without experience; wherefore, the proper point of time, must be some particular point between the two extremes, in which a sufficiency of the former remains, and a proper increase of the latter is obtained: And that point of time is the present time.

The reader will pardon this digression, as it does not properly come under the head I first set out with, and to which I again return by the following position, viz.:

Should affairs be patched up with Britain, and she to remain the governing and sovereign power of America, (which, as matters are now circumstanced, is giving up the point entirely) we shall deprive ourselves of the very means of sinking the debt we have, or may contract. The value of the back lands, which some of the provinces are clandestinely deprived of, by the unjust extension of the limits of Canada, valued only at five pounds sterling per hundred acres, amount to upwards of twenty-five millions, Pennsylvania currency; and the quit-rents, at one penny sterling per acre, to two millions yearly.

It is by the sale of those lands that the debt may be sunk, without burthen to any, and the quit-rent reserved thereon will always lessen, and in time will wholly support, the yearly expense of government. It matters not how long the debt is in paying, so that the lands when sold be applied to the discharge of it, and for the execution of which the Congress for the time being will be the continental trustees.

I proceed now to the second head, viz. Which is the easiest and most practicable plan, Reconciliation or Independence; with some occasional remarks.

He who takes nature for his guide, is not easily beaten out of his argument, and on that ground, I answer generally—*That* independance *being a* single simple line, *contained within ourselves; and reconciliation, a matter exceedingly perplexed and complicated, and in which a treacherous capricious court is to interfere, gives the answer without a doubt.*

The present state of America is truly alarming to every man who is capable of reflection. Without law, without government, without any other mode of power than what is founded on, and granted by, courtesy. Held together by an unexampled occurrence of sentiment, which is nevertheless subject to change, and which every secret enemy is endeavoring to dissolve. Our present condition is, Legislation without law; wisdom without a plan; a constitution without a name; and, what is strangely astonishing, perfect independance contending for dependance. The instance is without a precedent, the case never existed before, and who can tell what may be the event? The property of no man is secure in the present unbraced system of things. The mind of the multitude is left at random, and seeing no fixed object before them, they pursue such as fancy or opinion presents. Nothing is criminal; there is no such thing as treason; wherefore, every one thinks himself at liberty to act as he pleases. The Tories would not have dared to assemble offensively, had they known that their lives, by that act, were forfeited to the laws of the state. A line of distinction should be drawn between English soldiers taken in battle, and inhabitants of America taken in arms. The first are prisoners, but the latter traitors. The one forfeits his liberty, the other his head.

Notwithstanding our wisdom, there is a visible feebleness in some of our proceedings which gives encouragement to dissentions. The Continental Belt is too loosely buckled: And if something is not done in time, it will be too late to do any thing, and we shall fall into a state, in which neither Reconciliation nor Independence will be practicable. The king and his worthless adherents are got at their old game of dividing the Continent, and there are not wanting among us Printers who will be busy in spreading specious falsehoods. The artful and hypocritical letter which appeared a few months ago in two of the New-York papers, and likewise in two others, is an evidence that there are men who want both judgment and honesty.

It is easy getting into holes and corners, and talking of reconciliation: But do such men seriously consider how difficult the task is, and how dangerous it may prove, should the Continent divide thereon? Do they take within their view all the various orders of men whose situation and circumstances, as well as their own, are to be considered therein? Do they put themselves in the place of the sufferer whose *all* is *already* gone, and of the soldier, who hath quitted *all* for the defence of his country? If their ill-judged moderation be suited to their own private situations *only*, regardless of others, the event will convince them that "they are reckoning without their host."

Put us, say some, on the footing we were in the year 1763: To which I answer, the request is not now in the power of Britain to comply with, neither will she propose it; but if it were, and even should be granted, I ask, as a reasonable question, By what means is such a corrupt and faithless court to be kept to its engagements? Another parliament, nay, even the present, may hereafter repeal the obligation, on the pretence of its being violently obtained, or unwisely granted; and, in that case, Where is our redress? No going to law with nations; cannon are the barristers of crowns; and the sword, not of justice, but of war, decides the suit. To be on the footing of 1763, it is not sufficient, that the laws only be put in the same state, but, that our circumstances likewise be put in the same state; our burnt and destroyed towns repaired or built up, our private losses made good, our public debts (contracted for defence) discharged; otherwise we shall be millions worse than we were at that enviable period. Such a request, had it been complied with a year ago, would have won the heart and soul of the Continent, but now it is too late. "The Rubicon is passed."

Besides, the taking up arms, merely to enforce the repeal of a pecuniary law, seems as unwarrantable by the divine law, and as repugnant to human feelings, as the taking up arms to enforce obedience thereto. The object, on either side, doth not justify the means; for the lives of men are too valuable to be cast away on such trifles. It is the violence which is done and threatened to our persons; the destruction of our property by an armed force; the invasion of our country by fire and sword, which conscientiously qualifies the use of arms: and the instant in which such mode of defence became necessary, all subjection to Britain ought to have ceased; and the independance of America should have been considered as dating its era from, and published by, *the first musket that was fired against her*. This line is a line of consistency; neither drawn by caprice, nor extended by ambition; but produced by a chain of events, of which the colonies were not the authors.

I shall conclude these remarks, with the following timely and well-intended hints. We ought to reflect, that there are three different ways by which an independancy may hereafter be effected; and that *one* of those *three*, will, one day or other, be the fate of America, viz. By the legal voice of the people in Congress; by a military power; or by a mob: It may not always happen that our soldiers are citizens, and the multitude a body of reasonable men; virtue, as I have already remarked, is not hereditary, neither is it perpetual. Should an independancy be brought about by the first of those means, we have every opportunity and every encouragement before us, to form the noblest, purest constitution on the face of the earth. We have it in our power to begin the world over again. A situation, similar to the present, hath not happened since the days of Noah until now. The birthday of a new world is at hand, and a race of men, perhaps as numerous as all Europe contains, are to receive their portion of freedom from the events of a few months. The reflection is awful, and in this point of view, how trifling, how ridiculous, do the little paltry cavilings of a few weak or interested men appear, when weighed against the business of a world.

Should we neglect the present favorable and inviting period, and independance be hereafter effected by any other means, we must charge the consequence to ourselves, or to those rather whose narrow and prejudiced souls are habitually opposing the measure, without either inquiring or reflecting. There are reasons to be given in support of independance which men should rather privately think of, than be publicly told of. We ought not now to be debating whether we shall be independant or not, but anxious to accomplish it on a firm, secure, and honorable basis, and uneasy rather that it is not yet began upon. Every day convinces us of its necessity. Even the Tories (if such beings yet remain among us) should, of all men, be the most solicitous to promote it; for as the appointment of committees at first protected them from popular rage, so, a wise and well established form of government will be the only certain means of continuing it securely to them. Wherefore, if they have not virtue enough to be WHIGS, they ought to have prudence enough to wish for independance.

In short, Independance is the only BOND that tye and keep us together. We shall then see our object, and our ears will be legally shut against the schemes of an intriguing, as well as cruel, enemy. We shall then, too, be on a proper footing to treat with Britain; for there is reason to conclude, that the pride of that court will be less hurt by treating with the American states for terms of peace, than with those, whom she denominates "rebellious subjects," for terms of accommodation. It is our delaying in that, encourages her to hope for conquest, and our backwardness tends only to prolong the war. As we have, without any good effect therefrom, withheld our trade to obtain a redress of our grievances, let us now try the alternative, by independantly redressing them ourselves, and then offering to open the trade. The mercantile and reasonable part of England, will be still with us; because, peace, with trade, is preferable to war without it. And if this offer be not accepted, other courts may be applied to.

On these grounds I rest the matter. And as no offer hath yet been made to refute the doctrine contained in the former editions of this pamphlet, it is a negative proof, that either the doctrine cannot be refuted, or, that the party in favor of it are too numerous to be opposed. WHEREFORE, instead of gazing at each other with suspicious or doubtful curiosity, let each of us hold out to his neighbor the hearty hand of friendship, and unite in drawing a line, which, like an act of oblivion, shall bury in forgetfulness every former dissention. Let the names of Whig and Tory be extinct; and let none other be heard among us, than those of *a good citizen; an open and resolute friend;* and *a virtuous supporter of the* RIGHTS *of* MANKIND, *and of the* FREE AND INDEPENDANT STATES OF AMERICA.

# THE AMERICAN CRISIS (NUMBER I)

These are the times that try men's souls. The summer soldier and the sunshine patriot will, in this crisis, shrink from the service of their country; but he that stands it *now*, deserves the love and thanks of man and woman. Tyranny, like hell, is not easily conquered; yet we have this consolation with us, that the harder the conflict, the more glorious the triumph. What we obtain too cheap, we esteem too lightly: it is dearness only that gives every thing its value. Heaven knows how to put a proper price upon its goods; and it would be strange indeed if so celestial an article as FREEDOM should not be highly rated. Britain, with an army to enforce her tyranny, has declared that she has a right (*not only to* TAX) but "to BIND *us in* ALL CASES WHATSOEVER," and if being *bound in that manner*, is not slavery, then is there not such a thing as slavery upon earth. Even the expression is impious; for so unlimited a power can belong only to God.

Whether the independence of the continent was declared too soon, or delayed too long, I will not now enter into as an argument; my own simple opinion is, that had it been eight months earlier, it would have been much better. We did not make a proper use of last winter, neither could we, while we were in a dependant state. However, the fault, if it were one, was all our own* ; we have none to blame but ourselves. But no great deal is lost yet. All that Howe has been doing for this month past, is rather a ravage than a conquest, which the spirit of the Jerseys, a year ago, would have quickly repulsed, and which time and a little resolution will soon recover.

I have as little superstition in me as any man living, but my secret opinion has ever been, and still is, that God Almighty will not give up a people to military destruction, or leave them unsupportedly to perish, who have so earnestly and so repeatedly sought to avoid the calamities of war, by every decent method which wisdom could invent. Neither have I so much of the infidel in me, as to suppose that He has relinquished the government of the world, and given us up to the care of devils; and as I do not, I cannot see on what grounds the king of Britain can look up to heaven for help against us: a common murderer, a highwayman, or a house-breaker, has as good a pretence as he.

'Tis surprising to see how rapidly a panic will sometimes run through a country. All nations and ages have been subject to them: Britain has trembled like an ague at the report of a French fleet of flat bottomed boats; and in the fourteenth [fifteenth] century the whole English army, after ravaging the kingdom of France, was driven back like men petrified with fear; and this brave exploit was performed by a few broken forces collected and headed by a woman, Joan of Arc. Would that heaven might inspire some Jersey maid to spirit up her countrymen, and save her fair fellow sufferers from ravage and ravishment! Yet panics, in some cases, have their uses; they produce as much good as hurt. Their duration is always short; the mind soon grows through them, and acquires a firmer habit than before. But their peculiar advantage is, that they are the touchstones of sincerity and hypocrisy, and bring things and men to light, which might otherwise have lain forever undiscovered. In fact, they have the same effect on secret traitors, which an imaginary apparition would have upon a private murderer. They sift out the hidden thoughts of man, and hold them up in public to the world. Many a disguised tory has lately shown his head, that shall penitentially solemnize with curses the day on which Howe arrived upon the Delaware.

As I was with the troops at Fort Lee, and marched with them to the edge of Pennsylvania, I am well acquainted with many circumstances, which those who live at a distance know but little or nothing of. Our situation there was exceedingly cramped, the place being a narrow neck of land between the North River and the Hackensack. Our force was inconsiderable, being not one fourth so great as Howe could bring against us. We had no army at hand to have relieved the garrison, had we shut ourselves up and stood on our defence. Our ammunition, light artillery, and the best part of our stores, had been removed, on the apprehension that Howe would endeavor to penetrate the Jerseys, in which case fort Lee could be of no use to us; for it must occur to every thinking man, whether in the army or not, that these kind of field forts are only for temporary purposes, and last in use no longer than the enemy directs his force against the particular object, which such forts are raised to defend. Such was our situation and condition at fort Lee on the morning of the 20th of November, when an officer arrived with information that the enemy with 200 boats had landed about seven miles above: Major General [Nathaniel] Green, who commanded the garrison, immediately ordered them under arms, and sent express to General Washington at the town of Hackensack, distant by the way of the ferry = six miles. Our first object was to secure the bridge over the Hackensack, which laid up the river between the enemy and us, about six miles from us, and three from them. General Washington arrived in about three quarters of an hour, and marched at the head of the troops towards the bridge, which place I expected we should have a brush for; however, they did not choose to dispute it with us, and the greatest part of our troops went over the bridge, the rest over the ferry, except some which passed at a mill on a small creek, between the bridge and the ferry, and made their way through some marshy grounds up to the town of Hackensack, and there passed the river. We brought off as much baggage as the wagons could contain, the rest was lost. The simple object was to bring off the garrison, and march them on till they could be strengthened by the Jersey or Pennsylvania militia, so as to be enabled to make a stand. We staid four days at Newark, collected our out-posts with some of the Jersey militia, and marched out twice to meet the enemy, on being informed that they were advancing, though our numbers were greatly inferior to theirs. Howe, in my little opinion, committed a great error in generalship in not throwing a body of forces off from Staten Island through Amboy, by which means he might have seized all our stores at Brunswick, and intercepted our march into Pennsylvania; but if we believe the power of hell to be limited, we must likewise believe that their agents are under some providential controul.

I shall not now attempt to give all the particulars of our retreat to the Delaware; suffice it for the present to say, that both officers and men, though greatly harassed and fatigued, frequently without rest, covering, or provision, the inevitable consequences of a long retreat, bore it with a manly and martial spirit. All their wishes centred in one, which was, that the country would turn out and help them to drive the enemy back. Voltaire has remarked that king William never appeared to full advantage but in difficulties and in action; the same remark may be made on General Washington, for the character fits him. There is a natural firmness in some minds which cannot be unlocked by trifles, but which, when unlocked, discovers a cabinet of fortitude; and I reckon it among those kind of public blessings, which we do not immediately see, that God hath blessed him with uninterrupted health, and given him a mind that can even flourish upon care.

I shall conclude this paper with some miscellaneous remarks on the state of our affairs; and shall begin with asking the following question, Why is it that the enemy have left the New-England provinces, and made these middle ones the seat of war? The answer is easy: New-England is not infested with tories, and we are. I have been tender in raising the cry against these men, and used numberless arguments to show them their danger, but it will not do to sacrifice a world either to their folly or their baseness. The period is now arrived, in which either they or we must change our sentiments, or one or both must fall. And what is a tory? Good God! what is he? I should not be afraid to go with a hundred whigs against a thousand tories, were they to attempt to get into arms. Every tory is a coward; for servile, slavish, self-interested fear is the foundation of toryism; and a man under such influence, though he may be cruel, never can be brave.

But, before the line of irrecoverable separation be drawn between us, let us reason the matter together: Your conduct is an invitation to the enemy, yet not one in a thousand of you has heart enough to join him. Howe is as much deceived by you as the American cause is injured by you. He expects you will all take up arms, and flock to his standard, with muskets on your shoulders. Your opinions are of no use to him, unless you support him personally, for 'tis soldiers, and not tories, that he wants.

I once felt all that kind of anger, which a man ought to feel, against the mean principles that are held by the tories: a noted one, who kept a tavern at Amboy, was standing at his door, with as pretty a child in his hand, about eight or nine years old, as I ever saw, and after speaking his mind as freely as he thought was prudent, finished with this unfatherly expression, *"Well! give me peace in my day."* Not a man lives on the continent but fully believes that a separation must some time or other finally take place, and a generous parent should have said, *"If there must be trouble, let it be in my day, that my child may have peace;"* and this single reflection, well applied, is sufficient to awaken every man to duty. Not a place upon earth might be so happy as America. Her situation is remote from all the wrangling world, and she has nothing to do but to trade with them. A man can distinguish himself between temper and principle, and I am as confident, as I am that God governs the world, that America will never be happy till she gets clear of foreign dominion. Wars, without ceasing, will break out till that period arrives, and the continent must in the end be conqueror; for though the flame of liberty may sometimes cease to shine, the coal can never expire.

America did not, nor does not want force; but she wanted a proper application of that force. Wisdom is not the purchase of a day, and it is no wonder that we should err at the first setting off. From an excess of tenderness, we were unwilling to raise an army, and trusted our cause to the temporary defence of a well-meaning militia. A summer's experience has now taught us better; yet with those troops, while they were collected, we were able to set bounds to the progress of the enemy, and, thank God! they are again assembling. I always considered militia as the best troops in the world for a sudden exertion, but they will not do for a long campaign. Howe, it is probable, will make an attempt on this city; should he fail on this side the Delaware, he is ruined: if he succeeds, our cause is not ruined. He stakes all on his side against a part on ours; admitting he succeeds, the consequence will be, that armies from both ends of the continent will march to assist their suffering friends in the middle states; for he cannot go everywhere, it is impossible. I consider Howe as the greatest enemy the tories have; he is bringing a war into their country, which, had it not been for him and partly for themselves, they had been clear of. Should he now be expelled, I wish with all the devotion of a Christian, that the names of whig and tory may never more be mentioned; but should the tories give him encouragement to come, or assistance if he come, I as sincerely wish that our next year's arms may expel them from the continent, and the congress appropriate their possessions to the relief of those who have suffered in well-doing. A single successful battle next year will settle the whole. America could carry on a two years war by the confiscation of the property of disaffected persons, and be made happy by their expulsion. Say not that this is revenge, call it rather the soft resentment of a suffering people, who, having no object in view but the *good* of *all*, have staked their *own all* upon a seemingly doubtful event. Yet it is folly to argue against determined hardness; eloquence may strike the ear, and the language of sorrow draw forth the tear of compassion, but nothing can reach the heart that is steeled with prejudice.

Quitting this class of men, I turn with the warm ardor of a friend to those who have nobly stood, and are yet determined to stand the matter out: I call not upon a few, but upon all: not on *this* state or *that* state, but on *every* state: up and help us; lay your shoulders to the wheel; better have too much force than too little, when so great an object is at stake. Let it be told to the future world, that in the depth of winter, when nothing but hope and virtue could survive, that the city and the country, alarmed at one common danger, came forth to meet and to repulse it. Say not that thousands are gone, turn out your tens of thousands; throw not the burden of the day upon Providence, but *"show your faith by your works,"* that God may bless you. It matters not where you live, or what rank of life you hold, the evil or the blessing will reach you all. The far and the near, the home counties and the back, the rich and the poor, will suffer or rejoice alike. The heart that feels not now, is dead: the blood of his children will curse his cowardice, who shrinks back at a time when a little might have saved the whole, and made *them* happy. I love the man that can smile in trouble, that can gather strength from distress, and grow brave by reflection. 'Tis the business of little minds to shrink; but he whose heart is firm, and whose conscience approves his conduct, will pursue his principles unto death. My own line of reasoning is to myself as straight and clear as a ray of light. Not all the treasures of the world, so far as I believe, could have induced me to support an offensive war, for I think it murder; but if a thief breaks into my house, burns and destroys my property, and kills or threatens to kill me, or those that are in it, and to *"bind me in all cases whatsoever"* to his absolute will, am I to suffer it? What signifies it to me, whether he who does it is a king or a common man; my countryman or not my countryman; whether it be done by an individual villain, or an army of them? If we reason to the root of things we shall find no difference; neither can any just cause be assigned why we should punish in the one case and pardon in the other. Let them call me rebel, and welcome, I feel no concern from it; but I should suffer the misery of devils, were I to make a whore of my soul by swearing allegiance to one whose character is that of a sottish, stupid, stubborn, worthless, brutish man. I conceive likewise a horrid idea in receiving mercy from a being, who at the last day shall be shrieking to the rocks and mountains to cover him, and fleeing with terror from the orphan, the widow, and the slain of America.

There are cases which cannot be overdone by language, and this is one. There are persons, too, who see not the full extent of the evil which threatens them; they solace themselves with hopes that the enemy, if he succeed, will be merciful. It is the madness of folly, to expect mercy from those who have refused to do justice; and even mercy, where conquest is the object, is only a trick of war; the cunning of the fox is as murderous as the violence of the wolf, and we ought to guard equally against both. Howe's first object is, partly by threats and partly by promises, to terrify or seduce the people to deliver up their arms and receive mercy. The ministry recommended the same plan to Gage, and this is what the tories call making their peace, *"a peace which passeth all understanding"* indeed! A peace which would be the immediate forerunner of a worse ruin than any we have yet thought of. Ye men of Pennsylvania, do reason upon these things! Were the back counties to give up their arms, they would fall an easy prey to the Indians, who are all armed: this perhaps is what some tories would not be sorry for. Were the home counties to deliver up their arms, they would be exposed to the resentment of the back counties, who would then have it in their power to chastise their defection at pleasure. And were any one state to give up its arms, *that* state must be garrisoned by all Howe's army of Britons and Hessians to preserve it from the anger of the rest. Mutual fear is the principal link in the chain of mutual love, and woe be to that state that breaks the compact. Howe is mercifully inviting you to barbarous destruction, and men must be either rogues or fools that will not see it. I dwell not upon the vapours of imagination: I bring reason to your ears, and, in language as plain as A, B, C, hold up truth to your eyes.

I thank God, that I fear not. I see no real cause for fear. I know our situation well, and can see the way out of it. While our army was collected, Howe dared not risk a battle; and it is no credit to him that he decamped from the White Plains, and waited a mean opportunity to ravage the defenceless Jerseys; but it is great credit to us, that, with a handful of men, we sustained an orderly retreat for near an hundred miles, brought off our ammunition, all our field pieces, the greatest part of our stores, and had four rivers to pass. None can say that our retreat was precipitate, for we were near three weeks in performing it, that the country might have time to come in. Twice we marched back to meet the enemy, and remained out till dark. The sign of fear was not seen in our camp, and had not some of the cowardly and disaffected inhabitants spread false alarms through the country, the Jerseys had never been ravaged. Once more we are again collected and collecting; our new army at both ends of the continent is recruiting fast, and we shall be able to open the next campaign with sixty thousand men, well armed and clothed. This is our situation, and who will may know it. By perseverance and fortitude we have the prospect of a glorious issue; by cowardice and submission, the sad choice of a variety of evils—a ravaged country—a depopulated city—habitations without safety, and slavery without hope—our homes turned into barracks and bawdy-houses for Hessians, and a future race to provide for, whose fathers we shall doubt of. Look on this picture and weep over it! and if there yet remains one thoughtless wretch who believes it not, let him suffer it unlamented.

# ALEXANDER HAMILTON
## (1755/57-1804)

# ALEXANDER HAMILTON
## (1755/57-1804)

ALEXANDER HAMILTON WAS BORN IN THE British West Indies, on the island of Nevis, on January 11, 1755 or 1757 (the exact date is unknown, as it is believed that Hamilton lied about his age). Hamilton's mother was married to the highly abusive John Lavien. Lavien had her imprisoned and, upon her release, she fled to St. Kitts and met Hamilton's father, James Hamilton. Together, they had two children: James and Alexander. Though, it wasn't soon after that James Sr. deserted the family and left them in poverty.

Hamilton wanted to improve his standing in life and acquired his first job as a clerk when he was 11 years old. In 1768, his mother died of illness. Hamilton continued to work diligently and impressed his employer with his intelligence and eagerness to learn. Given this, he was taught much about money and trading. Nicolas Cruger, Hamilton's boss, and other businessmen worked together to have Hamilton sent to America for an education.

In 1773, around the age of 16, Hamilton arrived in New York. He then enrolled in King's College (now Columbia University). In 1774, he wrote a political article that defended the idea of a revolution. He believed so fiercely in the cause that he left King's College early, without graduating, in order to join the effort of the patriots. In 1775, Hamilton became part of the New York Provincial Artillery Company and fought in multiple battles. In 1777, he was promoted to lieutenant colonel and became Washington's advisor and assistant. Hamilton remained in this position for five years, writing important documents for Washington and helping reform the Continental Army.

Hamilton married Elizabeth "Eliza" Schulyer, the daughter of Philip Schuyler and Catherine Van Rensselaer, on December 14, 1780.

They maintained a strong marriage until Hamilton's death, despite the fact that Hamilton had an affair with Maria Reynolds, a young woman that claimed to be seeking help because her husband left her destitute, which became one of the nation's first sex scandals.

In 1781, Hamilton began to grow restless working behind a desk and asked Washington to let him return to action. Washington allowed it, and Hamilton led troops during the Battle of Yorktown, which ultimately led to the surrender of the British. During his time as Washington's advisor, Hamilton came to see some of the weaknesses within Congress, such as tension between states. Many of these, he thought, were brought on by the Articles of Confederation. In 1782, Hamilton left his role as advisor and focused his attention on practicing law.

Hamilton's practice began in New York City and many of his clients were British loyalists, as the patriots fled their homes during the war and the abandoned buildings became populated with loyalists. Upon their return home, the patriots sued the Loyalists for compensation and Hamilton defended them. Stemming from this, Hamilton took on the *Rutgers v. Waddington* case in 1784, which resulted in the creation of the judicial review system. This same year, he helped found the Bank of New York. After taking on 45 more trespassing cases, Hamilton assisted in repealing the Trespass Act (1783), which was a law that permitted patriots to collect damages from the loyalists that had been occupying their homes.

In 1787, Hamilton served as a New York Delegate and in his work on the Constitution, he argued for a stronger central government. It was then that he joined John Jay and James Madison to write *The Federalist Papers*. In 1788, he went to the New York Ratification Convention. Facing bleak odds, with two-thirds of the delegates in opposition to the Constitution, Hamilton argued diligently and ended up helping to sway enough votes for New York to ratify the Constitution.

When Washington was elected President in 1789, he appointed Hamilton to be the first Secretary of Treasury. Hamilton was constantly at odds with other cabinet members, such as Secretary of State Thomas Jefferson, who opposed a strong central government. Hamilton turned down the opportunity for New York to be the home of the nation's capital, preferring to secure funds for one of his economic programs. He had the federal government assume state debts, initiated the payment of federal war bonds, created a system for federal tax collection, and later helped the U.S. establish credit with foreign nations. Eventually, in 1790, Hamilton and Madison agreed to a compromise: Hamilton would support having the nation's capital be near the Potomac river, and Madison would stop blocking Hamilton's policies in Congress. Hamilton stepped down from his position in 1795.

The election of 1800 consisted of Democratic-Republican Thomas Jefferson running against Federalist John Adams. Jefferson ended up tying Aaron Burr for the presidency and Hamilton, who saw Jefferson as the lesser of two evils, went against other Federalists by helping Jefferson secure the presidency. Given the contested race, Jefferson lost trust in Burr and left him out of important discussions during the presidency. Jefferson ran again without Burr in 1804 and won. Burr became increasingly frustrated with Hamilton, as Hamilton's constant public attacks on Burr were damaging to his political career. Eventually fed up, Burr challenged Hamilton to a duel, which he accepted.

On the morning of July 11, 1804, in Weehawken, NJ, Hamilton and Burr dueled. As a result, Hamilton was mortally wounded and brought back to New York City where he died the next day. The exact details of the duel are unknown, and some speculate that Hamilton deliberately missed Burr. Hamilton's wife lived for another 50 years without him, dedicating her life to preserving his legacy.

# A Full Vindication of the Measures of the Congress

FRIENDS and COUNTRYMEN,

IT was hardly to be expected that any man could be so presump-tuous, as openly to controvert the equity, wis|dom, and authority of the measures, adopted by the congress: an assembly truly respectable on every ac|count!—Whether we consider the characters of the men, who composed it; the number, and dignity of their constituents, or the important ends for which they were appointed. But, however improb-able such a degree of pre|sumption might have seemed, we find there are some, in whom it exists. Attempts are daily making to diminish the influence of their decisions, and prevent the salutary effects, in-tended by them.—The impotence of such insidious efforts is evident from the general indignation they are treated with; so that no mate|rial ill-consequences can be dreaded from them. But left they should have a tendency to mislead, and prejudice the minds of a few; it cannot be deemed altogether useless to bestow some notice upon them.

And first, let me ask these restless spirits, whence arises that vio-lent antipathy they seem to entertain, not only to the natu|ral rights of mankind; but to common sense and common mo|desty. That they are enemies to the natural rights of mankind is manifest, because they wish to see one part of their species enslaved by another. That they have an invincible aversion to common sense is apparent in many respects: They endea|vour to persuade us, that the absolute sovereignty of parlia|ment does not imply our absolute slavery; that it is a Christian duty to submit to be plundered of all we have, merely because some of our fellow-sub-jects are wicked enough to require it of us, that slavery, so far from being a great evil, is a great bless|ing; and even, that our contest with Britain is founded entire|ly upon the petty duty of 3 pence per pound on East India tea; whereas the whole world knows, it is built upon this inter-esting question, whether the inhabitants of Great-Britain have a right to dispose of the lives and properties of the inhabitants of Ame|rica, or not? And lastly, that these men have discarded all pretension to common modesty, is clear from hence, first, be|cause they, in the plainest terms, call an august body of men, famed for their patriotism and abilities, fools or knaves, and of course the people whom they represented cannot be exempt from the same opprobrious appellations: and secondly, because they set themselves up as standards of wisdom and probity, by contradicting and censuring the public voice in favour of those men.

A little consideration will convince us, that the congress in|stead of having "ignorantly misunderstood, carelessly neglected, or basely betrayed the interests of the colonies," have, on the contrary, devised and recommended the only effectual means to secure the freedom, and establish the future prosperity of Ame|rica upon a solid basis. If we are not free and happy hereafter, it must proceed from the want of integrity and resolution, in executing what they have concerted; not from the temerity or impolicy of their determinations.

Before I proceed to confirm this assertion by the most obvious arguments, I will premise a few brief remarks. The only dis|tinction between freedom and slavery consists in this: In the former state, a man is governed by the laws to which he has given his consent, either in person, or by his representative: In the latter, he is governed by the will of another. In the one case his life and property are his own, in the other, they de|pend upon the pleasure of a master. It is easy to discern which of these two states is preferable. No man in his senses can he|sitate in choosing to be free, rather than a slave.

That Americans are intitled to freedom, is incontestible upon every rational principle. All men have one common original: they participate in one common nature, and consequently have one common right. No reason can be assigned why one man should exercise any power, or pre eminence over his fellow crea|tures more than another; unless they have voluntarily vested him with it. Since then, Americans have not by any act of their's impowered the British Parliament to make laws for them, it follows they can have no just authority to do it.

Besides the clear voice of natural justice in this respect, the fundamental principles of the English constitution are in our favour. It has been repeatedly demonstrated, that the idea of legislation, or taxation, when the subject is not represented, is inconsistent with *that*. Nor is this all, our charters, the express conditions on which our progenitors relinquished their native countries, and came to settle in this, preclude every claim of ruling and taxing us without our assent.

Every subterfuge that sophistry has been able to invent, to evade or obscure this truth, has been refuted by the most con|clusive reasonings; so that we may pronounce it a matter of undeniable certainty, that the pretensions of Parliament are contradictory to the law of nature, subversive of the British con|stitution, and destructive of the faith of the most solemn com|pacts.

What then is the subject of our controversy with the mother country?—It is this, whether we shall preserve that security to our lives and properties, which the law of nature, the genius of the British constitution, and our charters afford us; or whe|ther we shall resign them into the hands of the British House of Commons, which is no more privileged to dispose of them than the Grand Mogul?—What can actuate those men, who labour to delude any of us into an opinion, that the object of contention between the parent state and the colonies is only three pence duty upon tea? or that the commotions in America ori|ginate in a plan, formed by some turbulent men to erect it into a republican government? The parliament claims a right to tax us in all cases whatsoever: Its late acts are in virtue of that claim.—How ridiculous then is it to affirm, that we are quarrelling for the trifling sum of three pence a pound on tea; when it is evi|dently the principle against which we contend.

The design of electing members to represent us in general congress, was, that the wisdom of America might be collected in devising the most proper and expedient means to repel this atro|cious invasion of our rights. It has been accordingly done. Their decrees are binding upon all, and demand a religious ob|servance.

We did not, especially in this province, circumscribe them by any fixed boundary, and therefore as they cannot be said to have exceeded the limits of their authority, their act must be esteemed the act of their constituents. If it should be objected, that they have not answered the end of their election; but have fallen up|on an improper and ruinous mode of proceeding: I reply, by asking, Who shall be the judge? Shall any individual oppose his private sentiment to the united counsels of men, in whom America has reposed so high a confidence? The attempt must argue no small degree of arrogance and self-sufficiency.

Yet this attempt has been made, and it is become in some measure necessary to vindicate the conduct of this venerable as|sembly from the aspersions of men, who are their adversaries, on|ly because they are foes to America.

When the political salvation of any community is depending, it is incumbent upon those who are set up as its guardians, to embrace such measures, as have justice, vigour, and a probability of success to recommend them: If instead of this, they take those methods which are in themselves feeble, and little likely to suc|ceed; and may, through a defect in vigour, involve the com|munity in still greater danger; they may be justly considered as its betrayers. It is not enough in times of eminent peril to use only possible means of preservation: Justice and found policy dictate the use of probable means.

The only scheme of opposition, suggested by those, who have been, and are averse from a non-importation and non-exportation agreement, is, by REMONSTRANCE and PETITION. The au|thors and abettors of this scheme, have never been able to *invent* a single argument to prove the likelihood of its succeeding. On the other hand, there are many standing facts, and valid conside|rations against it.

In the infancy of the present dispute, we had recourse to this method only. We addressed the throne in the most loyal and respectful manner, in a legislative capacity; but what was the consequence? Our address was treated with contempt and ne|glect. The first American congress did the same, and met with similar treatment. The total repeal of the stamp act, and the partial repeal of the revenue acts took place, not because the complaints of America were deemed just and reasonable; but because these acts were found to militate against the commercial interests of Great Britain: This was the declared motive of the repeal.

These instances are sufficient for our purpose; but they de|rive greater validity and force from the following:

The legal assembly of Massachusetts Bay, presented, not long since, a most humble, dutiful, and earnest petition to his Ma|jesty, requesting the dismission of a governor, highly odious to the people, and whose misrepresentations they regarded as one chief source of all their calamities. Did they succeed in their request? No, it was treated with the greatest indignity, and stigmatized as "a seditious, vexatious, and scandalous libel."

I know the men I have to deal with will acquiesce in this stigma. Will they also dare to calumniate the noble and spirit|ed petition that came from the Mayor and Aldermen of the city of London? Will they venture to justify that unparalelled stride of power, by which popery and arbitrary dominion were esta|blished in Canada? The citizens of London remonstrated against it, they signified its repugnancy to the principles of the revolution; but like ours, their complaints were unattended to. From thence we may learn how little dependence ought to be placed on this method of obtaining the redress of grievances.

There is less reason now than ever to expect deliverance, in this way, from the hand of oppression. The system of slavery, fabricated against America, cannot at this time be considered as the effect of inconsideration and rashness. It is the offspring of mature deliberation. It has been fostered by time, and strength|ened by every artifice human subtilty is capable of. After the claims of parliament had lain dormant for awhile, they are again resumed and prosecuted with more than common ardour. The Premier has advanced too far to recede with safety: He is deep|ly interested to execute his purpose, if possible: we know he has declared, that he will never desist, till he has brought America to his feet; and we may conclude, nothing but necessity will induce him to abandon his aims. In common life, to retract an error even in the beginning, is no easy talk:—Perseverance confirms us in it, and rivets the difficulty; but in a public sta|tion, to have been in an error, and to have persisted in it, when it is detected, ruins both reputation and fortune. To this we may add, that disappointment and opposition inflame the minds of men, and attach them, still more, to their mistakes.

What can we represent which has not already been represented? what petitions can we offer, that have not already been offered? The rights of America, and the injustice of parliamentary pretensions have been clearly and repeatedly stated, both in and out of parliament. No new arguments can be framed to operate in our favour. Should we even resolve the errors of the mini|stry and parliament into the falibility of human understand|ing, if they have not yet been convinced, we have no prospect of being able to do it by any thing further we can say. But if we impute their conduct to a wicked thirst of domination and disregard to justice, we have no hope of prevailing with them to alter it, by expatiating on our rights, and suing to their compassion for relief;

especially since we have sound, by various experiments, the inefficacy of such methods.

Upon the whole, it is morally certain, this mode of oppo|sition would be fruitless and defective. The exigency of the times requires vigorous and probable remedies; not weak and improbable.—It would therefore be the extreme of folly to place any confidence in, much less, confine ourselves wholly to it.

This being the case, we can have no resource but in a restric|tion of our trade, or in a resistance *vi & armis*. It is impossible to conceive any other alternative. Our congress, therefore, have imposed what restraint they thought necessary. Those, who condemn or clamour against it, do nothing more, nor less, than advise us to be slaves.

I shall now examine the principal measures of the congress, and vindicate them fully from the charge of injustice or impo|licy.

Were I to argue in a philosophical manner, I might say, the obligation to a mutual intercourse in the way of trade with the inhabitants of Great-Britain, Ireland and the West-Indies is of the *imperfect* kind. There is no law, either of nature, or of the civil society in which we live, that obliges us to purchase, and make use of the products and manufactures of a different land, or people. It is indeed a dictate of humanity to con|tribute to the support and happiness of our fellow creatures and more especially those who are allied to us by the ties of blood, interest, and mutual protection; but humanity does not require us to sacrifice our own security and welfare to the convenience, or advantage of others. Self preservation is the first principle of our nature. When our lives and properties are at stake, it would be foolish and unnatural to refrain from such measures as might preserve them, because they would be detrimental to others.

But we are justified upon another principle besides this.—Though the manufacturers of Great Britain and Ireland, and the Inhabitants of the West Indies are not chargeable with any actual crime towards America, they may, in a political view, be esteemed criminal. In a civil society, it is the du|ty of each particular branch to promote, not only the good of the whole community, but the good of every other parti|cular branch: If one part endeavours to violate the rights of another, the rest ought to assist in preventing the injury:—When they do not, but remain nutral, they are deficient in their duty, and may be regarded, in some measure, as ac|complices.

The reason of this is obvious, from the design of civil so|ciety, which is, that the united strength of the several mem|bers might give stability and security to the whole body; and each respective member; so that one part cannot encroach up|on another, without becoming a common enemy, and event|ually endangering the safety and happiness of all the other parts.

Since then the persons who will be distressed by the me|thods we are using for our own protection, have by their neu|trality first committed to breach of an obligation, similar to that which bound us to consult their emolument, it is plain, the obligation upon us is annulled, and we are blameless in what we are about to do.

With respect to the manufacturers of Great Britain, they are criminal in a more particular sense. Our oppression arises from that member of the great body politic, of which they compose a considerable part. So far as their influence has been wanting to counteract the iniquity of their rulers, so far they acquiesced in it, and are to be deemed confederates in their guilt. It is impossible to exculpate a people, that suffers its rulers to abuse and tyrannize over others.

It may not be amiss to add, that we are ready to receive with open arms, any who may be sufferers by the operation of our measures, and recompense them with every blessing our country affords to honest industry. We will receive them as brethren, and make them sharers with us in all the advantages we are struggling for.

From these plain and indisputable principles, the mode of opposition we have chosen is reconcileable to the strictest max|ims of Justice. It remains now to be examined, whether it, has also the sanction of good policy.

To render it agreeable to good policy, three things are re|quisite. First, that the necessity of the times require it: Se|condly, that it be not the probable source of greater evils, than those it pretends to remedy: And lastly, that it have a probability of success.

That the necessity of the times demands it needs but lit|tle elucidation. We are threatened with absolute slavery; it has been proved, that resistance by means of REMONSTRANCE and PETITION, would not be efficacious, and of course, that a restriction on our trade, is the only peaceable method, in our power, to avoid the impending mischief: It follows there|fore, that such a restriction is necessary.

That it is not the probable source of greater evils than those it pretends to remedy, may easily be determined. The most abject slavery, which comprehends almost every species of hu|man misery, is what it is designed to prevent.

The consequences of the means are a temporary stagnation of commerce, and thereby a deprivation of the luxuries and some of the conveniencies of life. The necessaries, and many of conveniencies, our own fertile and propitious soil affords us.

No person, that has enjoyed the sweets of liberty, can be in|sensible of its infinite value, or can reflect on its reverse, with|out horror and detestation. No person, that is not lost to eve|ry generous feeling of humanity, or that is not stupidly blind to his own interest, could bear to offer himself and posterity as victims at the shrine of despotism, in preference to endur|ing the short lived inconveniencies that may result from an abridgment, or even entire suspension of commerce.

Were not the disadvantages of slavery too obvious to stand in need of it, I might enumerate and describe the tedious train of calamities, inseparable from it. I might shew that it is fatal to religion and morality; that it tends to debase the mind, and corrupt its noblest springs of action. I might shew, that it relaxes the sinews of industry, clips the wings of com|merce, and introduces misery and indigence in every shape.

Under the auspices of tyranny, the life of the subject is of|ten sported with: and the fruits of his daily toil are con|sumed in oppressive taxes, that serve to gratify the ambition, avarice and lusts of his superiors. Every court minion riots in the spoils of the honest labourer, and despises the hand by which he is fed. The page of history is replete with instances that loudly warn us to beware of slavery.

Rome was the nurse of freedom. She was celebrated for her justice and lenity; but in what manner did she govern her dependent provinces? They were made the continual scene of rapine and cruelty. From thence let us learn, how little confidence is due to the wisdom and equity of the most exem|plary nations.

Should Americans submit to become the vassals of their fel||low-subjects in Great Britain, their yoke will be peculiarly grievous and intolerable. A vast majority of mankind is in|tirely biassed by motives of self-interest. Most men are glad to remove any burthens off themselves, and place them upon the necks of their neighbours. We cannot therefore doubt, but that the British Parliament, with a view to the ease and advan|tage of itself, and its constituents, would oppress and grind the Americans as much as possible. Jealousy would concur with self|ishness; and for fear of the future independence of America, if it should be permitted to rise to too great a height of splendor and opulence, every method would be taken to drain it of its wealth and restrain its prosperity. We are already suspected of aiming at independence, and that is one principal cause of the severity we experience. The same cause will always operate against us, and produce an uniform severity of treatment.

The evils which may flow from the execution of our mea|sures, if we consider them with respect to their extent and du|ration, are comparatively nothing. In all human probability they will scarcely be felt. Reason and experience teach us, that the consequences would be too fatal to Great Britain to admit of delay. There is an immense trade between her and the colo|nies. The revenues arising from thence are prodigious. The consumption of her manufactures in these colonies supplies the means of subsistence to a vast number of her most useful inhabi|tants. The experiment we have made heretofore, shews us of how much importance our commercial connexion is to her; and gives us the highest assurance of obtaining immediate redress by suspending it.

From these considerations it is evident, she must do something decisive. She must either listen to our complaints, and restore us to a peaceful enjoyment of our violated rights; or she must exert herself to enforce her despotic claims by fire and sword. To imagine she would prefer the latter, implies a charge of the grossest infatuation of madness itself. Our numbers are very con|siderable; the courage of Americans has been tried and proved. Contests for liberty have ever been found the most bloody, im|placable and obstinate. The disciplined troops Great Britain could send against us, would be but few, Our superiority in number would over balance our inferiority in discipline. If would be a hard, if not an impracticable task to subjugate us by force.

Besides, while Great Britain was engaged in carrying on an unnatural war against us, her commerce would be in a state of decay. Her revenues would be decreasing. An armament, sufficient to enslave America, would put her to an insupportable expence.

She would be laid open to the attacks of foreign enemies, Ruin, like a deluge, would pour in from every quarter. After lavishing her blood and treasure to reduce us to a state of vassa|lage, she would her-self become a prey to some triumphant neighbour.

These are not imaginary mischiefs. The colonies contain above three millions of people. Commerce flourishes with the most rapid progress throughout them. This commerce Great|Britain has hither-to regulated to her own advantage. Can we think the annihilation of so exuberant a source of wealth, a matter of trifling import. On the contrary, must it not be pro|ductive of the most disastrous effects? It is evident it must. It is equally evident, that the conquest of so numer-ous a people, armed in the animating cause of liberty could not be accom|plished without inconceivable expence of blood and treasure.

We cannot therefore suspect Great-Britain to be capable of such frantic extravagance as to hazard these dreadful conse|quences; without which she must necessarily desist from her un|just pretensions, and leave us in the undisturbed possession of our privileges.

Those, who affect to ridicule the resistance America might make to the military force of Great-Britain, and represent its humiliation as a matter the most easily to be atchieved, betray either a mind clouded by the most irrational prejudices, or a total ignorance of human nature. However, it must be the with of every honest man never to see a trial.

But should we admit a possibility of a third course, as our pam-phleteer supposes, that is, the endeavouring to bring us to a compli-ance by putting a stop to our whole trade: Even this would not be so terrible as be pretends. We can live without trade of any kind. Food and clothing we have within ourselves. Our climate produces cotton, wool, flax and hemp, which, with proper cultivation would furnish us with summer apparel in abundance. The article of cotton indeed would do more, it would contribute to defend us from the inclemen-cy of winter. We have sheep, which, with due care in improving and increas|ing them, would soon yield a sufficiency of wool. The large quantity of skins, we have among us, would never let us want a warm and comfortable suit. It would be no unbecoming employment for our daughters to provide silks of their own country. The silk-worm answers as well here as in any part of the world. Those hands, which may be deprived of business by the cessation of commerce, may be oc-cupied in various kinds of manufactures and other internal improve-ments. If by the necessity of the thing, manufactures should once be established and take root among us, they will pave the way, still more, to the future grandeur and glory of America, and by lessening its need of external commerce, will render it still securer against the encroachments of tyranny.

It is however, chimerical to imagine that the circumstances of Great-Britain will admit of such a tardy method of subjecting us, for reasons, which have been already given, and which shall be corroborated by others equally forcible.

I come now to consider the last and principal engredient that constitutes the policy of a measure, which is a probability of success. I have been obliged to anticipate this part of my sub|ject, in considering the second requisite, and indeed what I have already said seems to me to leave no room for doubting, that the means we have used will be successful, but I shall here examine the matter more thoroughly, and endeavour to evince it more fully.

The design of the Congress in their proceedings, it cannot, and need not be desired, was either, by a prospect of the evil consequences, to influence the ministry to give up their enter|prize; or should they prove inflexible, to affect the inhabitants of Great-Britain, Ireland and the West-Indies in such a manner, as to rouse them from their state of neutrality, and engage them to unite with us in opposing the lawless hand of tyranny, which is extended to ravish our liberty from us, and might soon be extended for the same purpose against them.

The BARMER mentions, as one probable consequence of our measures, "clamours, discord, confusion, mobs, riots, insur|rections, rebellions in Great-Britain, Ireland and the West-Indies;" though at the same time that he thinks *it is*, he also thinks *it is not* a probable consequence. For my part, without hazarding any such seeming contradictions, I shall, in a plain way, assert, that I verily believe a non-importation and non|exportation will effect all the purposes they are intended for.

It is no easy matter to make any tolerably exact estimate of the advantages that acrue to Great-Britain, Ireland and the West-Indies from their commercial intercourse with the colonies, nor indeed is it necessary. Every man, the least acquainted with the state and extent of our trade, must be convinced, it is the source of immense revenues to the parent state, and gives employment and bread to a vast number of his

Majesty's sub|jects. It is impossible but that a suspension of it for any time, must introduce beggary and wretchedness in an eminent degree, both in England and Ireland; and as to the West-India planta|tions, they could not possibly subsist without us. I am the more confident of this, because I have a pretty general acquaintance with their circumstances and dependencies.

We are told, "that it is highly improbable, we shall succeed in distressing the people of Great-Britain, Ireland and the West-Indies, so far as to oblige them to join with us in getting the acts of Parliament, which we complain of, repealed: The first distress (it is said) will fall on ourselves; it will be more severely felt by us, than any part of all his Majesty's dominions, and will affect us the longest. The fleets of Great-Britain command respect throughout the globe. Her influence extends to every part of the earth. Her manufactures are equal to any: Superior to most in the world. Her wealth is great. Her people enter|prizing and persevering in their attempts to extend, and enlarge, and protect her trade. The total loss of our trade will be felt only for a time. Her merchants would turn their attention another way: New sources of trade and wealth would be opened: New schemes pursued. She would soon find a vent for all her manufactures in spite of all we could do. Our malice would hurt only ourselves. Should our schemes distress some branches of her trade, it would be only for a time; and there is ability and humanity enough in the nation to relieve those, that are distressed by us, and put them in some other way of getting their living."

The omnipotence and all sufficiency of Great-Britain may be pretty good topics for her passionate admirers to exercise their declamatory powers upon, for amusement and trial of skill; but they ought not to be proposed to the world as matters of truth and reality. In the calm, unprejudiced eye of reason, they are altogether visionary. As to her wealth, it is notorious that she is oppressed with a heavy national debt, which it re|quires the utmost policy and aeconomy ever to discharge. Luxury has arrived to a great pitch; and it is an universal maxim that luxury indicates the declension of a state. Her subjects are loaded with the most enormous taxes: All circumstances agree in declaring their distress. The continual emigrations, from Great-Britain and Ireland, to the continent, are a glaring symptom, that those kingdoms are a good deal impoverished.

The attention of Great-Britain has hitherto been constantly awake to expand her commerce. She has been vigilant to ex|plore every region, with which it might be her interest to trade. One of the principal branches of her commerce is with the co|lonies. These colonies, as they are now settled and peopled, have been the work of near two centuries: They are blessed with every advantage of soil, climate and situation. They have advanced with an almost incredible rapidity. It is therefore an egregious piece of absurdity to affirm, that the loss of our trade would be felt for a time (which must signify a short time.) No new schemes could be pursued that would not require, at least, as much time to repair the less of our trade, as was spent in bringing it to its present degree of perfection, which is near two centuries. Nor can it be reasonably imagined, that the total and sudden loss of so extensive and lucrative a branch, would not produce the most violent effects to a nation that sub|sists entirely upon its commerce.

It is said, "there is ability and humanity enough in the nation to relieve those that are distressed by us; and to put them into some other way of getting their living."—I wish the gentleman had obliged his readers so much, as to have pointed out this other way; I must confess, I have racked my brains to no pur|pose to discover it, and am fully of opinion it is purely ideal.—Besides the common mechanic arts, which are subservient to the ordinary uses of life, and which are the instruments of commerce; know no other ways in time of peace, in which men can be em|ployed, except in agriculture and the liberal arts. Persons em|ployed in the mechanic arts, are those, whom the abridgment of commerce would immediately affect, and as to such branch|es as might be less affected, they are already sufficiently stocked with workmen, and could give bread to no more; not only so, but I can't see by what legerdemain, a weaver, or clothier could be at once converted into a carpenter of black-smith. With respect to agriculture. the lands of Great Britain and Ire|land have been long ago distributed and taken up; nor do they require any additional labourers to till them; so that there could be no employment in this way. The liberal arts cannot maintain those who are already devoted to them; not to say, it is more than probable, the generality of mechanics, would make but indifferent philosophers, poets, painters and musicians.

What poor shifts is sophistry obliged to have recourse to! we are threatened with the resentment of those against whem our measures will operate. It is said, that "instead of conciliating, we shall alienate the affections of the people of Great-Britain, of friends, we shall make them our enemies;" and further, that "we shall excite the resentment of the government at home against which will do us no good, but, on the contrary, much harm."

Soon after, we are told that "we shall probably raise the re|sentment of the Irish and West-Indians: The passions of human nature" it is said, "are much the same in all countries. If they find us disposed wantonly to distress them, to serve our own purposes, they will look out for some method to do without us: will they not look elsewhere for a supply of those articles, they used to take from us? They would deserve to be despised for their meanness did they not."

To these objections I reply, first with respect to the inhabi|tants of Great-Britain, that if they are our friends, as is sup|posed, and as we have reason to believe; they cannot, without being destitute of rationality, be incensed against us for using the only peaceable and probable means, in our power, to pre|serve our invaded rights: They know by their own experience how fruitless remonstrances and petitions are: They know, we have tried them over and over to no purpose: They know also, how dangerous to their liberties, the loss of ours must be.—What then could exite their resentment if they have the least re|gard to common justice? The calamities, that threaten them, proceed from the weakness, or wickedness of their own rulers; which compels us to take the measures we do. The insinuation, that we *wantonly* distress them to serve our own purposes, is fu|tile and unsupported by a single argument. I have shewn, we could have no other resource; nor can they think our conduct such, without a degree of infatuation, that it would be impos|sible to provide against, and therefore useless to consult. It is most reasonable to believe, they will revenge the evils they may feel on the true authors of them, on an aspiring and ill-judging ministry; not on us, who act out of a melancholy necessity, and are the innocent causes in self-defence.

With respect to the ministry, it is certain, that any thing, which has a tendency to frustrate their designs, will not fail to excite their displeasure; but since we have nothing to expect from their justice and lenity, it can be no objection to a mea|sure, that it tends to stir up their resent-

ment. But their re|sentment (it is often said) may ruin us. The impos-
sibility of doing that, without at the same time, ruining Great-Britain,
is a sufficient security.

The same may be said with regard to the Irish and the West-Indi-
ans, which has been said concerning the people of Great|Britain. The
Irish, in particular, by their own circumstances will be taught to sym-
pathise with us, and commend our conduct. Justice will direct their
resentment to its proper objects.

It is true self-love will prompt both the Irish and the West-Indi-
ans to take every method in their power, to escape the mi|series they
are in danger of; but what methods can they take? "The Irish (it is
said) may be supplied with flax-seed from Holland, the Baltic, and
the river St. Lawrence: Canada pro|duces no inconsiderable quantity
already." And as to the West|Indies, "they produce now many of the
necessaries of life. The quantity may be easily increased. Canada will
furnish them with many articles they now take from us; flour, lum-
ber, hors|es, &c. Georgia, the Floridas, and the Mississippi abound in
lumber: Nova Scotia in fish."

The Dutch are rivals to the English in their commerce. They
make large quantities of fine linens, gause, laces, &c. which re|quire
the flax to be picked before it comes to seed; for which reason, it is
not in their power to raise much more seed than they want for their
own use. Ireland has always had the sur|plus from them. They could,
if they were ever so willing, en|large their usual supplies but very lit-
tle. It is indeed probable they may withold them. They may choose to
improve the oc|casion for the advancement of their own trade: They
may take advantage of the scarcity of materials in Ireland, to increase
and put off their own manufactures.

The Baltic has ever supplied Ireland with its flax, and she has been
able to consume that, with all she could derive from other quarters.

As to Canada, I am well informed it could at present afford, but a very
inconsiderable quantity. It has had little encourage|ment, hitherto, to raise
that article, and of course has not much attended to it. The instances mentioned, of seed being "bought up there at a low price, brought to New-York,
and sold to the Irish factors at a great advance," does not prove there is any
quantity raised there. Its cheapness proceeds from there being no demand for
it; and where there was no demand, there was no inducement to cultivate it.

Upon the whole, it appears, that the supplies of flax-seed, which Ireland might draw elsewhere, could be trifling in com|parison with those received from us, and not at all equivalent to her wants. But if this were not the case, if she might pro|cure a sufficiency without our help, yet could she not do without us. She would want purchasers for her linens after they were manufactured; and where could she find any so numerous and wealthy as we are? I must refer it to the profound sagacity of Mr. A. W. Farmer, to explore them, it is too arduous a task for me.

Much less could the West-Indies subsist independent of us. Not-withstanding the continual imports from hence, there is sel|dom or ever, in any of the islands, a sufficient stock of provisions to last six months, which may give us an idea, how great the consumption is. The necessaries they produce within them|selves, when compared with the consumption, are scarcely worth mentioning. Very small portions of the lands are ap|propriated to the productions of such necessaries, indeed it is too valuable to admit of it. Nor could the quantity be increased to any material degree, without applying the whole of the land to it. It is alledged, that Canada will furnish them with flour, lumber, horses, &c. and that Georgia, the Floridas and Mississipi abound in lumber; Nova Scotia in fish." These countries have been all-along carrying on a trade to the West-Indies, as well as we; and can it be imagined that alone, they will be able to supply them tolerably? The Canadians have been indolent, and have not improved their country as they ought to have done. The wheat they raise at present, over and above what they have occasion for themselves, would be found to go but little way among the islands. Those, who think the contrary, must have mistaken notions of them. They must be unapprized of the number of souls they contain: Almost every 150 or 200 acres of land, exclusive of populous towns, comprehend a hundred people. It is not a small quantity of food that will suf|fice for so many. Ten or fifteen years diligence, I grant, might enable Canada to perform what is now expected from her; but, in the mean time, the West-Indians might have the satisfaction of starving.

To suppose the best, which is, that by applying their cane|lands to the purpose of procuring sustenance, they may pre|serve themselves from starving: still the consequences must be very serious or perni-cious. The wealthy planters would but ill relish the loss of their crops, and such of them as were consider|ably in debt would be ruined. At any rate, the revenues of Great-Britain would suffer a vast diminution.

The FARMER, I am inclined to hope, builds too much upon the present disunion of Canada, Georgia, the Floridas, the Mis|sissip-pi, and Nova Scotia from other colonies.—A little time. I trust, will awaken them from their slumber, and bring them to a proper sense of their indiscretion. I please myself with the flattering prospect, that they will, ere long, unite in one indisso|luble chain with the rest of the colonies.—I cannot believe they will persist in such a conduct as must exclude them from the se|cure enjoyment of those heaven-descended immunities we are contending for.

There is one argument I have frequently heard urged, which it may be of some use to invalidate. It is this, that if the mo|ther country should be inclined to an accommodation of our dis|putes, we have by our rash procedure thrown an insurmount|able obstacle in her way; we have made it disgraceful to her to comply with our requisitions, because they are proposed in a hostile manner.

Our present measures, I have proved, are the only peaceable ones we could place the least confidence in. They are the least exceptionable, upon the score of irritating Great-Bri|tain, of anyour circumstances would permit. The congress have petitioned his Majesty for the re-dress of grievances. They have, no doubt, addressed him in the most humble, respectful and affectionate terms; assured him, of their own loyalty, and fidelity and of the loyalty and fidelity; of his American subjects in general; endeavoured to convince him, that we have been misrepresented and abused; and ex|pressed an earnest desire to see an amicable termination of the unhappy differences now existing. Can a pretext be wanting, in this case, to preserve the dignity of this parent state, and yet remove the complaints of the colonies? How easy would it be to overlook our particular agreements, and grant us redress in consequence of our petitions? It is easy to perceive there would be no difficulty in this respect.

I have omitted many considerations, which might be adduced to shew the impolicy of Great-Britains, delaying to accommo|date mat-ters, and attempting to enforce submission by cutting off all external sources of trade. To say all the subject allows, would spin out this piece to an immoderate length; I shall, therefore content myself with men-

tioning only three things more. First, it would be extremely hurtful
to the commerce of Great-Britain to drive us to the necessity of laying a regular foundation for manufactories of our own; which, if once
estab|lished, could not easily, if at all, be undermined, or abolished.
Secondly, it would be very expensive to the nation to maintain a fleet
for the purpose of blocking up our ports, and destroying our trade:
nor could she interrupt our intercourse with foreign climes without, at
the same time, retrenching her own reve|nues; for she must then lose
the duties and customs upon the articles we are wont to export to, and
import from them.—Added to this, it would not be prudent to risk the
displeasure of those nations, to whom our trade is useful and beneficial.
And lastly, a perseverance in ill-treatment would naturally beget such
deep-rooted animosities in America, as might never be eradicated; and
which might operate to the prejudice of the empire to the latest period.

Thus have I clearly proved, that the plan of opposition con|certed
by our congress is perfectly consonant with justice and sound policy;
and will, in all human probability, secure our freedom against the as-
saults of our enemies.

But, after all, it may be demanded why they have adopted a
non-exportation; seeing many arguments tend to shew that a non-importation alone would accomplish the end desired?

I answer, that the continuance of our exports is the only thing
which could lessen, or retard the efficacy of a non-im|portation. It is
not indeed probable it should do that to any great degree; but it was
adviseable to provide against every possible obstruction. Besides this,
the prospect of its taking place, and of the evils attendant upon it, will
be a prevailing motive with the ministry to abandon their malignant
schemes. It will also serve to convince them, that we are not afraid of
putting ourselves to any inconveniencies, sooner than be the victims of
their lawless ambition.

The execution of this measure has been wisely deserted to a future
time, because we have the greatest reason to think affairs will be settled
without it, and because its consequences would be too fatal to be justified
by any thing but absolute necessity. This necessity there will be, should not
our disputes terminate be|fore the time allotted for its commencement.

Before I conclude this part of my address, I will answer two very
singular interrogatories proposed by the FARMER, "Can we think

(says he) to threaten, and bully, and frighten the su|preme government of the nation into a compliance with our de|mands? Can we expect to force submission to our peevish and petulant humours, by exciting clamours and riots in England?" No, gentle Sir.—We neither desire, nor endeavour to threaten, bully, or frighten any persons into a compli-ance with our de|mands. We have no peevish and petulant humours to be sub|mitted to.—All we aim at, is to convince your high and mighty masters, the ministry, that we are not such asses as to let them ride us as they please. We are determined to shew them, that we know the value of freedom; nor shall their rapacity extort, that inestimable jewel from us, without a manly and virtuous struggle. But for your part, sweet Sir! tho' we cannot much applaud your wisdom, yet we are compelled to admire your valour, which leads you to hope you may be able to *swear*, threaten, bully and frighten all America into a compliance with your sinister designs. When properly accoutered and armed with your for-midable hic|cory cudgel, what may not the ministry expect from such a cham|pion? alas! for the poor committee gentlemen, how I trem|ble when I reflect on the many wounds and sears they must re|ceive from your tremendous arm! Alas! for their supporters and abettors; a very large part indeed of the continent; but what of that? they must all be soundly drubbed with that con|founded hiccory cudgel; for surely you would not undertake to drub one of them, without knowing yourself able to treat all their friends and adherents in the same manner; since 'tis plain you would bring them all upon your back.

I am now to address myself in particular to the Farmers of New-York.

*My good Countrymen,*

THE reason address myself to you, in particular, is, because I am one of your number, or connected with your in interest more than with any other branch of the community. I love to speak the truth, and would scorn to prejudice you in favour of what I have to say, by taking upon me a fictitious character as other people have done. I can venture to assure you, the true writer of the piece signed A. W. FARMER, is not in reality a Farmer. He is some ministerial emissary, that has assumed the name to deceive you, and make you swallow the intoxicating po-tion he has prepared for you. But I have a better opinion of you than to think he will be able to succeed. I am persuad|ed you love yourselves and children better than to let any de|signing men cheat you out of your liberty and property, to serve their own purposes. You would be a disgrace to your ancestors, and the bitterest enemies to yourselves and to your posterity, if you did not act like men, in protecting and defending those rights you have hitherto enjoyed.

I say, my friends, I do not address you in particular, be|cause I have any greater connexion with you, than with other people. I despise all false pretensions, and mean arts. Let those have recourse to dissimulation and falshood, who can't de|fend their cause without it. 'Tis my maxim to let the plain naked truth speak for itself; and if men won't listen to it, 'tis their own fault: they must be contented to suffer for it. I am neither merchant, nor farmer. I address you, because I wish well to my country, and of course to you, who are one chief sup|port of it; and because an attempt has been made to lead you astray in particular. You are the men too who would lose most should you be foolish enough to counteract the prudent measures our worthy congress has taken for the preservation of our liber|ties. Those, who advise you to do it, are not your friends, but your greatest foes. They would have you made slaves, that they may pamper themselves with the fruits of your honest labour. 'Tis the Farmer who is most oppressed in all countries where slavery prevails.

You have seen how clearly I have proved, that a non-impor|tation and non-exportation are the only peaceable means in our power to save ourselves from the most dreadful state of slavery. I have shewn there is not the least hope, to be placed in any thing else. I have confuted all the principal cavils raised by the pretended Farmer, and I hope, before I finish, to satisfy you, that he has attempted to frighten you with the prospect of evils, which will never happen. This indeed I have, in a great mea|sure, done already, by making appear the great probability, I may almost say certainty, that our measures will procure us the most speedy redress.

Are you willing then to be slaves without a single struggle? Will you give up your freedom, or, which is the same thing, will you resign all security for your life and property, rather than endure some small present inconveniencies? Will you not take a little trouble to transmit the advantages you now possess to those, who are to come after you?

I cannot doubt it. I would not suspect you of so much baseness and stupidity, as to suppose the contrary.

Pray who can tell me why a farmer in America, is not as honest and good a man, as a farmer in England? or why has not the one as good a right to what he has earned by his labour, as the other? I can't, for my life, see any distinction between them. And yet it seems the English farmers are to be governed and taxed by their own Assembly, or Parliament; and the Ame|rican farmers are not. The former are to choose their own Re|presentatives from among themselves, whose interest is connected with theirs, and over whom they have proper controul. The latter are to be loaded with taxes by men three thousand miles off; by men, who have no interest, or connexions among them; but whose interest it will be to burden them as much as possible; and over whom they cannot have the least restraint. How do you like this doctrine my friends? Are you ready to own the English farmers for your masters? Are you willing to acknow|ledge their right to take your property from you, and when they please? I know you scorn the thought. You had rather die, than submit to it.

But some people try to make you believe, we are disputing about the foolish trifle of three pence duty upon tea. They may as well tell you, that black is white. Surely you can judge for yourselves. Is a dispute, whether the Parliament of Great|Britain shall make what laws, and impose what taxes they please upon us, or not; I say, is this a dispute about three pence duty upon tea? The man that affirms it, deserves to be laughed at.

It is true, we are denying to pay the duty upon tea; but it is not for the value of the thing itself. It is because we cannot submit to that, without acknowledging the principle upon which it is founded, and that principle is *a right to tax us in all cases whatsoever.*

You have, heretofore experienced the benefit of being taxed by your own Assemblies only. Your burdens are so light, that you scarcely feel them. You'd soon find the difference if you were once to let the Parliament have the management to these matters.

How would you like to pay four shillings a year, out of every pound your farms are worth, to be squandered, (at least a great part of it) upon ministerial tools and court sycophants? What would you think of giving a tenth part of the yearly products of your lands to the clergy?

Would you not think it very hard to pay 10s. sterling per annum, for every wheel of your waggons and other carriages, a shilling or two for every pane of glass in your houses, and two or three shillings for every one of your hearths? I might mention taxes upon your mares, cows, and many other things; but those I have already men|tioned are sufficient. Methinks I see you stare, and hear you ask how you could live, if you were to pay such heavy taxes? Indeed my friends I can't tell you— You are to look out for that, and take care you do not run yourselves in the way of danger, by following the advice of those, who want to betray you. This you may depend upon, if ever you let the Parliament carry its point, you will have these and more to pay. Perhaps before long, your tables, and chairs, and platters, and dishes, and knives and forks, and every thing else would be taxed.—Nay, I don't know but they would find means to tax you for every child you got, and for every kiss your daughters received from their sweet-hearts, and God knows, that would soon ruin you. The people of England would pull down the Parliament House, if their present heavy burdens were not transferred from them to you. Indeed there is no reason to think the Parliament would have any inclination to spare you: The contrary is evident.

But being ruined by taxes is not the worst you have to fear. What security would you have for your lives? How can any of you be sure you would have the free enjoyment of your religion long? would you put your religion in the power of any set of men living? Remember civil and religious liberty always go together, if the foundation of the one be sapped, the other will fall of course.

Call to mind one of our sister colonies, Boston. Reflect up|on the situation of Canada, and then tell me whether you are Inclined to place any confidence in the justice and humanity of the parliament. The port of Boston is blocked up, and an ar|my planted in the town. An act has been passed to alter its charter, to prohibit its assemblies, to license the murder of its inhabitants, and to convey them from their own country to Great Britain, to be tried for their lives. What was all this for? Just because a small number of people, provoked by an open and dangerous attack upon their liberties, destroyed a parcel of Tea be|longing to the East India Company. It was not public but private property they destroyed. It was not the act of the whole province, but the act of a part of the citizens; instead of trying to dis-co|ver the perpetrators, and commencing a legal prosecution against them; the parliament of Great-Britain interfered in an unprecedented manner, and inflicted a punishment upon a whole province, "untried, unheard, unconvicted of any crime." This may be justice, but it looks so much like cruelty, that a man of a humane heart would be more apt to call it by the latter, than the former name."

The affair of Canada, if possible, is still worse. The English laws have been superceded by the French laws. The Romish faith is made the established religion of the land, and his Ma|jesty is placed at the head of it. The free exercise of the pro|testant faith depends upon the pleasure of the Governor and Council. The subject is divested of the right of trial by jury, and an innocent man may be imprisoned his whole life, without being able to obtain any trial at all. The parliament was not contented with introducing arbitrary power and popery in Cana|da, with its former limits, but they have annexed to it the vast tracts of land that surround all the colonies.

Does not your blood run cold, to think an English parliament should pass an act for the establishment of arbitrary power and pop-ery in such an extensive country? If they had had any re|gard to the freedom and happiness of mankind, they woud ne|ver have done it. If they had been friends to the protestant cause, they would never have provided such a nursery for its great enemy: They would not have given such encouragement to popery. The thought of their conduct, in this particular shocks me. It must shock you too my friends. Beware of trusting yourselves to men, who are capable of such an action! They may as well establish popery in New-York and the other colonies as they did in Canada. They had no more right to do it there than here.

Is it not better, I ask, to suffer a few present inconveniencies, than to put yourselves in the way of losing every thing that is pre-cious. Your lives, your property, your religion are all at stake. I do my duty. I warn you of your danger. If you should still be so mad, as to bring destruction upon yourselves; if you should still neglect what you owe to God and man, you cannot plead ignorance in your excuse. Your consciences will reproach you for your folly, and your children's children will curse you.

You are told, the schemes of our Congress will ruin you. You are told, they have not considered your interest; but have neglected, or betrayed you. It is endeavoured to make you look upon some of the wisest and best men in the America, as rogues and rebels. What will not wicked men attempt! They will scruple nothing, that may serve their purposes. In truth, my friends, it is very unlikely any of us shall suffer much; but let the word happen, the farmers will be better off, than other people.

Many of those that made up the Congress have large posses|sions in land, and may, therefore be looked upon as farmers themselves. Can it be supposed, they would be careless about the farmer's interest, when they could not injure that, without in|juring themselves?—You see the absurdity of such a supposition.

The merchants and a great part of the tradesmen get their living by commerce. These are the people that would be hurt most, by putting a stop to it. As to the farmers, "they furnish food for the merchant and mechanic; the raw materials for most manufactures are the produce of their industry." The merchants and mechanics are already dependent upon the farmers for their food, and if the non-importation should continue any time, they would be dependent upon them for their cloaths also.

It is a false assertion, that the merchants have imported more than usual this year. That report has been raised by your ene|mies to poison your minds with evil suspicions. If our disputes be not settled within eighteen months, the goods we have among us will be consumed; and then the materials for making cloaths must be had from you. Manufactures must be promoted with vigour, and a high price will be given for your wool, flax and hemp. It will be your interest to pay the greatest care and atten|tion to your sheep. Increase and improve the breed as much as possible: *Kill them sparingly*, and such only as will not be of use towards the increase and improvement of them. In a few months we shall know what we have to trust to. If matters be not ac|commodated by spring, enlarge the quantity of your flax and hemp. You will experience the benefit of it. All those articles will be very much wanted: They will bring a great deal higher price than they used to do. And while you are supplying the wants of the community, you will be enriching yourselves.

Should we hereafter, find it necessary to stop our exports, you can apply more of your land to raising flax and hemp, and less of it to wheat, rye, &c. By which means, you will not have any of those latter articles to lie upon hand. There will be a consumption for as much of the former as you can raise, and the great demand they will be in, will make them very profitable to you.

Patience good Mr. Critic! *Kill them sparingly, I said,* what objection have you to the phrase? You'll tell me, it is not *classi|cal;* but I affirm it is, and if you will condescend to look into Mr. Johnson's dictionary, you will find I have his authority for it. Pray then, for the future, *spare* your wit, upon such occa|sions, otherwise the world will not be disposed to *spare* its ridi|cule. And though the man that *spares* nobody does not deserve to be *spared* himself, yet will I *spare* you, for the present, and proceed to things of more importance.

Pardon me, my friends, for taking up your time with this digression; but I could not forbear stepping out of the way a little, to shew the world, I am as able a critic, and as good a punster as Mr. Farmer. I now return to the main point with pleasure.

It is insinuated, "That the bustle about non-importation, &c. has its rise, not from patriotism, but selfishness;" and is only made by the merchants, that they may get a high price for their goods.

By this time, I flatter myself you are convinced, that we are not disputing about trifles. It has been clearly proved to you, that we are contending for every thing dear in life, and that the measures adopted by the congress, are the only ones which can save us from ruin. This is sufficient to confute that insinuation. But to confirm it, let me observe to you, that the merchants have not been the foremost to bring about a non-importation. All the members of the congress were unanimous in it; and *many* of them were no merchants. The warmest advocates for it, every where, are not concerned in trade, and, as I before re|marked, the traders will be the principal sufferers, if it should continue any time.

But it is said it will not continue, because, "when the stores are like to become empty, they will have weight enough to break up the agreement." I don't think they would attempt it; but if they should, it is impossible a few mercenary men could have influence enough to make the whole body of the peo|ple give up the only plan their circumstances admit of for the preservation of their rights, and, of course, to forfeit all they have been so long striving to secure. The making of a non-im|portation agreement did not depend upon the merchants;

nei|ther will the breaking of it depend upon them. The congress have provided against the breach of the non-importation, by the non-con-sumption agreement. They have resolved for themselves and us their constituents, "not to purchase, or use any East|India Tea whatsoever; nor any goods, wares, or merchandize, from Great-Britain or Ireland, imported after the first of Decem|ber, nor molasses, &c. from the West Indies, nor wine from Madeira, or the Western Islands, nor foreign In-digo. If we do not purchase or use these things, the merchant will have no in|ducement to import them.

Hence you may perceive the reason of a non-consumption agree-ment. It is to put it out of the power of dishonest men, to break the non importation. *Is this a slavish regulation?* Or is it a hardship upon us to submit to it? Surely not. Every sensible, every good man must approve of it. Whoever tries to disaffect you to it, ought to meet with your contempt.

Take notice, my friends, how these men are obliged to con|tradict themselves. In one place you are told, that all the bustle about non-im-portation, &c. has its rise, no from patriotism, but from selfishness, "or, in other words, that it is made by the merchants to get a higher price for their goods. In another place it is said, that all we are doing is instigated by some tur|bulent men, who want to establish a republican form of Govern|ment among us."

The Congress is censured for appointing committees to carry their measures into execution, and directing them "to establish such further regulations, as they may think proper for that pur|pose."— Pray, did we not appoint our Delegates to make regu|lations for us? What signified making them, if they did not provide some persons to see them executed?—Must a few bad men be left to do what they please, contrary to the general sense of the people, without any per-sons to controul them, or to look into their behaviour and mark them out to the public?—The man that desires to screen his knavery from the public eye, will answer yes; but the honest man, that is de-termined to do nothing hurtful to his country, and who is conscious his actions will bear the light, will heartily answer no.

The high prices of goods are held up to make you dissatisfied with the non-importation. If the argument on this head were true, it would be much better to subject yourselves to that dis|advantage, for a time, than to bring upon yourselves all the mischiefs I have pointed out to you. Should you submit to claims of the Parliament, you will not only be oppressed with the taxes upon your lands, &c. which I have already mentioned; but you will have to pay heavy taxes upon all the goods we import from Great-Britain. Large duties will be laid upon them at home; and the merchants, of course, will have a greater price for them, or it would not be worth their while to carry on trade. The duty laid upon paper, glass, painter's colours, &c. was a beginning of this kind. The present duty upon tea is preparatory to the imposition of duties upon all other articles. Do you think the Parliament would make such a serious matter of three pence a pound upon tea, if it intended to stop there? It is absurd to imagine it. You would soon find your mistake if you did. For fear of paying somewhat a higher price to the merchants for a year or two, you would have to pay an endless list of taxes, within and without, as long as you live, and your children after you.

But I trust, there is no danger that the prices of goods will rise much, if at all. The same congress that put a stop to the importation of them, has also forbid raising the prices of them. The same committee that is to regulate the one, is also to re|gulate the other. All care will be taken to give no cause of dissatisfaction. Confide in the men whom you, and the rest of the continent have chosen the guardians of our common li|berties. They are men of sense and virtue. They will do no|thing but what is really necessary for the security of your lives and properties.

A sad pother is made too about prohibiting the exportation of sheep, without excepting weathers. The poor Farmer is at a mighty loss to know how weathers can improve, or increase the breed. Truly I am not such a conjurer, as to be able to inform him; but if you please, my friends, I can give you two pretty good reasons, why the congress has not excepted weathers. One is, that for some time, we shall have occasion for all the wool we can raise; so that it would be imprudent to export sheep of any kind: and the other is, that, if you confine yourself chiefly to killing weathers, as you ought to do, you will have none to ex|port. The gentleman who made the objection, must have known these things, as well as myself; but he loves to crack a jest, and could not pass by so fair an opportunity.

He takes notice of the first of these reasons himself; but in order to weaken its force, cries, "let me ask you, brother far|mers, which of you would keep a flock of sheep, barely, for the sake of their wool?" To this he answers, "not one of you. If you cannot sell your sheep to advantage, at a certain age, you cannot keep them to any profit." He thinks, because he calls you brother farmers, that he can cajole you into believing what he pleaser; but you are not the fools he takes you for. You know what is for your own interest better than he can tell you. And we all know, that in a little time, if our affairs be not settled, the demand for wool will be very great. You will be able to obtain such a price, as will make it worth your while to bestow the greatest attention upon your sheep.

In another place, this crafty writer tells you, that, "from the day our exports, from this province are stopped, the farmers may date the commencement of their ruin." He asks, "will the shop-keeper give you his goods? will the weaver, since|maker, black smith, carpenter work for you without pay!" I make no doubt, you are satisfied, from what I have said, that we shall never have occasion to stop our exports; but if things turn out contrary to our expectation, and it should become ne|cessary to take that step, you will find no difficulty in getting what you want from the merchants and mechanics. They will not be able to do without you, and, consequently, they cannot refuse to supply you with what you stand in need of from them. Where will the merchants and mechanics get food and materials for clothing, if not from the farmer? And if they are depen|dent upon you, for those two grand supports of life, how can they withold what they have from you?

I repeat it (my friends) we shall know, how matters are like to be settled by the spring. If our disputes be not terminated to our satisfaction by that time, it will your business to plant large parts of your lands with flax and hemp. Those articles will be wanted for manufactures, and they will yield you a greater pro|fit than any thing else. In the interim, take good care of your sheep.

I heartily concur with the farmer, in condemning all illicit trade. Perjury is, no doubt, a most heineous and detestable crime; and for my part, I had rather suffer any thing, than have my wants relieved at the expence of truth and integrity. I know, there are many pretended friends to liberty, who will take of|fence at this declaration; but I speak the sentiments of my heart without reserve. I do not write for a party. I should scorn to be of any. All I say, is from a disinterested regard to the public weal.

The congress, I am persuaded, were of the same opinion: They, like honest men, have, as much as was in their power, provided against this kind of trade, by agreeing to use no East-India tea whatever, after the first day of March next.

I shall now consider what has been said, with respect to the payment of debts, and stopping of the courts of justice. Let what will happen, it will be your own faults, if you are not able to pay your debts. I have told you, in what manner you may make as much out of your lands as ever: by bestowing more of your attention upon raising flax and hemp, and less upon other things. Those articles (as I have more than once ob|served) will be in the highest demand: There will be no doing without them; and, of course, you will be able to get a very pro|fitable price for them. How can it be, that the farmers should be at a loss for money to pay their debts, at a time, when the whole community must buy, not only their food, but all the materials for their cloaths from them? You have no reason to be uneasy on that account.

As to the courts of justice; no violence can, or will be used to shut them up; but, if it should be found necessary, we may enter into solemn agreement to cease from all litigations at law, except particular cases. We may regulate law suits, in such a manner, as to prevent any mischief that might arise from them. Restrictions may be laid on to hinder merciless creditors, from taking advantage of the times, to oppress and ruin their deb|tors but, at the same time, not to put it in the power of the debtors, *wantonly*, to withold their just dues from their credi|tors, when they are able to pay them. The law ruins many a good honest family. Disputes may be settled in a more friendly way; one or two virtuous neighbours may be chosen by each party to decide them. If the next congress should think any regulations concerning the courts of justice requisite, they will make them; and proper persons will be appointed to carry them into execution, and to see, that no individuals deviate from them. It will be your duty to elect persons, whose fidelity and zeal for your interest you can't depend upon, to represent you in *that* congress; which is to meet at Philadelphia, in May ensuing.

The Farmer cries, "tell me not of delegates, congresses com|mittees, mobs, riots, insurrections, associations, a plague on them all. Give me the steady, uniform, unbiassed influence of the courts of justice. I have been happy under their protection, and I trust in God, I shall be so again."

I say, tell me not of the British Commons, Lords, ministry, ministerial tools, placemen, pensioners, parasites. I scorn to let my life and
property depend upon the pleasure of any of them. Give me the steady,
uniform, unshaken security of constitutional freedom; give me the
right to be tried by a jury of my own neighbours, and to be taxed by
my own representatives only. What will become of the law and courts
of justice without this? The shadow may remain, but the substance will
be gone. I would die to preserve the law upon a solid foundation; but
take away liberty, and the foundation is destroyed.

The last thing I shall take notice of, is the complaint of the Farmer,
that the congress will not allow you "a dish of tea to please your wives
with, nor a glass of Madeira to cheer your spirits, nor a spoonful of
molasses, to sweeten your butter milk with." You would have a right to
complain, if the use of these things had been forbidden to you alone;
but it has been equally forbidden to all sorts of people. The members
of the congress themselves are no more permitted to please their wives
with a dish of tea, or to cheer their spirits with a glass of wine, or to
sweeten their butter milk with a spoonful of molasses, than you are.
They are upon a footing with you in this respect.

By him! but, with your leave, my friends, we'll try, if we can, to do
without swearing. I say, it is enough to make a man mad, to hear such
ridiculous quibbles offered instead of found argument; but so it is, the
piece I am writing against contains nothing else.

When a man grows warm, he has a confounded itch for swear|ing.
I have been going, above twenty times, to rap out an oath, *by him that
made me*, but I have checked myself, with this reflection, that it is
rather *unmannerly*, to treat him that made us with so much freedom.

Thus have I examined and confuted, all the cavils and ob|jections,
of any consequence, stated by this Farmer. I have on|ly passed over
such things, as are of little weight, the fallacy of which will easily appear. I have shewn, that the congress have neither "ignorantly misun-
derstood, carelesly neglected, nor basely betrayed you;" but that they
have desired and recom|mended the *only* effectual means to preserve
your invaluable pri|vileges. I have proved, that their measures cannot
fail of suc|cess; but will procure the most speedy relief for us. I have also
proved, that the farmers are the people who would suffer least, should
we be obliged to carry all our measures into execution.

Will you then, my friends, allow yourselves, to be duped by this artful enemy? will you follow his advices, disregard the authority of your congress, and bring ruin on yourselves and posterity? will you act in such a manner as to deserve the hatred and resentment of all the rest of America? I am sure you will not. I should be sorry to think, any of my countrymen would be so mean, so blind to their own interest, so lost to every ge|nerous and manly seeling.

The sort of men I am opposing give you fair words, to per|suade you to serve their own turns; but they think and speak of you in common in a very disrespectful manner. I have heard some of their party talk of you, as the most ignorant and mean|spirited set of people in the world. They say, that you have no sense of honour or generosity, that you don't care a farthing about your country, children or any body else, but yourselves; and that you are so ignorant, as not to be able to look beyond the present; so that if you can once be persuaded to believe the measures of your congress will involve you in some little present perplexities, you will be glad to do any thing to avoid them; without considering the much greater miseries that await you at a little distance off. This is the character they give of you. Bad men are apt to paint others like themselves. For my part, I will never entertain such an opinion of you, unless you should verify their words, by wilfully falling into the pit they have prepared for you. I flatter myself you will convince them of their error, by shewing the world, you are capable of judging what is right and left, and have resolution to pursue it.

All I ask is, that you will judge for yourselves. I don't de|sire you to take my opinion or any man's opinion, as the guide of your actions. I have stated a number of plain arguments; I have support-ed them with several well-known facts: It is your business to draw a conclusion and act accordingly.

I caution you, again and again, to beware of the men who advise you to forsake the plain path, marked out for you by the congress. They only mean to deceive and betray you. Our representatives in general assembly cannot take any wiser or better course to settle our differences, than our representa|tives in the continental congress have taken. If you join with the rest of America in the same common measure, you will be sure to preserve your liberties inviolate; but if you separate from them, and seek for redress alone, and unseconded, you will certainly fall a prey to your enemies, and repent your folly as long as you live.

May God give you wisdom to see what is your true interest, and inspire you with becoming zeal for the cause of virtue and mankind.

A Friend to America.

# The Federalist Papers

## #1 (General Introduction)

To the People of the State of New York:

AFTER an unequivocal experience of the inefficiency of the subsisting federal government, you are called upon to deliberate on a new Constitution for the United States of America. The subject speaks its own importance; comprehending in its consequences nothing less than the existence of the UNION, the safety and welfare of the parts of which it is composed, the fate of an empire in many respects the most interesting in the world. It has been frequently remarked that it seems to have been reserved to the people of this country, by their conduct and example, to decide the important question, whether societies of men are really capable or not of establishing good government from reflection and choice, or whether they are forever destined to depend for their political constitutions on accident and force. If there be any truth in the remark, the crisis at which we are arrived may with propriety be regarded as the era in which that decision is to be made; and a wrong election of the part we shall act may, in this view, deserve to be considered as the general misfortune of mankind.

This idea will add the inducements of philanthropy to those of patriotism, to heighten the solicitude which all considerate and good men must feel for the event. Happy will it be if our choice should be directed by a judicious estimate of our true interests, unperplexed and unbiased by considerations not connected with the public good. But this is a thing more ardently to be wished than seriously to be expected. The plan offered to our deliberations affects too many particular interests, innovates upon too many local institutions, not to involve in its discussion a variety of objects foreign to its merits, and of views, passions and prejudices little favorable to the discovery of truth.

Among the most formidable of the obstacles which the new Constitution will have to encounter may readily be distinguished the obvious interest of a certain class of men in every State to resist all changes which may hazard a diminution of the power, emolument, and consequence of the offices they hold under the State establishments; and the perverted ambition of another class of men, who will either hope to aggrandize themselves by the confusions of their country, or will flatter themselves with fairer prospects of elevation from the subdivision of the empire into several partial confederacies than from its union under one government.

It is not, however, my design to dwell upon observations of this nature. I am well aware that it would be disingenuous to resolve indiscriminately the opposition of any set of men (merely because their situations might subject them to suspicion) into interested or ambitious views. Candor will oblige us to admit that even such men may be actuated by upright intentions; and it cannot be doubted that much of the opposition which has made its appearance, or may hereafter make its appearance, will spring from sources, blameless at least, if not respectable--the honest errors of minds led astray by preconceived jealousies and fears. So numerous indeed and so powerful are the causes which serve to give a false bias to the judgment, that we, upon many occasions, see wise and good men on the wrong as well as on the right side of questions of the first magnitude to society. This circumstance, if duly attended to, would furnish a lesson of moderation to those who are ever so much persuaded of their being in the right in any controversy. And a further reason for caution, in this respect, might be drawn from the reflection that we are not always sure that those who advocate the truth are influenced by purer principles than their antagonists. Ambition, avarice, personal animosity, party opposition, and many other motives not more laudable than these, are apt to operate as well upon those who support as those who oppose the right side of a question. Were there not even these inducements to moderation, nothing could be more ill-judged than that intolerant spirit which has, at all times, characterized political parties. For in politics, as in religion, it is equally absurd to aim at making proselytes by fire and sword. Heresies in either can rarely be cured by persecution.

And yet, however just these sentiments will be allowed to be, we have already sufficient indications that it will happen in this as in all former cases of great national discussion. A torrent of angry and malignant passions will be let loose. To judge from the conduct of the opposite parties, we shall be led to conclude that they will mutually hope to evince the justness of their opinions, and to increase the number of their converts by the loudness of their declamations and the bitterness of their invectives. An enlightened zeal for the energy and efficiency of government will be stigmatized as the offspring of a temper fond of despotic power and hostile to the principles of liberty. An over-scrupulous jealousy of danger to the rights of the people, which is more commonly the fault of the head than of the heart, will be represented as mere pretense and artifice, the stale bait for popularity at the expense of the public good. It will be forgotten, on the one hand, that jealousy is the usual concomitant of love, and that the noble enthusiasm of liberty is apt to be infected with a spirit of narrow and illiberal distrust. On the other hand, it will be equally forgotten that the vigor of government is essential to the security of liberty; that, in the contemplation of a sound and well-informed judgment, their interest can never be separated; and that a dangerous ambition more often lurks behind the specious mask of zeal for the rights of the people than under the forbidden appearance of zeal for the firmness and efficiency of government. History will teach us that the former has been found a much more certain road to the introduction of despotism than the latter, and that of those men who have overturned the liberties of republics, the greatest number have begun their career by paying an obsequious court to the people; commencing demagogues, and ending tyrants.

In the course of the preceding observations, I have had an eye, my fellow-citizens, to putting you upon your guard against all attempts, from whatever quarter, to influence your decision in a matter of the utmost moment to your welfare, by any impressions other than those which may result from the evidence of truth. You will, no doubt, at the same time, have collected from the general scope of them, that they proceed from a source not unfriendly to the new Constitution. Yes, my countrymen, I own to you that, after having given it an attentive consideration, I am clearly of opinion it is your interest to adopt it. I am convinced that this is the safest course for your liberty, your dignity, and your happiness. I affect not reserves which I do not feel. I will not amuse you with an appearance of deliberation when I have decided. I frankly acknowledge to you my convictions, and I will freely lay before you the reasons on which they are founded. The consciousness of good intentions disdains ambiguity. I shall not, however, multiply professions on this head. My motives must remain in the depository of my own breast. My arguments will be open to all, and may be judged of by all. They shall at least be offered in a spirit which will not disgrace the cause of truth.

I propose, in a series of papers, to discuss the following interesting particulars: THE UTILITY OF THE UNION TO YOUR POLITICAL PROSPERITY THE INSUFFICIENCY OF THE PRESENT CONFEDERATION TO PRESERVE THAT UNION THE NECESSITY OF A GOVERNMENT AT LEAST EQUALLY ENERGETIC WITH THE ONE PROPOSED, TO THE ATTAINMENT OF THIS OBJECT THE CONFORMITY OF THE PROPOSED CONSTITUTION TO THE TRUE PRINCIPLES OF REPUBLICAN GOVERNMENT ITS ANALOGY TO YOUR OWN STATE CONSTITUTION and lastly, THE ADDITIONAL SECURITY WHICH ITS ADOPTION WILL AFFORD TO THE PRESERVATION OF THAT SPECIES OF GOVERNMENT, TO LIBERTY, AND TO PROPERTY.

In the progress of this discussion I shall endeavor to give a satisfactory answer to all the objections which shall have made their appearance, that may seem to have any claim to your attention.

It may perhaps be thought superfluous to offer arguments to prove the utility of the UNION, a point, no doubt, deeply engraved on the hearts of the great body of the people in every State, and one, which it may be imagined, has no adversaries. But the fact is, that we already hear it whispered in the private circles of those who oppose the new Constitution, that the thirteen States are of too great extent for any general system, and that we must of necessity resort to separate confederacies of distinct portions of the whole.1 This doctrine will, in all probability, be gradually propagated, till it has votaries enough to countenance an open avowal of it. For nothing can be more evident, to those who are able to take an enlarged view of the subject, than the alternative of an adoption of the new Constitution or a dismemberment of the Union. It will therefore be of use to begin by examining the advantages of that Union, the certain evils, and the probable dangers, to which every State will be exposed from its dissolution. This shall accordingly constitute the subject of my next address.

*PUBLIUS.*

# The Federalist Papers

## #9 (The Union as a Safeguard Against Domestic Faction and Insurrection)

To the People of the State of New York:

A FIRM Union will be of the utmost moment to the peace and liberty of the States, as a barrier against domestic faction and insurrection. It is impossible to read the history of the petty republics of Greece and Italy without feeling sensations of horror and disgust at the distractions with which they were continually agitated, and at the rapid succession of revolutions by which they were kept in a state of perpetual vibration between the extremes of tyranny and anarchy. If they exhibit occasional calms, these only serve as short-lived contrast to the furious storms that are to succeed. If now and then intervals of felicity open to view, we behold them with a mixture of regret, arising from the reflection that the pleasing scenes before us are soon to be overwhelmed by the tempestuous waves of sedition and party rage. If momentary rays of glory break forth from the gloom, while they dazzle us with a transient and fleeting brilliancy, they at the same time admonish us to lament that the vices of government should pervert the direction and tarnish the lustre of those bright talents and exalted endowments for which the favored soils that produced them have been so justly celebrated.

From the disorders that disfigure the annals of those republics the advocates of despotism have drawn arguments, not only against the forms of republican government, but against the very principles of civil liberty. They have decried all free government as inconsistent with the order of society, and have indulged themselves in malicious exultation over its friends and partisans. Happily for mankind, stupendous fabrics reared on the basis of liberty, which have flourished for ages, have, in a few glorious instances, refuted their gloomy sophisms. And, I trust, America will be the broad and solid foundation of other edifices, not less magnificent, which will be equally permanent monuments of their errors.

But it is not to be denied that the portraits they have sketched of republican government were too just copies of the originals from which they were taken. If it had been found impracticable to have devised models of a more perfect structure, the enlightened friends to liberty would have been obliged to abandon the cause of that species of government as indefensible. The science of politics, however, like most other sciences, has received great improvement. The efficacy of various principles is now well understood, which were either not known at all, or imperfectly known to the ancients. The regular distribution of power into distinct departments; the introduction of legislative balances and checks; the institution of courts composed of judges holding their offices during good behavior; the representation of the people in the legislature by deputies of their own election: these are wholly new discoveries, or have made their principal progress towards perfection in modern times. They are means, and powerful means, by which the excellences of republican government may be retained and its imperfections lessened or avoided. To this catalogue of circumstances that tend to the amelioration of popular systems of civil government, I shall venture, however novel it may appear to some, to add one more, on a principle which has been made the foundation of an objection to the new Constitution; I mean the ENLARGEMENT of the ORBIT within which such systems are to revolve, either in respect to the dimensions of a single State or to the consolidation of several smaller States into one great Confederacy. The latter is that which immediately concerns the object under consideration. It will, however, be of use to examine the principle in its application to a single State, which shall be attended to in another place.

The utility of a Confederacy, as well to suppress faction and to guard the internal tranquillity of States, as to increase their external force and security, is in reality not a new idea. It has been practiced upon in different countries and ages, and has received the sanction of the most approved writers on the subject of politics. The opponents of the plan proposed have, with great assiduity, cited and circulated the observations of Montesquieu on the necessity of a contracted territory for a republican government. But they seem not to have been apprised of the sentiments of that great man expressed in another part of his work, nor to have adverted to the consequences of the principle to which they subscribe with such ready acquiescence.

When Montesquieu recommends a small extent for republics, the standards he had in view were of dimensions far short of the limits of almost every one of these States. Neither Virginia, Massachusetts, Pennsylvania, New York, North Carolina, nor Georgia can by any means be compared with the models from which he reasoned and to which the terms of his description apply. If we therefore take his ideas on this point as the criterion of truth, we shall be driven to the alternative either of taking refuge at once in the arms of monarchy, or of splitting ourselves into an infinity of little, jealous, clashing, tumultuous commonwealths, the wretched nurseries of unceasing discord, and the miserable objects of universal pity or contempt. Some of the writers who have come forward on the other side of the question seem to have been aware of the dilemma; and have even been bold enough to hint at the division of the larger States as a desirable thing. Such an infatuated policy, such a desperate expedient, might, by the multiplication of petty offices, answer the views of men who possess not qualifications to extend their influence beyond the narrow circles of personal intrigue, but it could never promote the greatness or happiness of the people of America.

Referring the examination of the principle itself to another place, as has been already mentioned, it will be sufficient to remark here that, in the sense of the author who has been most emphatically quoted upon the occasion, it would only dictate a reduction of the SIZE of the more considerable MEMBERS of the Union, but would not militate against their being all comprehended in one confederate government. And this is the true question, in the discussion of which we are at present interested.

So far are the suggestions of Montesquieu from standing in opposition to a general Union of the States, that he explicitly treats of a CONFEDERATE REPUBLIC as the expedient for extending the sphere of popular government, and reconciling the advantages of monarchy with those of republicanism.

"It is very probable," (says he) "that mankind would have been obliged at length to live constantly under the government of a single person, had they not contrived a kind of constitution that has all the internal advantages of a republican, together with the external force of a monarchical government. I mean a CONFEDERATE REPUBLIC.

"This form of government is a convention by which several smaller STATES agree to become members of a larger ONE, which they intend to form. It is a kind of assemblage of societies that constitute a new one, capable of increasing, by means of new associations, till they arrive to such a degree of power as to be able to provide for the security of the united body.

"A republic of this kind, able to withstand an external force, may support itself without any internal corruptions. The form of this society prevents all manner of inconveniences.

"If a single member should attempt to usurp the supreme authority, he could not be supposed to have an equal authority and credit in all the confederate states. Were he to have too great influence over one, this would alarm the rest. Were he to subdue a part, that which would still remain free might oppose him with forces independent of those which he had usurped and overpower him before he could be settled in his usurpation.

"Should a popular insurrection happen in one of the confederate states the others are able to quell it. Should abuses creep into one part, they are reformed by those that remain sound. The state may be destroyed on one side, and not on the other; the confederacy may be dissolved, and the confederates preserve their sovereignty.

"As this government is composed of small republics, it enjoys the internal happiness of each; and with respect to its external situation, it is possessed, by means of the association, of all the advantages of large monarchies."

I have thought it proper to quote at length these interesting passages, because they contain a luminous abridgment of the principal arguments in favor of the Union, and must effectually remove the false impressions which a misapplication of other parts of the work was calculated to make. They have, at the same time, an intimate connection with the more immediate design of this paper; which is, to illustrate the tendency of the Union to repress domestic faction and insurrection.

A distinction, more subtle than accurate, has been raised between a CONFEDERACY and a CONSOLIDATION of the States. The essential characteristic of the first is said to be, the restriction of its authority to the members in their collective capacities, without reaching to the individuals of whom they are composed. It is contended that the national council ought to have no concern with any object of internal administration. An exact equality of suffrage between the members has also been insisted upon as a leading feature of a confederate government. These positions are, in the main, arbitrary; they are supported neither by principle nor precedent. It has indeed happened, that governments of this kind have generally operated in the manner which the distinction taken notice of, supposes to be inherent in their nature; but there have been in most of them extensive exceptions to the practice, which serve to prove, as far as example will go, that there is no absolute rule on the subject. And it will be clearly shown in the course of this investigation that as far as the principle contended for has prevailed, it has been the cause of incurable disorder and imbecility in the government.

The definition of a CONFEDERATE REPUBLIC seems simply to be "an assemblage of societies," or an association of two or more states into one state. The extent, modifications, and objects of the federal authority are mere matters of discretion. So long as the separate organization of the members be not abolished; so long as it exists, by a constitutional necessity, for local purposes; though it should be in perfect subordination to the general authority of the union, it would still be, in fact and in theory, an association of states, or a confederacy. The proposed Constitution, so far from implying an abolition of the State governments, makes them constituent parts of the national sovereignty, by allowing them a direct representation in the Senate, and leaves in their possession certain exclusive and very important portions of sovereign power. This fully corresponds, in every rational import of the terms, with the idea of a federal government.

In the Lycian confederacy, which consisted of twenty-three CITIES or republics, the largest were entitled to THREE votes in the COMMON COUNCIL, those of the middle class to TWO, and the smallest to ONE. The COMMON COUNCIL had the appointment of all the judges and magistrates of the respective CITIES. This was certainly the most, delicate species of interference in their internal administration; for if there be any thing that seems exclusively appropriated to the local jurisdictions, it is the appointment of their own officers. Yet Montesquieu, speaking of this association, says: "Were I to give a model of an excellent Confederate Republic, it would be that of Lycia." Thus we perceive that the distinctions insisted upon were not within the contemplation of this enlightened civilian; and we shall be led to conclude, that they are the novel refinements of an erroneous theory.

*PUBLIUS.*

# The Federalist Papers

## #28 (The Same Subject Continued: The Idea of Restraining the Legislative Authority in Regard to the Common Defense Considered)

To the People of the State of New York:

THAT there may happen cases in which the national government may be necessitated to resort to force, cannot be denied. Our own experience has corroborated the lessons taught by the examples of other nations; that emergencies of this sort will sometimes arise in all societies, however constituted; that seditions and insurrections are, unhappily, maladies as inseparable from the body politic as tumors and eruptions from the natural body; that the idea of governing at all times by the simple force of law (which we have been told is the only admissible principle of republican government), has no place but in the reveries of those political doctors whose sagacity disdains the admonitions of experimental instruction.

Should such emergencies at any time happen under the national government, there could be no remedy but force. The means to be employed must be proportioned to the extent of the mischief. If it should be a slight commotion in a small part of a State, the militia of the residue would be adequate to its suppression; and the national presumption is that they would be ready to do their duty. An insurrection, whatever may be its immediate cause, eventually endangers all government. Regard to the public peace, if not to the rights of the Union, would engage the citizens to whom the contagion had not communicated itself to oppose the insurgents; and if the general government should be found in practice conducive to the prosperity and felicity of the people, it were irrational to believe that they would be disinclined to its support.

If, on the contrary, the insurrection should pervade a whole State, or a principal part of it, the employment of a different kind of force might become unavoidable. It appears that Massachusetts found it necessary to raise troops for repressing the disorders within that State; that Pennsylvania, from the mere apprehension of commotions among a part of her citizens, has thought proper to have recourse to the same measure. Suppose the State of New York had been inclined to re-establish her lost jurisdiction over the inhabitants of Vermont, could she have hoped for success in such an enterprise from the efforts of the militia alone? Would she not have been compelled to raise and to maintain a more regular force for the execution of her design? If it must then be admitted that the necessity of recurring to a force different from the militia, in cases of this extraordinary nature, is applicable to the State governments themselves, why should the possibility, that the national government might be under a like necessity, in similar extremities, be made an objection to its existence? Is it not surprising that men who declare an attachment to the Union in the abstract, should urge as an objection to the proposed Constitution what applies with tenfold weight to the plan for which they contend; and what, as far as it has any foundation in truth, is an inevitable consequence of civil society upon an enlarged scale? Who would not prefer that possibility to the unceasing agitations and frequent revolutions which are the continual scourges of petty republics?

Let us pursue this examination in another light. Suppose, in lieu of one general system, two, or three, or even four Confederacies were to be formed, would not the same difficulty oppose itself to the operations of either of these Confederacies? Would not each of them be exposed to the same casualties; and when these happened, be obliged to have recourse to the same expedients for upholding its authority which are objected to in a government for all the States? Would the militia, in this supposition, be more ready or more able to support the federal authority than in the case of a general union? All candid and intelligent men must, upon due consideration, acknowledge that the principle of the objection is equally applicable to either of the two cases; and that whether we have one government for all the States, or different governments for different parcels of them, or even if there should be an entire separation of the States, there might sometimes be a necessity to make use of a force constituted differently from the militia, to preserve the peace of the community and to maintain the just authority of the laws against those violent invasions of them which amount to insurrections and rebellions.

Independent of all other reasonings upon the subject, it is a full answer to those who require a more peremptory provision against military establishments in time of peace, to say that the whole power of the proposed government is to be in the hands of the representatives of the people. This is the essential, and, after all, only efficacious security for the rights and privileges of the people, which is attainable in civil society.

If the representatives of the people betray their constituents, there is then no resource left but in the exertion of that original right of self-defense which is paramount to all positive forms of government, and which against the usurpations of the national rulers, may be exerted with infinitely better prospect of success than against those of the rulers of an individual state. In a single state, if the persons intrusted with supreme power become usurpers, the different parcels, subdivisions, or districts of which it consists, having no distinct government in each, can take no regular measures for defense. The citizens must rush tumultuously to arms, without concert, without system, without resource; except in their courage and despair. The usurpers, clothed with the forms of legal authority, can too often crush the opposition in embryo. The smaller the extent of the territory, the more difficult will it be for the people to form a regular or systematic plan of opposition, and the more easy will it be to defeat their early efforts. Intelligence can be more speedily obtained of their preparations and movements, and the military force in the possession of the usurpers can be more rapidly directed against the part where the opposition has begun. In this situation there must be a peculiar coincidence of circumstances to insure success to the popular resistance.

The obstacles to usurpation and the facilities of resistance increase with the increased extent of the state, provided the citizens understand their rights and are disposed to defend them. The natural strength of the people in a large community, in proportion to the artificial strength of the government, is greater than in a small, and of course more competent to a struggle with the attempts of the government to establish a tyranny. But in a confederacy the people, without exaggeration, may be said to be entirely the masters of their own fate. Power being almost always the rival of power, the general government will at all times stand ready to check the usurpations of the state governments, and these will have the same disposition towards the general government. The people, by throwing themselves into either scale, will infallibly make it preponderate. If their rights are invaded by either, they can make use of the other as the instrument of redress. How wise will it be in them by cherishing the union to preserve to themselves an advantage which can never be too highly prized!

It may safely be received as an axiom in our political system, that the State governments will, in all possible contingencies, afford complete security against invasions of the public liberty by the national authority. Projects of usurpation cannot be masked under pretenses so likely to escape the penetration of select bodies of men, as of the people at large. The legislatures will have better means of information. They can discover the danger at a distance; and possessing all the organs of civil power, and the confidence of the people, they can at once adopt a regular plan of opposition, in which they can combine all the resources of the community. They can readily communicate with each other in the different States, and unite their common forces for the protection of their common liberty.

The great extent of the country is a further security. We have already experienced its utility against the attacks of a foreign power. And it would have precisely the same effect against the enterprises of ambitious rulers in the national councils. If the federal army should be able to quell the resistance of one State, the distant States would have it in their power to make head with fresh forces. The advantages obtained in one place must be abandoned to subdue the opposition in others; and the moment the part which had been reduced to submission was left to itself, its efforts would be renewed, and its resistance revive.

We should recollect that the extent of the military force must, at all events, be regulated by the resources of the country. For a long time to come, it will not be possible to maintain a large army; and as the means of doing this increase, the population and natural strength of the community will proportionably increase. When will the time arrive that the federal government can raise and maintain an army capable of erecting a despotism over the great body of the people of an immense empire, who are in a situation, through the medium of their State governments, to take measures for their own defense, with all the celerity, regularity, and system of independent nations? The apprehension may be considered as a disease, for which there can be found no cure in the resources of argument and reasoning.

*PUBLIUS.*

# THE FEDERALIST PAPERS

## #85 (CONCLUDING REMARKS)

To the People of the State of New York:

ACCORDING to the formal division of the subject of these papers, announced in my first number, there would appear still to remain for discussion two points: "the analogy of the proposed government to your own State constitution," and "the additional security which its adoption will afford to republican government, to liberty, and to property." But these heads have been so fully anticipated and exhausted in the progress of the work, that it would now scarcely be possible to do any thing more than repeat, in a more dilated form, what has been heretofore said, which the advanced stage of the question, and the time already spent upon it, conspire to forbid.

It is remarkable, that the resemblance of the plan of the convention to the act which organizes the government of this State holds, not less with regard to many of the supposed defects, than to the real excellences of the former. Among the pretended defects are the re-eligibility of the Executive, the want of a council, the omission of a formal bill of rights, the omission of a provision respecting the liberty of the press. These and several others which have been noted in the course of our inquiries are as much chargeable on the existing constitution of this State, as on the one proposed for the Union; and a man must have slender pretensions to consistency, who can rail at the latter for imperfections which he finds no difficulty in excusing in the former. Nor indeed can there be a better proof of the insincerity and affectation of some of the zealous adversaries of the plan of the convention among us, who profess to be the devoted admirers of the government under which they live, than the fury with which they have attacked that plan, for matters in regard to which our own constitution is equally or perhaps more vulnerable.

The additional securities to republican government, to liberty and to property, to be derived from the adoption of the plan under consideration, consist chiefly in the restraints which the preservation of the Union will impose on local factions and insurrections, and on the ambition of powerful individuals in single States, who may acquire credit and influence enough, from leaders and favorites, to become the despots of the people; in the diminution of the opportunities to foreign intrigue, which the dissolution of the Confederacy would invite and facilitate; in the prevention of extensive military establishments, which could not fail to grow out of wars between the States in a disunited situation; in the express guaranty of a republican form of government to each; in the absolute and universal exclusion of titles of nobility; and in the precautions against the repetition of those practices on the part of the State governments which have undermined the foundations of property and credit, have planted mutual distrust in the breasts of all classes of citizens, and have occasioned an almost universal prostration of morals.

Thus have I, fellow-citizens, executed the task I had assigned to myself; with what success, your conduct must determine. I trust at least you will admit that I have not failed in the assurance I gave you respecting the spirit with which my endeavors should be conducted. I have addressed myself purely to your judgments, and have studiously avoided those asperities which are too apt to disgrace political disputants of all parties, and which have been not a little provoked by the language and conduct of the opponents of the Constitution. The charge of a conspiracy against the liberties of the people, which has been indiscriminately brought against the advocates of the plan, has something in it too wanton and too malignant, not to excite the indignation of every man who feels in his own bosom a refutation of the calumny. The perpetual changes which have been rung upon the wealthy, the well-born, and the great, have been such as to inspire the disgust of all sensible men. And the unwarrantable concealments and misrepresentations which have been in various ways practiced to keep the truth from the public eye, have been of a nature to demand the reprobation of all honest men. It is not impossible that these circumstances may have occasionally betrayed me into intemperances of expression which I did not intend; it is certain that I have frequently felt a struggle between sensibility and moderation; and if the former has in some instances prevailed, it must be my excuse that it has been neither often nor much.

Let us now pause and ask ourselves whether, in the course of these papers, the proposed Constitution has not been satisfactorily vindicated from the aspersions thrown upon it; and whether it has not been shown to be worthy of the public approbation, and necessary to the public safety and prosperity. Every man is bound to answer these questions to himself, according to the best of his conscience and understanding, and to act agreeably to the genuine and sober dictates of his judgment. This is a duty from which nothing can give him a dispensation. This is one that he is called upon, nay, constrained by all the obligations that form the bands of society, to discharge sincerely and honestly. No partial motive, no particular interest, no pride of opinion, no temporary passion or prejudice, will justify to himself, to his country, or to his posterity, an improper election of the part he is to act. Let him beware of an obstinate adherence to party; let him reflect that the object upon which he is to decide is not a particular interest of the community, but the very existence of the nation; and let him remember that a majority of America has already given its sanction to the plan which he is to approve or reject.

I shall not dissemble that I feel an entire confidence in the arguments which recommend the proposed system to your adoption, and that I am unable to discern any real force in those by which it has been opposed. I am persuaded that it is the best which our political situation, habits, and opinions will admit, and superior to any the revolution has produced.

Concessions on the part of the friends of the plan, that it has not a claim to absolute perfection, have afforded matter of no small triumph to its enemies. "Why," say they, "should we adopt an imperfect thing? Why not amend it and make it perfect before it is irrevocably established?" This may be plausible enough, but it is only plausible. In the first place I remark, that the extent of these concessions has been greatly exaggerated. They have been stated as amounting to an admission that the plan is radically defective, and that without material alterations the rights and the interests of the community cannot be safely confided to it. This, as far as I have understood the meaning of those who make the concessions, is an entire perversion of their sense. No advocate of the measure can be found, who will not declare as his sentiment, that the system, though it may not be perfect in every part, is, upon the whole, a good one; is the best that the present views and circumstances of the country will permit; and is such an one as promises every species of security which a reasonable people can desire.

I answer in the next place, that I should esteem it the extreme of imprudence to prolong the precarious state of our national affairs, and to expose the Union to the jeopardy of successive experiments, in the chimerical pursuit of a perfect plan. I never expect to see a perfect work from imperfect man. The result of the deliberations of all collective bodies must necessarily be a compound, as well of the errors and prejudices, as of the good sense and wisdom, of the individuals of whom they are composed. The compacts which are to embrace thirteen distinct States in a common bond of amity and union, must as necessarily be a compromise of as many dissimilar interests and inclinations. How can perfection spring from such materials?

The reasons assigned in an excellent little pamphlet lately published in this city, are unanswerable to show the utter improbability of assembling a new convention, under circumstances in any degree so favorable to a happy issue, as those in which the late convention met, deliberated, and concluded. I will not repeat the arguments there used, as I presume the production itself has had an extensive circulation. It is certainly well worthy the perusal of every friend to his country. There is, however, one point of light in which the subject of amendments still remains to be considered, and in which it has not yet been exhibited to public view. I cannot resolve to conclude without first taking a survey of it in this aspect.

It appears to me susceptible of absolute demonstration, that it will be far more easy to obtain subsequent than previous amendments to the Constitution. The moment an alteration is made in the present plan, it becomes, to the purpose of adoption, a new one, and must undergo a new decision of each State. To its complete establishment throughout the Union, it will therefore require the concurrence of thirteen States. If, on the contrary, the Constitution proposed should once be ratified by all the States as it stands, alterations in it may at any time be effected by nine States. Here, then, the chances are as thirteen to nine in favor of subsequent amendment, rather than of the original adoption of an entire system.

This is not all. Every Constitution for the United States must inevitably consist of a great variety of particulars, in which thirteen independent States are to be accommodated in their interests or opinions of interest. We may of course expect to see, in any body of men charged with its original formation, very different combinations of the parts upon different points. Many of those who form a majority on one question, may become the minority on a second, and an association dissimilar to either may constitute the majority on a third. Hence the necessity of moulding and arranging all the particulars which are to compose the whole, in such a manner as to satisfy all the parties to the compact; and hence, also, an immense multiplication of difficulties and casualties in obtaining the collective assent to a final act. The degree of that multiplication must evidently be in a ratio to the number of particulars and the number of parties.

But every amendment to the Constitution, if once established, would be a single proposition, and might be brought forward singly. There would then be no necessity for management or compromise, in relation to any other point no giving nor taking. The will of the requisite number would at once bring the matter to a decisive issue. And consequently, whenever nine, or rather ten States, were united in the desire of a particular amendment, that amendment must infallibly take place. There can, therefore, be no comparison between the facility of affecting an amendment, and that of establishing in the first instance a complete Constitution.

In opposition to the probability of subsequent amendments, it has been urged that the persons delegated to the administration of the national government will always be disinclined to yield up any portion of the authority of which they were once possessed. For my own part I acknowledge a thorough conviction that any amendments which may, upon mature consideration, be thought useful, will be applicable to the organization of the government, not to the mass of its powers; and on this account alone, I think there is no weight in the observation just stated. I also think there is little weight in it on another account. The intrinsic difficulty of governing thirteen States at any rate, independent of calculations upon an ordinary degree of public spirit and integrity, will, in my opinion constantly impose on the national rulers the necessity of a spirit of accommodation to the reasonable expectations of their constituents. But there is yet a further consideration, which proves beyond the possibility of a doubt, that the observation is futile. It is this that the national rulers, whenever nine States concur, will have no option upon the subject. By the fifth article of the plan, the Congress will be obliged "on the application of the legislatures of two thirds of the States (which at present amount to nine), to call a convention for proposing amendments, which shall be valid, to all intents and purposes, as part of the Constitution, when ratified by the legislatures of three fourths of the States, or by conventions in three fourths thereof." The words of this article are peremptory. The Congress "shall call a convention." Nothing in this particular is left to the discretion of that body. And of consequence, all the declamation about the disinclination to a change vanishes in air. Nor however difficult it may be supposed to unite two thirds or three fourths of the State legislatures, in amendments which may affect local interests, can there be any room to apprehend any such difficulty in a union on points which are merely relative to the general liberty or security of the people. We may safely rely on the disposition of the State legislatures to erect barriers against the encroachments of the national authority.

If the foregoing argument is a fallacy, certain it is that I am myself deceived by it, for it is, in my conception, one of those rare instances in which a political truth can be brought to the test of a mathematical demonstration. Those who see the matter in the same light with me, however zealous they may be for amendments, must agree in the propriety of a previous adoption, as the most direct road to their own object.

The zeal for attempts to amend, prior to the establishment of the Constitution, must abate in every man who is ready to accede to the truth of the following observations of a writer equally solid and ingenious: "To balance a large state or society Usays hee, whether monarchical or republican, on general laws, is a work of so great difficulty, that no human genius, however comprehensive, is able, by the mere dint of reason and reflection, to effect it. The judgments of many must unite in the work; experience must guide their labor; time must bring it to perfection, and the feeling of inconveniences must correct the mistakes which they INEVITABLY fall into in their first trials and experiments." These judicious reflections contain a lesson of moderation to all the sincere lovers of the Union, and ought to put them upon their guard against hazarding anarchy, civil war, a perpetual alienation of the States from each other, and perhaps the military despotism of a victorious demagoguery, in the pursuit of what they are not likely to obtain, but from time and experience. It may be in me a defect of political fortitude, but I acknowledge that I cannot entertain an equal tranquillity with those who affect to treat the dangers of a longer continuance in our present situation as imaginary. A nation, without a national government, is, in my view, an awful spectacle. The establishment of a Constitution, in time of profound peace, by the voluntary consent of a whole people, is a prodigy, to the completion of which I look forward with trembling anxiety. I can reconcile it to no rules of prudence to let go the hold we now have, in so arduous an enterprise, upon seven out of the thirteen States, and after having passed over so considerable a part of the ground, to recommence the course. I dread the more the consequences of new attempts, because I know that powerful individuals, in this and in other States, are enemies to a general national government in every possible shape.

*PUBLIUS.*

# Benjamin Franklin
## (1706-1790)

# BENJAMIN FRANKLIN
## (1706-1790)

BORN ON JANUARY 17, 1706, IN Boston, Benjamin Franklin was the 15th child of Josiah Franklin, a soap and candlemaker. Franklin's mother, Abiah Folger, was the second wife of Josiah. Franklin learned to read while he was young and was highly successful in school, but he stopped schooling at the age of 10 in order to work for his father. This did not appeal to young Franklin, so his father had him apprenticed at his brother James' print shop at the age of 12.

James was hard on Franklin and often beat him, but Franklin was still able to learn much about printing and began writing his own works. When he was 16, Franklin became fed up with James' unwillingness to publish any of his writings, so he established a pseudonym: Mrs. Silence Dogood. He published 14 of these letters, which found some success. However, James was furious when he found out that Franklin had written them. In 1723, Franklin was fed up with James' treatment of him, so he left Boston for New York and eventually settled in Pennsylvania, where he began working with another printer. While living with a man named John Read, Franklin met John's daughter, Deborah, who he married in 1730.

In 1724, Franklin journeyed to England in order to purchase supplies to start his own print shop. While there, he read often, chatted with the locals, and attended theatrical performances. In 1725, he published "A Dissertation upon Liberty and Necessity, Pleasure and Pain," which claimed that humans didn't have free will and, therefore, shouldn't be blamed for their actions. He later grew to question this argument, so he burned almost all copies of the pamphlet. Franklin returned to Philadelphia in 1726 and found that Deborah had already married, but she was abandoned by her husband soon after, allowing them to marry in 1730. Franklin fathered three children: William, a child out of wedlock around 1730, Francis, born in 1732 but died at the age of four, and Sarah, in 1743. Franklin moved to London once in 1757, and once more in 1764. Deborah never joined him in Europe and she died in Philadelphia of a stroke in 1774.

During his time in Philadelphia, Franklin worked several different jobs: shopkeeper, bookkeeper, and others. In 1728, he began printing paper currency in New Jersey before opening up his own print shop. His business mainly published government books and pamphlets, which led to him being named the official printer of Pennsylvania in 1730. Around this time, Franklin created a group called "Junto," which was a study group for young men that met once a week to discuss morals, politics, and philosophy. Stemming from this, Franklin helped create the Library Company of Philadelphia in 1731.

In 1729, Franklin published a pamphlet called "A Modest Enquiry into The Nature and Necessity of a Paper Currency," which called for more money to help the economy grow. From this, Franklin earned enough to be able to purchase *The Pennsylvania Gazette,* which was failing, and turn it into the most-read newspaper in the colonies. Franklin also joined the Freemasons in 1731 and was elected grandmaster of the Masons of Pennsylvania. In 1732, Franklin began regularly publishing his *Poor Richard's Almanac,* which contained weather, astrology, poetry, proverbs, and witty maxims. He continued publishing it for 25 years.

During the 1740s, Franklin became more interested in science. He wrote a pamphlet called "A Proposal for Promoting Useful Knowledge," which became the founding document for the American Philosophy Society. By 1748, Franklin was one of the wealthiest men in Pennsylvania, and he turned his printing business over to a partner so that he had more time to conduct experiments as well as serve in the militia.

Franklin was responsible for the inventions of the Franklin stove, bifocals, the armonica, the rocking chair, the flexible catheter, and the American penny. In addition to this, he discovered the Gulf Stream in 1775. In recognition of his scientific achievements, Harvard, Yale, England's University of Oxford, and the University of St. Andrews in Scotland all granted Franklin honorary degrees. In 1749, Franklin wrote a pamphlet that discussed the youth's education in Pennsylvania and led to the creation of the Academy of Philadelphia (now the University of Pennsylvania).

In 1752, Franklin's key-and-kite experiment proved that lightning was electricity, leading to his invention of the lightning rod and the 1751 publishing of his "Experiments and Observations on Electricity." Franklin coined terms that we still use today, including battery, charge, electrify, and conductor.

In 1748, Franklin had a couple of slaves working for him at his print shop, but he eventually saw slavery as wrong and freed his slaves in the 1760s. At one point, he became the president of the Pennsylvania Society for Promoting the Abolition of Slavery and penned several works that advocated for the abolishment of slavery. In the same year, Franklin became a member of Philadelphia's City Council and then a justice of the peace in 1750. The following year, he was elected a Philadelphia alderman and then as a representative to the Pennsylvania Assembly. He was re-elected annually for this position until 1764. Two years later, he received a royal appointment as Deputy Postmaster General of North America.

Franklin called for the colonies to band together when the French and Indian War began in 1754. To drive this point home, he published his famous "Join or Die" cartoon in *The Pennsylvania Gazette*. He was a representative of Pennsylvania at the Albany Congress, which adopted his proposal, called the "Plan of Union." However, the plan was never ratified by the colonies. Franklin was appointed by the Pennsylvania Assembly in 1757 to serve as the colony's agent in England where he remained until 1762. However, he returned to London in 1764 when he lost his seat in the Pennsylvania Assembly. Franklin spoke out in Parliament against the Stamp Act of 1765, which helped lead to its repeal in 1766.

Franklin soon wrote the pamphlet "Causes of the American Discontents before 1768," and also became an agent for Georgia, New Jersey, and Massachusetts. Soon after this, he sent private letters from the governor of Massachusetts, Thomas Hutchinson, to America, where they were published in Boston. These letters called for the colonists'

rights to be restricted. In light of their publication, an uproar exploded in the colonies and Franklin was stripped of his duty as Deputy Postmaster General. He began writing his autobiography in 1771, although it wouldn't be published until the 1790s. He returned to America in 1775, fully supporting the cause of the patriots. This same year, he was elected to the Second Continental Congress and appointed as the first Postmaster General for the colonies. In 1776, he was appointed as the commissioner to Canada and was one of the five men to help draft the Declaration of Independence. By the end of the year, Franklin was elected to be the commissioner to France where he aimed to negotiate a treaty that would help his country's military. In 1783, Franklin played a large role in the negotiation of the Treaty of Paris, which ended the Revolutionary War. He finally returned to America in 1785 after nearly a decade in France.

In 1787, Franklin represented Pennsylvania at the Constitutional Convention, which drafted the new constitution. During the Convention, he helped negotiate the Great Compromise, which led to representation based on population in the House of Representatives and equal representation in the Senate. This same year, he helped found the Society for Political Inquiries.

Benjamin Franklin died on April 17, 1790, at the home of his daughter, Sarah. The cause of his death was empyema, a condition in which pus gathers in the area between the lungs and the chest wall, which was brought on by pleurisy, an inflammation of the tissues that line the lungs and chest cavity. This condition caused an abscess in his lung to burst resulting in a coma that he remained in until he died.

# An Excerpt From Franklin's Autobiography

Plan For Attaining Moral Perfection:

IT was about this time I conceived the bold and arduous project of arriving at moral perfection. I wish'd to live without committing any fault at any time; I would conquer all that either natural inclination, custom, or company might lead me into. As I knew, or thought I knew, what was right and wrong, I did not see why I might not always do the one and avoid the other. But I soon found I had undertaken a task of more difficulty than I had imagined. While my care was employ'd in guarding against one fault, I was often surprised by another; habit took the advantage of inattention; inclination was sometimes too strong for reason. I concluded, at length, that the mere speculative conviction that it was our interest to be completely virtuous, was not sufficient to prevent our slipping; and that the contrary habits must be broken, and good ones acquired and established, before we can have any dependence on a steady, uniform rectitude of conduct. For this purpose I therefore contrived the following method.

In the various enumerations of the moral virtues I had met with in my reading, I found the catalogue more or less numerous, as different writers included more or fewer ideas under the same name. Temperance, for example, was by some confined to eating and drinking, while by others it was extended to mean the moderating every other pleasure, appetite, inclination, or passion, bodily or mental, even to our avarice and ambition. I propos'd to myself, for the sake of clearness, to use rather more names, with fewer ideas annex'd to each, than a few names with more ideas; and I included under thirteen names of virtues all that at that time occurr'd to me as necessary or desirable, and annexed to each a short precept, which fully express'd the extent I gave to its meaning.

These names of virtues, with their precepts, were:

1. Temperance
   Eat not to dullness; drink not to elevation.

2. Silence.
   Speak not but what may benefit others or yourself; avoid trifling conversation.

3. Order.
   Let all your things have their places; let each part of your business have its time.

4. Resolution.
   Resolve to perform what you ought; perform without fail what you resolve.

5. Frugality.
   Make no expense but to do good to others or yourself; i. e., waste nothing.

6. Industry.
   Lose no time; be always employ'd in something useful; cut off all unnecessary actions.

7. Sincerity.
   Use no hurtful deceit; think innocently and justly; and, if you speak, speak accordingly.

8. Justice.
   Wrong none by doing injuries, or omitting the benefits that are your Duty.

9. Moderation.
   Avoid extreams; forbear resenting injuries so much as you think they Deserve.

10. Cleanliness.
Tolerate no uncleanliness in body, cloaths, or habitation.

11. Tranquillity.
Be not disturbed at trifles, or at accidents common or unavoidable.

12. Chastity.

13. Humility.
Imitate Jesus and Socrates.

My intention being to acquire the *habitude* of all these virtues, I judg'd it would be well not to distract my attention by attempting the whole at once, but to fix it on one of them at a time; and, when I should be master of that, then to proceed to another, and so on, till I should have gone thro' the thirteen; and, as the previous acquisition of some might facilitate the acquisition of certain others, I arrang'd them with that view, as they stand above. Temperance first, as it tends to procure that coolness and clearness of head, which is so necessary where constant vigilance was to be kept up, and guard maintained against the unremitting attraction of ancient habits, and the force of perpetual temptations. This being acquir'd and establish'd, Silence would be more easy; and my desire being to gain knowledge at the same time that I improv'd in virtue, and considering that in conversation it was obtain'd rather by the use of the ears than of the tongue, and therefore wishing to break a habit I was getting into of prattling, punning, and joking, which only made me acceptable to trifling company, I gave *Silence* the second place. This and the next, *Order*, I expected would allow me more time for attending to my project and my studies. *Resolution*, once become habitual, would keep me firm in my endeavours to obtain all the subsequent virtues; *Frugality* and Industry freeing me from my remaining debt, and producing affluence and independence, would make more easy the practice of Sincerity and Justice, etc., etc. Conceiving then, that, agreeably to the advice of Pythagoras in his Golden Verses, daily examination would be necessary, I contrived the following method for conducting that examination.

I made a little book, in which I allotted a page for each of the virtues. I rul'd each page with red ink, so as to have seven columns, one for each day of the week, marking each column with a letter for the day. I cross'd these columns with thirteen red lines, marking the beginning of each line with the first letter of one of the virtues, on which line, and in its proper column, I might mark, by a little black spot, every fault I found upon examination to have been committed respecting that virtue upon that day.

*Form of the pages.*

| TEMPERANCE. | | | | | | |
|---|---|---|---|---|---|---|
| EAT NOT TO DULLNESS DRINK NOT TO ELEVATION. | | | | | | |
| | S. | M. | T. | W. | T. | F. | S. |
| T. | | | | | | | |
| S. | * | * | | * | | * | |
| O. | ** | * | * | | * | * | * |
| R. | | | * | | | * | |
| F. | | * | | | * | | |
| I. | | | * | | | | |
| S. | | | | | | | |
| J. | | | | | | | |
| M. | | | | | | | |
| C. | | | | | | | |
| T. | | | | | | | |
| C. | | | | | | | |
| H. | | | | | | | |
| J. | | | | | | | |

I determined to give a week's strict attention to each of the virtues successively. Thus, in the first week, my great guard was to avoid every the least offense against *Temperance*, leaving the other virtues to their ordinary chance, only marking every evening the faults of the day. Thus, if in the first week I could keep my first line, marked T, clear of spots, I suppos'd the habit of that virtue so much strengthen'd, and its opposite weaken'd, that I might venture extending my attention to include the next, and for the following week keep both lines clear of spots. Proceeding thus to the last, I could go thro' a course compleat in thirteen weeks, and four courses in a year. And like him who, having a garden to weed, does not attempt to eradicate all the bad herbs at once, which would exceed his reach and his strength, but works on one of the beds at a time, and, having accomplish'd the first, proceeds to a second, so I should have, I hoped, the encouraging pleasure of seeing on my pages the progress I made in virtue, by clearing successively my lines of their spots, till in the end, by a number of courses, I should be happy in viewing a clean book, after a thirteen weeks' daily examination.

This my little book had for its motto these lines from Addison's **Cato**:

> "Here will I hold. If there's a power above us
> (And that there is, all nature cries aloud
> Thro' all her works), He must delight in virtue;
> And that which he delights in must be happy."

Another from Cicero,

> "O vitæ Philosophia dux! O virtutum indagatrix expultrixque vitiorum! Unus dies, bene et ex præceptis tuis actus, peccanti immortalitati est anteponendus."

Another from the Proverbs of Solomon, speaking of wisdom or virtue:

> "Length of days is in her right hand, and in her left hand riches and honour. Her ways are ways of pleasantness, and all her paths are peace." iii. 16, 17.

And conceiving God to be the fountain of wisdom, I thought it right and necessary to solicit his assistance for obtaining it; to this end I formed the following little prayer, which was prefix'd to my tables of examination, for daily use.

*"O powerful Goodness! bountiful Father! merciful Guide! Increase in me that wisdom which discovers my truest interest. Strengthen my resolutions to perform what that wisdom dictates. Accept my kind offices to thy other children as the only return in my power for thy continual favours to me."*

I used also sometimes a little prayer which I took from Thomson's Poems, viz.:

"Father of light and life, thou Good Supreme!
O teach me what is good; teach me Thyself!
Save me from folly, vanity, and vice,
From every low pursuit; and fill my soul
With knowledge, conscious peace, and virtue pure;
Sacred, substantial, never-fading bliss!"

The precept of **Order** requiring that **every part of my business should have its allotted time**, one page in my little book contain'd the following scheme of employment for the twenty-four hours of a natural day.

| | | |
|---|---|---|
| The Morning.<br><br>*Question.* What good shall I do this day? | 5<br>6 | Rise, wash, and address ***Powerfull Goodness!*** Contrive day's business, and take the resolution of the day: prosecute the present study, and breakfast. |
| | 7 | |
| | 8<br>9<br>10<br>11 | Work. |
| Noon. | 12<br>1 | Read, or overlook my accounts, and dine. |
| | 2<br>3<br>4<br>5 | Work. |
| Evening<br><br>*Question.* What good have I done to-day? | 6<br>7<br>8<br>9 | Put things in their places. Supper.<br>Music or diversion, or conversation.<br>Examination of the day. |
| Night | 10<br>11<br>12<br>1<br>2<br>3<br>4 | Sleep. |

I enter'd upon the execution of this plan for self-examination, and continu'd it with occasional intermissions for some time. I was surpris'd to find myself so much fuller of faults than I had imagined; but I had the satisfaction of seeing them diminish. To avoid the trouble of renewing now and then my little book, which, by scraping out the marks on the paper of old faults to make room for new ones in a new course, became full of holes, I transferr'd my tables and precepts to the ivory leaves of a memorandum book, on which the lines were drawn with red ink, that made a durable stain, and on those lines I mark'd my faults with a blacklead pencil, which marks I could easily wipe out with a wet sponge. After a while I went thro' one course only in a year, and afterward only one in several years, till at length I omitted them entirely, being employ'd in voyages and business abroad, with a multiplicity of affairs that interfered; but I always carried my little book with me.

My scheme of Order gave me the most trouble; and I found that, tho' it might be practicable where a man's business was such as to leave him the disposition of his time, that of a journeyman printer, for instance, it was not possible to be exactly observed by a master, who must mix with the world, and often receive people of business at their own hours. *Order*, too, with regard to places for things, papers, etc., I found extreamly difficult to acquire. I had not been early accustomed to it, and, having an exceeding good memory, I was not so sensible of the inconvenience attending want of method. This article, therefore, cost me so much painful attention, and my faults in it vexed me so much, and I made so little progress in amendment, and had such frequent relapses, that I was almost ready to give up the attempt, and content myself with a faulty character in that respect, like the man who, in buying an ax of a smith, my neighbour, desired to have the whole of its surface as bright as the edge. The smith consented to grind it bright for him if he would turn the wheel; he turn'd, while the smith press'd the broad face of the ax hard and heavily on the stone, which made the turning of it very fatiguing. The man came every now and then from the wheel to see how the work went on, and at length would take his ax as it was, without farther grinding. "No," said the smith, "turn on, turn on; we shall have it bright by-and-by; as yet, it is only speckled." "Yes," says the man, "*but I think I like a speckled ax best.*" And I believe this may have been the case with many, who, having, for want of some such means as I employ'd, found the difficulty of obtaining good and breaking bad habits in other points of vice and virtue, have given up the struggle, and concluded that *"a speckled ax was best"*; for something, that pretended to be reason, was every now and then suggesting to me that such extream nicety as I exacted of myself might be a kind of foppery in morals, which, if it were known, would make me ridiculous; that a perfect character might be attended with the inconvenience of being envied and hated; and that a benevolent man should allow a few faults in himself, to keep his friends in countenance.

In truth, I found myself incorrigible with respect to Order; and now I am grown old, and my memory bad, I feel very sensibly the want of it. But, on the whole, tho' I never arrived at the perfection I had been so ambitious of obtaining, but fell far short of it, yet I was, by the endeavour, a better and a happier man than I otherwise should have been if I had not attempted it; as those who aim at perfect writing by imitating the engraved copies, tho' they never reach the wish'd-for excellence of those copies, their hand is mended by the endeavour, and is tolerable while it continues fair and legible.

It may be well my posterity should be informed that to this little artifice, with the blessing of God, their ancestor ow'd the constant felicity of his life, down to his 79th year, in which this is written. What reverses may attend the remainder is in the hand of Providence; but, if they arrive, the reflection on past happiness enjoy'd ought to help his bearing them with more resignation. To Temperance he ascribes his long-continued health, and what is still left to him of a good constitution; to Industry and Frugality, the early easiness of his circumstances and acquisition of his fortune, with all that knowledge that enabled him to be a useful citizen, and obtained for him some degree of reputation among the learned; to Sincerity and Justice, the confidence of his country, and the honorable employs it conferred upon him; and to the joint influence of the whole mass of the virtues, even in the imperfect state he was able to acquire them, all that evenness of temper, and that cheerfulness in conversation, which makes his company still sought for, and agreeable even to his younger acquaintance. I hope, therefore, that some of my descendants may follow the example and reap the benefit.

It will be remark'd that, tho' my scheme was not wholly without religion, there was in it no mark of any of the distinguishing tenets of any particular sect. I had purposely avoided them; for, being fully persuaded of the utility and excellency of my method, and that it might be serviceable to people in all religions, and intending some time or other to publish it, I would not have anything in it that should prejudice anyone, of any sect, against it. I purposed writing a little comment on each virtue, in which I would have shown the advantages of possessing it, and the mischiefs attending its opposite vice; and I should have called my book The Art of Virtue, because it would have shown the means and manner of obtaining virtue, which would have distinguished it from the mere exhortation to be good, that does not instruct and indicate the means, but is like the apostle's man of verbal charity, who only without showing to the naked and hungry how or where they might get clothes or victuals, exhorted them to be fed and clothed. — James ii. 15, 16.

But it so happened that my intention of writing and publishing this comment was never fulfilled. I did, indeed, from time to time, put down short hints of the sentiments, reasonings, etc., to be made use of in it, some of which I have still by me; but the necessary close attention to private business in the earlier part of my life, and public business since, have occasioned my postponing it; for, it being connected in my mind with *a great and extensive project*, that required the whole man to execute, and which an unforeseen succession of employs prevented my attending to, it has hitherto remain'd unfinish'd.

In this piece it was my design to explain and enforce this doctrine, that vicious actions are not hurtful because they are forbidden, but forbidden because they are hurtful, the nature of man alone considered; that it was, therefore, everyone's interest to be virtuous who wish'd to be happy even in this world; and I should, from this circumstance (there being always in the world a number of rich merchants, nobility, states, and princes, who have need of honest instruments for the management of their affairs, and such being so rare), have endeavoured to convince young persons that no qualities were so likely to make a poor man's fortune as those of probity and integrity.

My list of virtues contain'd at first but twelve; but a Quaker friend having kindly informed me that I was generally thought proud; that my pride show'd itself frequently in conversation; that I was not content with being in the right when discussing any point, but was overbearing, and rather insolent, of which he convinc'd me by mentioning several instances; I determined endeavouring to cure myself, if I could, of this vice or folly among the rest, and I added **Humility** to my list, giving an extensive meaning to the word.

I cannot boast of much success in acquiring the **reality** of this virtue, but I had a good deal with regard to the **appearance** of it. I made it a rule to forbear all direct contradiction to the sentiments of others, and all positive assertion of my own. I even forbid myself, agreeably to the old laws of our Junto, the use of every word or expression in the language that imported a fix'd opinion, such as c**ertainly, undoubtedly,** etc., and I adopted, instead of them, *I conceive, I apprehend,* or *I imagine* a thing to be so or so; or it *so appears to me at present*. When another asserted something that I thought an error, I deny'd myself the pleasure of contradicting him abruptly, and of showing immediately some absurdity in his proposition; and in answering I began by observing that in certain cases or circumstances his opinion would be right, but in the present case there *appear'd* or *seem'd* to me some difference, etc. I soon found the advantage of this change in my manner; the conversations I engag'd in went on more pleasantly. The modest way in which I propos'd my opinions procur'd them a readier reception and less contradiction; I had less mortification when I was found to be in the wrong, and I more easily prevail'd with others to give up their mistakes and join with me when I happened to be in the right.

And this mode, which I at first put on with some violence to natural inclination, became at length so easy, and so habitual to me, that perhaps for these fifty years past no one has ever heard a dogmatical expression escape me. And to this habit (after my character of integrity) I think it principally owing that I had early so much weight with my fellow-citizens when I proposed new institutions, or alterations in the old, and so much influence in public councils when I became a member; for I was but a bad speaker, never eloquent, subject to much hesitation in my choice of words, hardly correct in language, and yet I generally carried my points.

In reality, there is, perhaps, no one of our natural passions so hard to subdue as **pride**. Disguise it, struggle with it, beat it down, stifle it, mortify it as much as one pleases, it is still alive, and will every now and then peep out and show itself; you will see it, perhaps, often in this history; for, even if I could conceive that I had compleatly overcome it, I should probably be proud of my humility.

[Thus far written at Passy, 1784.]

[*"I am now about to write at home, August, 1788, but cannot have the help expected from my papers, many of them being lost in the war. I have, however, found the following."*]

Having mentioned *a great and extensive project* which I had con-ceiv'd, it seems proper that some account should be here given of that project and its object. Its first rise in my mind appears in the following little paper, accidentally preserv'd, viz.:

*Observations* on my reading history, in Library, May 19th, 1731.

"That the great affairs of the world, the wars, revolutions, etc., are carried on and effected by parties.

"That the view of these parties is their present general interest, or what they take to be such.

"That the different views of these different parties occasion all con-fusion.

"That while a party is carrying on a general design, each man has his particular private interest in view.

"That as soon as a party has gain'd its general point, each member becomes intent upon his particular interest; which, thwarting oth-ers, breaks that party into divisions, and occasions more confusion.

"That few in public affairs act from a mere view of the good of their country, whatever they may pretend; and, tho' their actings bring real good to their country, yet men primarily considered that their own and their country's interest was united, and did not act from a principle of benevolence.

"That fewer still, in public affairs, act with a view to the good of mankind.

"There seems to me at present to be great occasion for raising a United Party for Virtue, by forming the virtuous and good men of all nations into a regular body, to be govern'd by suitable good and wise rules, which good and wise men may probably be more unanimous in their obedience to, than common people are to common laws.

"I at present think that whoever attempts this aright, and is well qualified, cannot fail of pleasing God, and of meeting with success.

*B. F.*"


Revolving this project in my mind, as to be undertaken hereafter, when my circumstances should afford me the necessary leisure, I put down from time to time, on pieces of paper, such thoughts as occurr'd to me respecting it. Most of these are lost; but I find one purporting to be the substance of an intended creed, containing, as I thought, the essentials of every known religion, and being free of everything that might shock the professors of any religion. It is express'd in these words, viz.:

"That there is one God, who made all things.

"That he governs the world by his providence.

"That he ought to be worshiped by adoration, prayer, and thanksgiving.

"But that the most acceptable service of God is doing good to man.

"That the soul is immortal.

"And that God will certainly reward virtue and punish vice, either here or hereafter."


My ideas at that time were, that the sect should be begun and spread at first among young and single men only; that each person to be initiated should not only declare his assent to such creed, but should have exercised himself with the thirteen weeks' examination and practice of the virtues, as in the beforemention'd model; that the existence of such a society should be kept a secret, till it was become considerable, to prevent solicitations for the admission of improper persons, but that the members should each of them search among his acquaintance for ingenuous, well-disposed youths, to whom, with prudent caution, the scheme should be gradually communicated; that the members should engage to afford their advice, assistance, and support to each other in promoting one another's interests, business, and advancement in life; that, for distinction, we should be call'd *The Society of the Free and Easy*: free, as being, by the general practice and habit of the virtues, free from the dominion of vice; and particularly by the practice of industry and frugality, free from debt, which exposes a man to confinement, and a species of slavery to his creditors.

This is as much as I can now recollect of the project, except that I communicated it in part to two young men, who adopted it with some enthusiasm; but my then narrow circumstances, and the necessity I was under of sticking close to my business, occasioned my postponing the further prosecution of it at that time; and my multifarious occupations, public and private, induc'd me to continue postponing, so that it has been omitted till I have no longer strength or activity left sufficient for such an enterprise; though I am still of opinion that it was a practicable scheme, and might have been very useful, by forming a great number of good citizens; and I was not discourag'd by the seeming magnitude of the undertaking, as I have always thought that one man of tolerable abilities may work great changes, and accomplish great affairs among mankind, if he first forms a good plan, and, cutting off all amusements or other employments that would divert his attention, makes the execution of that same plan his sole study and business.

# GEORGE WASHINGTON
## (1732-1799)

# GEORGE WASHINGTON
## (1732-1799)

George Washington was born on February 22, 1732 at his family's plantation on Pope's Creek in the British colony of Virginia. Among the oldest of his siblings, and with his father passing while Washington was 11, it's plausible that he helped his mother in managing the family's plantation. While little is known about Washington's early education, many prominent families hired private tutors or had their children attend private schools. Washington likely finished his schooling around the age of 15. Having shown skill in mathematics, he became a surveyor and earned enough money to acquire land of his own. Making his only trip outside of the country in 1751, Washington journeyed to Barbados to try and help his older half-brother, Lawrence Washington, recover from tuberculosis. While there, Washington contracted smallpox, from which he recovered, but he developed facial scars that remained throughout his life. Washington eventually inherited Lawrence's estate in Virginia: Mount Vernon.

In December 1752, with no military experience, Washington was made a commander of Virginia's militia and, after seeing action in the French and Indian War, he was eventually put in charge of the entirety of the militia's forces. By 1759, Washington had resigned his commission, gotten married to Martha Dandridge Custis, a wealthy widow, who was a mother of two, and been elected to the Virginia House of Burgesses where he served until 1774.

Experiencing the discontent of having increasingly high taxes, Washington eventually came to desire the independence of the colonies from England. In 1774, he was a delegate to the First Continental Congress, the first governing body of the 13 colonies. By the time the Second Continental Congress met in 1775, the American

Revolution had already begun and he was named Commander in Chief of the Continental Army. While he was not a great military strategist, Washington was able to maintain the integrity of the ill-equipped army. He proved this in 1777-1778 at Valley Forge where he helped to train the army despite adverse conditions and, in doing so, instilled them with confidence.

When the war was officially over in 1783, Washington gave up his command of the army and intended to retire to his life as a farmer. In 1787, though, he was asked to attend the Constitutional Convention where his leadership convinced the delegates there that he was the most qualified man in the nation to be the first president. He hesitated to take on this role, but with strong public opinion swaying him, he eventually gave in and ran for the office.

Washington was aware that each decision he made would set a future precedent for those who would hold office after him. He took care to exhibit fairness, prudence, and integrity. He favored neutrality in foreign conflicts and had a cabinet of individuals with widely-differing opinions.

He finally retired in 1796. Three years later as he inspected his properties in the rain, Washington caught a cold and developed a throat infection that led to his death on December 14, 1799. He remains seen as the father of his country and there are universities and cities named after him. In honor of his birthday, his farewell address is read each February in the U.S. Senate.

# Inaugural Address of 1789

Fellow Citizens of the Senate and the House of Representatives.

Among the vicissitudes incident to life, no event could have filled me with greater anxieties than that of which the notification was transmitted by your order, and received on the fourteenth day of the present month. On the one hand, I was summoned by my Country, whose voice I can never hear but with veneration and love, from a retreat which I had chosen with the fondest predilection, and, in my flattering hopes, with an immutable decision, as the asylum of my declining years: a retreat which was rendered every day more necessary as well as more dear to me, by the addition of habit to inclination, and of frequent interruptions in my health to the gradual waste committed on it by time. On the other hand, the magnitude and difficulty of the trust to which the voice of my Country called me, being sufficient to awaken in the wisest and most experienced of her citizens, a distrustful scrutiny into his qualifications, could not but overwhelm with dispondence, one, who, inheriting inferior endowments from nature and unpractised in the duties of civil administration, ought to be peculiarly conscious of his own deficiencies. In this conflict of emotions, all I dare aver, is, that it has been my faithful study to collect my duty from a just appreciation of every circumstance, by which it might be affected. All I dare hope, is, that, if in executing this task I have been too much swayed by a grateful remembrance of former instances, or by an affectionate sensibility to this transcendent proof, of the confidence of my fellow-citizens; and have thence too little consulted my incapacity as well as disinclination for the weighty and untried cares before me; my error will be palliated by the motives which misled me, and its consequences be judged by my Country, with some share of the partiality in which they originated.

Such being the impressions under which I have, in obedience to the public summons, repaired to the present station; it would be peculiarly improper to omit in this first official Act, my fervent supplications to that Almighty Being who rules over the Universe, who presides in the Councils of Nations, and whose providential aids can supply every human defect, that his benediction may consecrate to the liberties and happiness of the People of the United States, a Government instituted by themselves for these essential purposes: and may enable every instrument employed in its administration to execute with success, the functions allotted to his charge. In tendering this homage to the Great Author of every public and private good I assure myself that it expresses your sentiments not less than my own; nor those of my fellow-citizens at large, less than either. No People can be bound to acknowledge and adore the invisible hand, which conducts the Affairs of men more than the People of the United States. Every step, by which they have advanced to the character of an independent nation, seems to have been distinguished by some token of providential agency. And in the important revolution just accomplished in the system of their United Government, the tranquil deliberations and voluntary consent of so many distinct communities, from which the event has resulted, cannot be compared with the means by which most Governments have been established, without some return of pious gratitude along with an humble anticipation of the future blessings which the past seem to presage. These reflections, arising out of the present crisis, have forced themselves too strongly on my mind to be suppressed. You will join with me I trust in thinking, that there are none under the influence of which, the proceedings of a new and free Government can more auspiciously commence.

By the article establishing the Executive Department, it is made the duty of the President "to recommend to your consideration, such measures as he shall judge necessary and expedient." The circumstances under which I now meet you, will acquit me from entering into that subject, farther than to refer to the Great Constitutional Charter under which you are assembled; and which, in defining your powers, designates the objects to which your attention is to be given. It will be more consistent with those circumstances, and far more congenial with the feelings which actuate me, to substitute, in place of a recommendation of particular measures, the tribute that is due to the talents, the rectitude, and the patriotism which adorn the characters selected to devise and adopt them. In these honorable qualifications, I behold the surest pledges, that as on one side, no local prejudices, or attachments; no seperate views, nor party animosities, will misdirect the comprehensive and equal eye which ought to watch over this great assemblage of communities and interests: so, on another, that the foundations of our National policy will be laid in the pure and immutable principles of private morality; and the pre-eminence of a free Government, be exemplified by all the attributes which can win the affections of its Citizens, and command the respect of the world.

I dwell on this prospect with every satisfaction which an ardent love for my Country can inspire: since there is no truth more thoroughly established, than that there exists in the economy and course of nature, an indissoluble union between virtue and happiness, between duty and advantage, between the genuine maxims of an honest and magnanimous policy, and the solid rewards of public prosperity and felicity: Since we ought to be no less persuaded that the propitious smiles of Heaven, can never be expected on a nation that disregards the eternal rules of order and right, which Heaven itself has ordained: And since the preservation of the sacred fire of liberty, and the destiny of the Republican model of Government, are justly considered as deeply, perhaps as finally staked, on the experiment entrusted to the hands of the American people.

Besides the ordinary objects submitted to your care, it will remain with your judgment to decide, how far an exercise of the occasional power delegated by the Fifth article of the Constitution is rendered expedient at the present juncture by the nature of objections which have been urged against the System, or by the degree of inquietude which has given birth to them. Instead of undertaking particular recommendations on this subject, in which I could be guided by no lights derived from official opportunities, I shall again give way to my entire confidence in your discernment and pursuit of the public good: For I assure myself that whilst you carefully avoid every alteration which might endanger the benefits of an United and effective Government, or which ought to await the future lessons of experience; a reverence for the characteristic rights of freemen, and a regard for the public harmony, will sufficiently influence your deliberations on the question how far the former can be more impregnably fortified, or the latter be safely and advantageously promoted.

To the preceeding observations I have one to add, which will be most properly addressed to the House of Representatives. It concerns myself, and will therefore be as brief as possible. When I was first honoured with a call into the Service of my Country, then on the eve of an arduous struggle for its liberties, the light in which I contemplated my duty required that I should renounce every pecuniary compensation. From this resolution I have in no instance departed. And being still under the impressions which produced it, I must decline as inapplicable to myself, any share in the personal emoluments, which may be indispensably included in a permanent provision for the Executive Department; and must accordingly pray that the pecuniary estimates for the Station in which I am placed, may, during my continuance in it, be limited to such actual expenditures as the public good may be thought to require.

Having thus imparted to you my sentiments, as they have been awakened by the occasion which brings us together, I shall take my present leave; but not without resorting once more to the benign parent of the human race, in humble supplication that since he has been pleased to favour the American people, with opportunities for deliberating in perfect tranquility, and dispositions for deciding with unparellelled unanimity on a form of Government, for the security of their Union, and the advancement of their happiness; so his divine blessing may be equally *conspicuous* in the enlarged views, the temperate consultations, and the wise measures on which the success of this Government must depend.

# Farewell Address

Friends and Fellow-Citizens:

The period for a new election of a citizen to administer the executive government of the United States being not far distant, and the time actually arrived when your thoughts must be employed in designating the person who is to be clothed with that important trust, it appears to me proper, especially as it may conduce to a more distinct expression of the public voice, that I should now apprise you of the resolution I have formed, to decline being considered among the number of those out of whom a choice is to be made.

I beg you, at the same time, to do me the justice to be assured that this resolution has not been taken without a strict regard to all the considerations appertaining to the relation which binds a dutiful citizen to his country—and that, in withdrawing the tender of service which silence in my situation might imply, I am influenced by no diminution of zeal for your future interest, no deficiency of grateful respect for your past kindness; but am supported by a full conviction that the step is compatible with both.

The acceptance of, and continuance hitherto in, the office to which your suffrages have twice called me, have been a uniform sacrifice of inclination to the opinion of duty and to a deference for what appeared to be your desire. I constantly hoped that it would have been much earlier in my power, consistently with motives which I was not at liberty to disregard, to return to that retirement from which I had been reluctantly drawn. The strength of my inclination to do this, previous to the last election, had even led to the preparation of an address to declare it to you; but mature reflection on the then perplexed and critical posture of our affairs with foreign nations, and the unanimous advice of persons entitled to my confidence, impelled me to abandon the idea.

I rejoice that the state of your concerns, external as well as internal, no longer renders the pursuit of inclination incompatible with the sentiment of duty or propriety, and am persuaded whatever partiality may be retained for my services, that in the present circumstances of our country, you will not disapprove my determination to retire.

The impressions with which I first undertook the arduous trust were explained on the proper occasion. In the discharge of this trust, I will only say that I have, with good intentions, contributed towards the organization and administration of the government, the best exertions of which a very fallible judgment was capable. Not unconscious in the outset of the inferiority of my qualifications, experience in my own eyes, perhaps still more in the eyes of others, has strengthened the motives to diffidence of myself; and every day the increasing weight of years admonishes me more and more that the shade of retirement is as necessary to me as it will be welcome. Satisfied that if any circumstances have given peculiar value to my services, they were temporary, I have the consolation to believe, that while choice and prudence invite me to quit the political scene, patriotism does not forbid it.

In looking forward to the moment which is intended to terminate the career of my public life, my feelings do not permit me to suspend the deep acknowledgment of that debt of gratitude which I owe to my beloved country for the many honors it has conferred upon me; still more for the steadfast confidence with which it has supported me; and for the opportunities I have thence enjoyed of manifesting my inviolable attachment, by services faithful and persevering, though in usefulness unequal to my zeal. If benefits have resulted to our country from these services, let it always be remembered to your praise, and as an instructive example in our annals that under circumstances in which the passions agitated in every direction were liable to mislead, amidst appearances sometimes dubious, vicissitudes of fortune often discouraging, in situations in which not unfrequently want of success has countenanced the spirit of criticism, the constancy of your support was the essential prop of the efforts, and a guarantee of the plans by which they were effected. Profoundly penetrated with this idea, I shall carry it with me to my grave, as a strong incitement to unceasing vows that Heaven may continue to you the choicest tokens of its beneficence; that your Union and brotherly affection may be perpetual; that the free constitution, which is the work of your hands, may be sacredly maintained; that its administration in every department may be stamped with wisdom and virtue; that, in fine, the happiness of the people of these states, under the auspices of liberty, may be made complete by so careful a preservation and so prudent a use of this blessing as will acquire to them the glory of recommending it to the applause, the affection, and adoption of every nation which is yet a stranger to it.

Here, perhaps, I ought to stop. But a solicitude for your welfare, which cannot end but with my life, and the apprehension of danger, natural to that solicitude, urge me on an occasion like the present, to offer to your solemn contemplation, and to recommend to your frequent review, some sentiments which are the result of much reflection, of no inconsiderable observation, and which appear to me all important to the permanency of your felicity as a people. These will be offered to you with the more freedom as you can only see in them the disinterested warnings of a parting friend, who can possibly have no personal motive to bias his counsel. Nor can I forget, as an encouragement to it, your indulgent reception of my sentiments on a former and not dissimilar occasion.

Interwoven as is the love of liberty with every ligament of your hearts, no recommendation of mine is necessary to fortify or confirm the attachment.

The unity of government which constitutes you one people is also now dear to you. It is justly so; for it is a main pillar in the edifice of your real independence, the support of your tranquility at home, your peace abroad, of your safety, of your prosperity, of that very liberty which you so highly prize. But as it is easy to foresee that, from different causes and from different quarters, much pains will be taken, many artifices employed, to weaken in your minds the conviction of this truth; as this is the point in your political fortress against which the batteries of internal and external enemies will be most constantly and actively (though often covertly and insidiously) directed, it is of infinite moment that you should properly estimate the immense value of your national Union to your collective and individual happiness; that you should cherish a cordial, habitual, and immovable attachment to it; accustoming yourselves to think and speak of it as of the palladium of your political safety and prosperity; watching for its preservation with jealous anxiety; discountenancing whatever may suggest even a suspicion that it can in any event be abandoned, and indignantly frowning upon the first dawning of every attempt to alienate any portion of our country from the rest, or to enfeeble the sacred ties which now link together the various parts.

For this you have every inducement of sympathy and interest. Citizens by birth or choice, of a common country, that country has a right to concentrate your affections. The name of American, which belongs to you, in your national capacity, must always exalt the just pride of patriotism more than any appellation derived from local discriminations.

With slight shades of difference, you have the same religion, manners, habits, and political principles. You have in a common cause fought and triumphed together. The independence and liberty you possess are the work of joint councils and joint efforts—of common dangers, sufferings, and successes.

But these considerations, however powerfully they address themselves to your sensibility, are greatly outweighed by those which apply more immediately to your interest. Here every portion of our country finds the most commanding motives for carefully guarding and preserving the Union of the whole.

The *North*, in an unrestrained intercourse with the *South*, protected by the equal laws of a common  government, finds in the productions of the latter great additional resources of maritime and commercial enterprise and precious materials of manufacturing industry. The *South* in the same intercourse, benefitting by the agency of the *North*, sees its agriculture grow and its commerce expand. Turning partly into its own channels the seamen of the *North*, it finds its particular navigation invigorated; and while it contributes, in different ways, to nourish and increase the general mass of the national navigation, it looks forward to the protection of a maritime strength, to which itself is unequally adapted. The *East*, in a like intercourse with the *West*, already finds, and in the progressive improvement of interior communications by land and water will more and more find a valuable vent for the commodities which it brings from abroad, or manufactures at home. The *West* derives from the *East* supplies requisite to its growth and comfort—and what is perhaps of still greater consequence, it must of necessity owe the secure enjoyment of indispensable *outlets* for its own productions to the weight, influence, and the future maritime strength of the Atlantic side of the Union, directed by an indissoluble community of interest as *one nation*. Any other tenure by which the *West* can hold this essential advantage, whether derived from its own separate strength, or from an apostate and unnatural connection with any foreign power, must be intrinsically precarious.

While then every part of our country thus feels an immediate and particular interest in union, all the parts combined cannot fail to find in the united mass of means and efforts greater strength, greater resource, proportionably greater security from external danger, a less frequent interruption of their peace by foreign nations; and, what is of inestimable value! they must derive from union an exemption from those broils and wars between themselves, which so frequently afflict neighboring countries not tied together by the same government; which their own rivalships alone would be sufficient to produce, but which opposite foreign alliances, attachments, and intrigues would stimulate and embitter. Hence likewise they will avoid the necessity of those overgrown military establishments which, under any form of government, are inauspicious to liberty, and which are to be regarded as particularly hostile to republican liberty. In this sense it is, that your Union ought to be considered as a main prop of your liberty, and that the love of the one ought to endear to you the preservation of the other.

These considerations speak a persuasive language to every reflecting and virtuous mind and exhibit the continuance of the Union as a primary object of patriotic desire. Is there a doubt whether a common government can embrace so large a sphere? Let experience solve it. To listen to mere speculation in such a case were criminal. We are authorized to hope that a proper organization of the whole, with the auxiliary agency of governments for the respective subdivisions, will afford a happy issue to the experiment. It is well worth a fair and full experiment. With such powerful and obvious motives to union affecting all parts of our country, while experience shall not have demonstrated its impracticability, there will always be reason to distrust the patriotism of those who in any quarter may endeavor to weaken its bands.

In contemplating the causes which may disturb our Union, it occurs as matter of serious concern that any ground should have been furnished for characterizing parties by *geographical* discriminations—*Northern* and *Southern*—*Atlantic* and *Western*; whence designing men may endeavor to excite a belief that there is a real difference of local interests and views.

One of the expedients of party to acquire influence within particular districts is to misrepresent the opinions and aims of other districts. You cannot shield yourselves too much against the jealousies and heart burnings which spring from these misrepresentations. They tend to render alien to each other those who ought to be bound together by fraternal affection. The inhabitants of our western country have lately had a useful lesson on this head. They have seen in the negotiation by the executive, and in the unanimous ratification by the Senate, of the treaty with Spain, and in the universal satisfaction at that event  throughout the United States, a decisive proof how unfounded were the suspicions propagated among them of a policy in the general government and in the Atlantic states unfriendly to their interests in regard to the Mississippi. They have been witnesses to the formation of two treaties, that with Great Britain and that with Spain, which secure to them everything they could desire, in respect to our foreign relations, towards confirming their prosperity. Will it not be their wisdom to rely for the preservation of these advantages on the Union by which they were procured? Will they not henceforth be deaf to those advisers, if such there are, who would sever them from their brethren and connect them with aliens?

To the efficacy and permanency of your Union, a government for the whole is indispensable. No alliances, however strict, between the parts can be an adequate substitute. They must inevitably experience the infractions and interruptions which all alliances in all times have experienced. Sensible of this momentous truth, you have improved upon your first essay by the adoption of a Constitution of government better calculated than your former for an intimate Union and for the efficacious management of your common concerns. This government, the offspring of our own choice uninfluenced and unawed, adopted upon full investigation and mature deliberation, completely free in its principles, in the distribution of its powers, uniting security with energy, and containing within itself a provision for its own amendment, has a just claim to your confidence and your support. Respect for its authority, compliance with its laws, acquiescence in its measures, are duties enjoined by the fundamental maxims of true liberty. The basis of our political systems is the right of the people to make and to alter their constitutions of government. But the Constitution which at any time exists, until changed by an explicit and authentic act of the whole people, is sacredly obligatory upon all. The very idea of the power and the right of the people to establish government presupposes the duty of every individual to obey the established government.

All obstructions to the execution of the laws, all combinations and associations under whatever plausible character, with the real design to direct, control, counteract, or awe the regular deliberation and action of the constituted authorities, are destructive of this fundamental principle and of fatal tendency. They serve to organize faction, to give it an artificial and extraordinary force—to put in the place of the delegated will of the nation the will of a party; often a small but artful and enterprising minority of the community; and, according to the alternate triumphs of different parties, to make the public administration the mirror of the ill concerted and incongruous projects of faction, rather than the organ of consistent and wholesome plans digested by common councils and modified by mutual interests. However combinations or associations of the above description may now and then answer popular ends, they are likely, in the course of time and things, to become potent engines by which cunning, ambitious, and unprincipled men will be enabled to subvert the power of the people and to usurp for themselves the reins of government, destroying afterwards the very engines which have lifted them to unjust dominion.

Towards the preservation of your government and the permanency of your present happy state, it is requisite, not only that you steadily discountenance irregular oppositions to its acknowledged authority, but also that you resist with care the spirit of innovation upon its principles, however specious the pretexts. One method of assault may be to effect in the forms of the Constitution alterations which will impair the energy of the system and thus to undermine what cannot be directly overthrown. In all the changes to which you may be invited, remember that time and habit are at least as necessary to fix the true character of governments as of other human institutions; that experience is the surest standard by which to test the real tendency of the existing constitution of a country; that facility in changes, upon the credit of mere hypotheses and opinion, exposes to perpetual change from the endless variety of hypotheses and opinion; and remember, especially, that for the efficient management of your common interests in a country so extensive as ours, a government of as much vigor as is consistent with the perfect security of liberty is indispensable. Liberty itself will find in such a government, with powers properly distributed and adjusted, its surest guardian. It is indeed little else than a name, where the government is too feeble to withstand the enterprises of faction, to confine each member of the society within the limits prescribed by the laws, and to maintain all in the secure and tranquil enjoyment of the rights of person and property.

I have already intimated to you the danger of parties in the state, with particular reference to the founding of them on geographical discriminations. Let me now take a more comprehensive view and warn you in the most solemn manner against the baneful effects of the spirit of party, generally.

This spirit, unfortunately, is inseparable from our nature, having its root in the strongest passions of the human mind. It exists under different shapes in all governments, more or less stifled, controlled, or repressed; but, in those of the popular form, it is seen in its greatest rankness and is truly their worst enemy.

The alternate domination of one faction over another, sharpened by the spirit of revenge natural to party dissension, which in different ages and countries has perpetrated the most horrid enormities, is itself a frightful despotism. But this leads at length to a more formal and permanent despotism. The disorders and miseries which result gradually incline the minds of men to seek security and repose in the absolute power of an individual; and sooner or later the chief of some prevailing faction, more able or more fortunate than his competitors, turns this disposition to the purposes of his own elevation on the ruins of public liberty.

Without looking forward to an extremity of this kind (which nevertheless ought not to be entirely out of sight) the common and continual mischiefs of the spirit of party are sufficient to make it the interest and the duty of a wise people to discourage and restrain it.

It serves always to distract the public councils and enfeeble the public administration. It agitates the community with ill founded jealousies and false alarms, kindles the animosity of one part against another, foments occasionally riot and insurrection. It opens the door to foreign influence and corruption, which find a facilitated access to the government itself through the channels of party passions. Thus the policy and the will of one country are subjected to the policy and will of another.

There is an opinion that parties in free countries are useful checks upon the administration of the government and serve to keep alive the spirit of liberty. This within certain limits is probably true—and in governments of a monarchical cast patriotism may look with indulgence, if not with favor, upon the spirit of party. But in those of the popular character, in governments purely elective, it is a spirit not to be encouraged. From their natural tendency, it is certain there will always be enough of that spirit for every salutary purpose. And there being constant danger of excess, the effort ought to be, by force of public opinion, to mitigate and assuage it. A fire not to be quenched, it demands a uniform vigilance to prevent its bursting into a flame, lest instead of warming it should consume.

It is important, likewise, that the habits of thinking in a free country should inspire caution in those entrusted with its administration, to confine themselves within their respective constitutional spheres, avoiding in the exercise of the powers of one department to encroach upon another. The spirit of encroachment tends to consolidate the powers of all the departments in one and thus to create, whatever the form of government, a real despotism. A just estimate of that love of power and proneness to abuse it which predominates in the human heart is sufficient to satisfy us of the truth of this position. The necessity of reciprocal checks in the exercise of political power, by dividing and distributing it into different depositories and constituting each the guardian of the public weal against invasions by the others, has been evinced by experiments ancient and modern, some of them in our country and under our own eyes. To preserve them must be as necessary as to institute them. If in the opinion of the people the distribution or modification of the constitutional powers be in any particular wrong, let it be corrected by an amendment in the way which the Constitution designates. But let there be no change by usurpation; for though this, in one instance, may be the instrument of good, it is the customary weapon by which free governments are destroyed. The precedent must always greatly overbalance in permanent evil any partial or transient benefit which the use can at any time yield.

Of all the dispositions and habits which lead to political prosperity, religion and morality are indispensable supports. In vain would that man claim the tribute of patriotism who should labor to subvert these great pillars of human happiness, these firmest props of the duties of men and citizens. The mere politician, equally with the pious man, ought to respect and to cherish them. A volume could not trace all their connections with private and public felicity. Let it simply be asked where is the security for property, for reputation, for life, if the sense of religious obligation *desert* the oaths, which are the instruments of investigation in courts of justice? And let us with caution indulge the supposition that morality can be maintained without religion. Whatever may be conceded to the influence of refined education on minds of peculiar structure, reason and experience both forbid us to expect that national morality can prevail in exclusion of religious principle.

It is substantially true that virtue or morality is a necessary spring of popular government. The rule indeed extends with more or less force to every species of free government. Who that is a sincere friend to it can look with indifference upon attempts to shake the foundation of the fabric?

Promote then, as an object of primary importance, institutions for the general diffusion of knowledge. In proportion as the structure of a government gives force to public opinion, it is essential that public opinion should be enlightened.

As a very important source of strength and security, cherish public credit. One method of preserving it is to use it as sparingly as possible, avoiding occasions of expense by cultivating peace, but remembering also that timely disbursements to prepare for danger frequently prevent much greater disbursements to repel it; avoiding likewise the accumulation of debt, not only by shunning occasions of expense, but by vigorous exertions in time of peace to discharge the debts which unavoidable wars may have occasioned, not ungenerously throwing upon posterity the burden which we ourselves ought to bear. The execution of these maxims belongs to your representatives, but it is necessary that public opinion should cooperate. To facilitate to them the performance of their duty, it is essential that you should practically bear in mind that towards the payment of debts there must be revenue; that to have revenue there must be taxes; that no taxes can be devised which are not more or less inconvenient and unpleasant; that the intrinsic embarrassment inseparable from the selection of the proper objects (which is always a choice of difficulties) ought to be a decisive motive for a candid construction of the conduct of the government in making it, and for a spirit of acquiescence in the measures for obtaining revenue which the public exigencies may at any time dictate.

Observe good faith and justice towards all nations; cultivate peace and harmony with all—religion and morality enjoin this conduct; and can it be that good policy does not equally enjoin it? It will be worthy of a free, enlightened, and, at no distant period, a great nation, to give to mankind the magnanimous and too novel example of a people always guided by an exalted justice and benevolence. Who can doubt that in the course of time and things the fruits of such a plan would richly repay any temporary advantages which might be lost by a steady adherence to it? Can it be, that Providence has not connected the permanent felicity of a nation with its virtue? The experiment, at least, is recommended by every sentiment which ennobles human nature. Alas! is it rendered impossible by its vices?

In the execution of such a plan nothing is more essential than that permanent, inveterate antipathies against particular nations and passionate attachments for others should be excluded and that in place of them just and amicable feelings towards all should be cultivated. The nation which indulges towards another an habitual hatred or an habitual fondness is in some degree a slave. It is a slave to its animosity or to its affection, either of which is sufficient to lead it astray from its duty and its interest. Antipathy in one nation against another disposes each more readily to offer insult and injury, to lay hold of slight causes of umbrage, and to be haughty and intractable when accidental or trifling occasions of dispute occur. Hence frequent collisions, obstinate, envenomed, and bloody contests. The nation, prompted by ill will and resentment, sometimes impels to war the government, contrary to the best calculations of policy. The government sometimes participates in the national propensity and adopts through passion what reason would reject; at other times, it makes the animosity of the nation subservient to projects of hostility instigated by pride, ambition and other sinister and pernicious motives. The peace often, sometimes perhaps the liberty, of nations has been the victim.

So likewise, a passionate attachment of one nation for another produces a variety of evils. Sympathy for the favorite nation, facilitating the illusion of an imaginary common interest in cases where no real common interest exists, and infusing into one the enmities of the other, betrays the former into a participation in the quarrels and wars of the latter  without adequate inducement or justification. It leads also to concessions to the favorite nation of privileges denied to others, which is apt doubly to injure the nation making the concessions—by unnecessarily parting with what ought to have been retained—and by exciting jealousy, ill will, and a disposition to retaliate in the parties from whom equal privileges are withheld. And it gives to ambitious, corrupted, or deluded citizens (who devote themselves to the favorite nation) facility to betray or sacrifice the interests of their own country without odium, sometimes even with popularity; gilding with the appearances of a virtuous sense of obligation a commendable deference for public opinion, or a laudable zeal for public good, the base or foolish compliances of ambition, corruption, or infatuation.

As avenues to foreign influence in innumerable ways, such attachments are particularly alarming to the truly enlightened and independent patriot. How many opportunities do they afford to tamper with domestic factions, to practice the arts of seduction, to mislead public opinion, to influence or awe the public councils! Such an attachment of a small or weak towards a great and powerful nation dooms the former to be the satellite of the latter.

Against the insidious wiles of foreign influence (I conjure you to believe me, fellow citizens) the jealousy of a free people ought to be *constantly* awake, since history and experience prove that foreign influence is one of the most baneful foes of republican government. But that jealousy to be useful must be impartial; else it becomes the instrument of the very influence to be avoided, instead of a defense against it. Excessive partiality for one foreign nation and excessive dislike of another cause those whom they actuate to see danger only on one side, and serve to veil and even second the arts of influence on the other. Real patriots, who may resist the intrigues of the favorite, are liable to become suspected and odious, while its tools and dupes usurp the applause and confidence of the people to surrender their interests.

The great rule of conduct for us in regard to foreign nations is, in extending our commercial relations, to have with them as little *political* connection as possible. So far as we have already formed engagements, let them be fulfilled with perfect good faith. Here let us stop.

Europe has a set of primary interests, which to us have none, or a very remote relation. Hence she must be engaged in frequent controversies, the causes of which are essentially foreign to our concerns. Hence therefore it must be unwise in us to implicate ourselves, by artificial ties, in the ordinary vicissitudes of her politics or the ordinary combinations and collisions of her friendships or enmities.

Our detached and distant situation invites and enables us to pursue a different course. If we remain  one people under an efficient government, the period is not far off when we may defy material injury from external annoyance; when we may take such an attitude as will cause the neutrality we may at any time resolve upon to be scrupulously respected; when belligerent nations, under the impossibility of making acquisitions upon us, will not lightly hazard the giving us provocation; when we may choose peace or war, as our interest, guided by justice, shall counsel.

Why forgo the advantages of so peculiar a situation? Why quit our own to stand upon foreign ground? Why, by interweaving our destiny with that of any part of Europe, entangle our peace and prosperity in the toils of European ambition, rivalship, interest, humor, or caprice?

It is our true policy to steer clear of permanent alliances with any portion of the foreign world—so far, I mean, as we are now at liberty to do it—for let me not be understood as capable of patronizing infidelity to existing engagements (I hold the maxim no less applicable to public than to private affairs, that honesty is always the best policy)—I repeat it therefore, let those engagements be observed in their genuine sense. But in my opinion it is unnecessary and would be unwise to extend them.

Taking care always to keep ourselves, by suitable establishments, on a respectably defensive posture, we may safely trust to temporary alliances for extraordinary emergencies.

Harmony, liberal intercourse with all nations, are recommended by policy, humanity, and interest. But even our commercial policy should hold an equal and impartial hand: neither seeking nor granting exclusive favors or preferences; consulting the natural course of things; diffusing and diversifying by gentle means the streams of commerce but forcing nothing; establishing with powers so disposed—in order to give to trade a stable course, to define the rights of our merchants, and to enable the government to support them—conventional rules of intercourse, the best that present circumstances and mutual opinion will permit, but temporary, and liable to be from time to time abandoned or varied, as experience and circumstances shall dictate; constantly keeping in view, that it is folly in one nation to look for disinterested favors from another—that it must pay with a portion of its independence for whatever it may accept under that character—that by such acceptance it may place itself in the condition of having given equivalents for nominal favors and yet of being reproached with ingratitude for not giving more. There can be no greater error than to expect or calculate upon real favors from nation to nation. It is an illusion which experience must cure, which a just pride ought to discard.

In offering to you, my countrymen, these counsels of an old and affectionate friend, I dare not hope they will make the strong and lasting impression I could wish—that they will control the usual current of the passions, or prevent our nation from running the course which has hitherto marked the destiny of nations. But if I may even flatter myself that they may be productive of some partial benefit, some occasional good, that they may now and then recur to moderate the fury of party spirit, to warn against the mischiefs of foreign intrigue, to guard against the impostures of pretended patriotism—this hope will be a full recompense for the solicitude for your welfare, by which they have been dictated.

How far in the discharge of my official duties I have been guided by the principles which have been delineated, the public records and other evidences of my conduct must witness to you and to the world. To myself, the assurance of my own conscience is that I have at least believed myself to be guided by them.

In relation to the still subsisting war in Europe, my proclamation of the 22d of April 1793 is the index to my plan. Sanctioned by your approving voice and by that of your representatives in both houses of Congress, the spirit of that measure has continually governed me, uninfluenced by any attempts to deter or divert me from it.

After deliberate examination with the aid of the best lights I could obtain, I was well satisfied that our country, under all the circumstances of the case, had a right to take—and was bound in duty and interest, to take—a neutral position. Having taken it, I determined, as far as should depend upon me, to maintain it with moderation, perseverence, and firmness.

The considerations which respect the right to hold this conduct it is not necessary on this occasion to detail. I will only observe that, according to my understanding of the matter, that right, so far from being denied by any of the belligerent powers, has been virtually admitted by all.

The duty of holding a neutral conduct may be inferred, without anything more, from the obligation which justice and humanity impose on every nation, in cases in which it is free to act, to maintain inviolate the relations of peace and amity towards other nations.

The inducements of interest for observing that conduct will best be referred to your own reflections and experience. With me, a predominant motive has been to endeavor to gain time to our country to settle and mature its yet recent institutions and to progress without interruption to that degree of strength and consistency which is necessary to give it, humanly speaking, the command of its own fortunes.

Though in reviewing the incidents of my administration I am unconscious of intentional error, I am nevertheless too sensible of my defects not to think it probable that I may have committed many errors. Whatever they may be, I fervently beseech the Almighty to avert or mitigate the evils to which they may tend. I shall also carry with me the hope that my country will never cease to view them with indulgence and that, after forty-five years of my life dedicated to its service with an upright zeal, the faults of incompetent abilities will be consigned to oblivion, as myself must soon be to the mansions of rest.

Relying on its kindness in this as in other things, and actuated by that fervent love towards it which is so natural to a man who views in it the native soil of himself and his progenitors for several generations, I anticipate with pleasing expectation that retreat in which I promise myself to realize without alloy the sweet enjoyment of partaking, in the midst of my fellow citizens, the benign influence of good laws under a free government—the ever favorite object of my heart, and the happy reward, as I trust, of our mutual cares, labors, and dangers.

*United States*
*19th September 1796*                    **G. Washington**

# Further Reading

*Archives.gov*, National Archives and Records Administration.

*Biography.com*, A&E Television Networks.

Chernow, Ron. *Alexander Hamilton*. Random House Large Print Publishing, 2004.

Chernow, Ron. *Washington: A Life*. Penguin Press, 2011.

Franklin, Benjamin. *The Autobiography of Benjamin Franklin*. Edited by Edmund S Morgan, Yale Univ. Press, 2003.

*Globalgreyebooks.com/Index.html*, Global Grey Ebooks.

*History.com*, A&E Television Networks.

Isaacson, Walter. *Benjamin Franklin: An American Life*. Simon & Schuster, 2004.

Keane, John. *Tom Paine: A Political Life*. Grove Press, 2003.

Ketcham, Ralph. *James Madison: A Biography*. Univ. Press of Virginia, 1990.

McCullough, David. *John Adams*. Simon & Schuster, 2008.

Meacham, Jon. *Thomas Jefferson: The Art of Power*. Random House, 2013.

*Oll.libertyfund.org*, Online Library of Liberty.

*ProjectGutenberg.com*, Project Gutenberg Editors.

"Research Guides." *Guides.loc.gov*, Library of Congress.

Stahr, Walter. *John Jay: Founding Father*. Diversion Books, 2017.

Text Creation Partnership. *Quod.lib.umich.edu/e/Evans*, Evans Early American Imprint Collection.

"Washington's Farewell Address." Senate.gov

*Special thanks to the OLL, Project Gutenberg, the Text Creation Partnership, and GlobalGray ebooks for assembling such a vast network of important documents that are in the public domain.

.

www.ingramcontent.com/pod-product-compliance
Lightning Source LLC
LaVergne TN
LVHW041152080426
835511LV00006B/563